INTERNATIONAL CUISINE

India

Cyrus Todiwala

Hodder Arnold

A MEMBER OF THE HODDER HEADLINE GROUP

Orders: please contact Bookpoint Ltd, 130 Milton Park, Abingdon, Oxon OX14 4SB. Telephone: (44) 01235 827720. Fax: (44) 01235 400454. Lines are open from 9.00 - 6.00, Monday to Saturday, with a 24-hour message answering service. You can also order through our website www.hoddereducation.co.uk.

British Library Cataloguing in Publication Data
A catalogue record for this title is available from the British Library

ISBN-10: 0 340 81301 6
ISBN-13: 978 0 340 81301 0

First published 2005

Impression number   10 9 8 7 6 5 4 3 2 1

Year   2100 2010 2009 2008 2007 2006 2005

Cover photo by Corbis

Typeset by Pantek Arts Ltd

Printed in Italy for Hodder Arnold, an imprint of Hodder Education, a member of the Hodder Headline Group, 338 Euston Road, London NW1 3BH

Contents

Publisher's Note   v
Acknowledgments   v

Introduction   vii

What is Indian food?   vii
Curry   x
Balance between spices, condiments and food ingredients   xi
Health applications and their connections   xiii
Key ingredients   xvi
Simplicity at the very heart of it   xxxix
Using nature's bounty to enhance and create seasonality   xxxix
Evolutions: Climatic implications on prepared foods   xli
Freshness and its importance   xlii
Family heirlooms   1
Menu planning and balancing   xlvii

1 Masalas and soups   1

What is a masala?   2

2 Chaats and Starters   29

3 Roasting   59

Roasting   60
Braising   61
Stewing   61
The tandoor   62

4 Seafood   103

On fish and seafood   104
Religion and religious occasions   105
Fish and seafood: eating habits, styles, etc.   105
What to look for in fresh fish/shellfish   106
Cooking techniques   106
Spicing and seasoning   107
Health   108

5   Vegetarian   150

Vegetables, vegetarian cooking and the vegetarian   151
Vegetables and health   153

6   Rice   193

7   Bread   219

8   Pickles and Chutneys   235

9   Sweets   247

10   Beverages   262

Glossary   273
Index   277

PUBLISHER'S NOTE

Please note that unless otherwise stated, all recipes are for four portions.

ACKNOWLEDGMENTS

The publishers would like to thank the following for use of copyright material:

Page vii photograph © Jeremy Horner/CORBIS

Pages 1, 216, 223, 247, 255 © CEPHAS/StockFood

All other photography by James Newell

Introduction

WHAT IS INDIAN FOOD?

Indian food in its entirety could be quite an in-depth or intricate topic to understand. To simplify matters, for the purpose of this book, the food from the sub-continent of India is considered to be Indian food, although the peoples of Pakistan and Bangladesh may feel otherwise. However, historically we were once all of the same land and are still very much the same people except for the imaginery lines that now divide the three nations. Also, most restaurants within the UK and globally, except perhaps those within the three countries themselves, consider or explain their individual cuisines as 'Indian'.

bouquet, quite like that of cinnamon. They are added to food for the scent rather than the flavour they may impart. This is no more evident than in the addition of bay leaves to water before boiling rice.

When buying bay leaves look for greener leaves and ensure that they are free from mould. This is not always possible as the leaves will very often be almost brown. These are not bad in any way, they may either be too old or may have been over exposed to the sun when drying.

Often in the monsoon season leaves can be damp and when packed these will eventually mould and smell and impart a musty flavour. They are available dried either whole or in pieces. They can be stored for up to six months in an airtight container. Since the use of bay leaves is limited and a few grams will yield a lot of leaves, an airtight jar placed in a dark area is most advisable.

Bay leaves are used in the clarifying process of many dyes and potpourri mixtures. The leaves contain an agent that has carminative properties. This is used to treat diarrhoea and colic. Bay leaves are also used in pickles and for preserving bottled fruits.

In the West bay leaves are used to flavour stuffings, roast meats, as part of a pot pourri and in some forms of preserving and sauces. In India they also make up a vital part of the indomitable garam masala. Used essentially in northern Indian rice and meat cookery, bay leaves are normally removed from the dish before serving due to their large ungainly presence. Bay leaves are often used in sizzling sauces and other dishes when they are added to hot oil before the main ingredients, since as with many other spices, frying releases their sweet perfume and the essential oils.

European bay leaves are not considered edible and therefore need to be removed before serving. Indian bay leaves on the other hand are not harmful and need not be removed except for aesthetic reasons.

In India, however, the leaves of both cinnamon and cassia trees are also often harvested and sold as bay leaves. Both possess a sweet scent and aroma and can be easily passed as the real thing. The leaves are also of a similar nature and very little difference is noticed.

Cardamom; (Elaichi); *Elettarai cardamomum*

There are many varieties of cardamom grown in south India. The major producers are India, Guatemala, Sri Lanka and Thailand. These tiny balloon-shaped green pods are the dried fruits of a herbaceous perennial

of the ginger family. The fruits are picked just before they are ripe and dried in the sun or drying houses.

Cardamom pods differ depending on the variety. The cardamom pod is oval in shape and contains between 10 and 40 hard dark brown seeds that stick together. The best variety is the green. Brown cardamom pods (some claim that these are not related) are bigger and hairy, but look like a small coconut and have rather a medicinal flavour. White cardamom pods, though looking bigger, are green before sulphur fumes are used to bleach them. If a seed is crushed, it releases a strong camphorus fragrance and a bittersweet perfumed taste when chewed. When cardamom seeds are whole they have a sweet flavour and a mild pleasant smell.

Cardamom can be bought in powdered form, but this is not recommended as it loses its potency quite quickly. It is best bought as whole pod since freshness is sealed in. Grind the seeds in a food processor or mortar. Better still, gently roast the pods and grind whole. Cardamom can be stored in dry clean jars in a dark place, or the refrigerator if not frequently used.

Gargling cardamom in water soothes sore throats. Boiling the spice in milk and sweetening with honey is thought to rectify impotency. Cardamom is also used to relieve stomach disorders and heartburn. It can be used in Indian mouth fresheners. Many Indians serve cardamoms coated in edible silver foil after heavy a meal, as a scented digestive. It is used for pharmaceutical purposes, in perfumery and to make liqueurs and bitters. Indians, particularly the Gujarati community, infuse it in their tea for an added spicy flavour.

The aromatic brown or black cardamom (*Badi elaichi*) spice is used in rich red curries and milky desserts in India and sometimes in tea and coffee. It is used in cakes and bread around the world. In savoury dishes mainly brown cardamom is used; rice dishes such as biryani may use both or one. It is an essential ingredient in garam masala along with green cardamom. In Sweden it is the most commonly used spice.

Cassia; (Jungli Dalchini); *Cinnamomum cassia*

The most ancient and largest producer of this spice was China, but cassia is native to north-east India and Burma. Often confused with cinnamon because of its appearance and name (cinnamon in Hindi is dalchini), the two are interchangeable. There are several varieties of cassia, all fairly similar, but the Chinese is considered the best.

Cassia comes from a tropical tree of the laurel family, which is cultivated in China, Central America, Burma, Indonesia and India. The bark of the tree is where the spice can be found. The cassia bark is brown rough layers on the outside and smooth and lighter layers on the inside. It is hard and coarse, unlike cinnamon, and does not come rolled. Cassia bark is sold dried,

complete with stalk and small round bud. The taste is bitter sweet and woody. The smell is similar to cinnamon but sweeter and less pronounced.

Cassia is available as small pieces or powder. When bought wholesale it has large dark stalks with unbroken tan-coloured buds. To keep the fragrance and flavour store cassia in an airtight jar away from light.

Cassia is used to treat diarrhoea, and to help relieve flatulence and colic. It is also added to pot-pourri, oils for aromatherapy and cosmetics. Oil extracted from cassia leaves is used in mosquito repellents.

In India, cassia is used like cinnamon in curries, rice and vegetables but is not added to sweets. Cassia buds are used in cooking and also in paan. It is also used in the blend of Chinese five-spice powder and garam masala.

Chillies

Chillies, surprisingly, are believed to have been unknown in India until about 400 years ago. The Portuguese take credit for having introduced this most essential of all ingredients used in Indian cooking, though for many of us, it is hard to believe. There are around 50 to 100 varieties of chilli grown on the sub-continent and it is hard to imagine all of these coming on a few ships that landed in very few places. It is believed that Columbus introduced the fruit to the Europeans and this is possibly true. This fruit belongs to the Solanaceae family, which includes the tomato and the aubergine. The chillies of Goa most definitely have a direct link to the South American varieties and are definitely a Portuguese introduction.

Chillies grow mainly in tropical and sub-tropical countries with India the largest producer and exporter. There are two major varieties – Capsicum annuum and Capsicum frutescens. Capsicum annuum fruits are large, mild and much like sweet peppers. Capsicum frutescent is smaller and has a pungent pod. The southeastern state of Andhra Pradesh takes credit for being the largest producer and consumer. Andhra food is perhaps the hottest food anywhere.

Unripe chillies come in various shades of green, from olive to lime. The ripe fruits are red, dark and crumpled looking. The Mexican chillies like the ancho, cascabel, jalapeno and serrano are short and thick. Habanera chillies are lantern shaped and are from the West Indies. Various Indian chillies are fat and long, round like cherries, or slender and small. Chilli tastes range from mild to hot and they have a strong smarting aroma.

Chillies are available fresh, dried, powdered and flaked, in sauce, bottled and pickled and in oil. Fresh chillies should be bought when they appear crisp, waxy, unwrinkled and green. Pungency can vary from the dried south Indian varieties, which are very hot, to mild Kashmiri. All ground spices including chilli powder lose their strength and appearance after a few months. There are several forms of chilli powder like paprika, which is mild but does not store well, and cayenne, which is hot. Indian chilli

powder is widely available and needs no alternative. Whole chillies will last up to a year stored in a dark dry place. Always remember that you may not get a consistent chilli powder in the markets as it could be made from different varieties and therefore recipes need to be regulated. Unless you use one kind of chilli only and grind it down you are likely to find you need to check each time.

Some chillies are good for colour and aroma or flavour like the Kashmiri, which is blended with others when grinding curry masalas for balance in flavour and heat.

Chillies are very high in vitamins A and C and have more vitamin C per gram than many oranges. Capsicum preparations are used for lumbago and rheumatic disorders, and are added to medicines for sore throats. Taken in excess chillies can burn the lining of the stomach. Capsicum plaster is an old remedy for aches and pains, pioneered commercially by a leading pharmaceutical company and known as Belladona Plaster. It has also been proven that chillies aid in releasing an enzyme in the body that gives us a kind of high and that leads to an addiction of a sort. This was the result of a study carried out in Singapore a few years ago.

Chillies or chilli powder are used in virtually every savoury dish in India. The capsaicin in chillies can irritate the skin, so be careful when preparing them. To increase pungency slice the chillies and leave, and do not remove the seeds. To reduce pungency discard the seeds and soak the chillies in cold salted water before use. This process also softens the chilli and therefore one must not leave them soaking for more than an hour or so. Dried chillies can also be washed in cold water, dried, then the stems and seeds removed. However, this is not necessary, as the seeds will come out quite easily in dry chillies. They can be soaked in warm water, or vinegar as you will see in certain recipes and ground into a paste. Always watch out for the little devils, though, as more often than not, it is the smallest and slimmest ones that are the hottest. A tiny one is known as 'Little Flea' and it stings like one too.

Cinnamon; (Dalchini); *Cinnamomum verum/Cinnamonmum zeylanicum*

Cinnamon is native to Sri Lanka. Sri Lanka was colonised by the Portuguese for its cinnamon, but then defeated by the Dutch. They limited its supply to control world prices. Cinnamon is also grown in India, leading from Goa to the southern tip.

Sri Lanka and the Seychelles are the largest producers of cinnamon, which is an evergreen tree of the laurel family.

The inner dried bark of the tree is the spice used in cooking. The bark is rolled into compact curls and dried. These are called quills. During

processing quills are sometimes damaged and pieces break off; these are sold as quillings. The art of making the quills or separating the bark from the trunk of the tree is unique and is a treat to watch. The spice is quite special and it is easy to recognise the sweet, woody scent. This is the main flavouring in many desserts.

Cinnamon is available as quills, quillings or ground into powder; the buds are sometimes used. Ground cinnamon loses its taste fairly quickly, within a month, and becomes musty. Like other spices it is best to keep it in a dark place well sealed or in the refrigerator. Quills can be ground.

Cinnamon bark oil is used in some pharmaceuticals, germicides and soaps. Cinnamon leaf oil is also used in perfumery and mosquito repellents. Another effective way of using cinnamon is to put it in warm water. This helps cure common colds, prevents nervous tension, checks nausea and stimulates digestion. It is also used as an inhalant for sinusitis and colds. It is often applied to localised areas to relieve rheumatic pain.

Cinnamon is used to flavour curries, rice, meats and desserts. Garam masala is the spice mixture that gives many Indian dishes the rich fragrance. Though cinnamon is an essential part of this, along with cardamom, cloves and peppercorns, it is not always used and cassia is most commonly used. Cinnamon is also used to lace the flavours of Masala Chai (Spiced Tea).

Cinnamon leaves are most often used in India as bay leaves and have a similar flavour and aroma. The difference is the size. Cinnamon leaves are longer.

Cloves; *Eugenia caryophyllus/ Syzgium aromaticum*

Clove trees love the tropical environment. The clove is the air-dried bud of a tropical tree. Cloves grow in clusters. The unopened buds are picked when they are fully grown and green, then dried in the sun until they turn dark brown and woody.

Cloves have a very powerful flavour; if too many are used in a dish the other flavours are completely lost. They are dark brown in colour and cylindrical. Richly aromatic cloves tend to leave a spectrum of sensation on the palate if chewed on their own, starting with a sharp tingling, and going on to taste woody and bitter and leaving the mouth feeling warm and numb.

Almost always used whole they form an important ingredient of garam masala, a blend of mixed spices ground to powder. Good cloves when pinched hard should leave a trace of oil on your fingers. Cloves will store well for up to a year, sealed well in a jar, in a dark place or better still in your refrigerator.

Clove oil is widely used to cure aches and pains such as toothache. The anaesthetic action of cloves helps numb the digestive system and reduce gastric irritability. Cholera and asthma symptoms are kept in check by clove water and clove infused steam inhalations. Clove oil is used in a number of perfumes, soaps, bath salts and in dentistry and medicines.

Cloves are used in mulled wine, baked/cured ham, breads and cakes all over the world. In India they are added to meats, rice and sweets, chutneys and pickles.

Coconut; (Narial); *Cocos nucifera*

Coconut trees grow in tropical climates in salty sandy soil or normal loamy soil to a height of 20 m (70 ft) or more depending on the variety. They grow all over the coasts of most regions of the globe. The fruit starts off being green and tender; when ripe they are picked after the outer shell or husk covering dries until hard and brown. Different breeds have different sizes both in the height of the tree as well as the fruit itself.

Coconuts used in cookery are large, hairy brown fruits removed after splitting open the outer layers of husk, to expose an almost round fruit with a woody shell which has within it a creamy white kernel. The best part is the white flesh or kernel, which is obtained after breaking the woody brown shell. The liquid inside the ripe coconut, which is slightly cloudy, makes a refreshing drink. Coconut has a subtle, oily aroma and a sweet nutty flavour.

Coconut can be bought fresh for its water only, or desiccated, as milk or creamed with water, or as a shelled hard round nut. It is also sold opened on the half shell in India. There are several brands of dehydrated coconut milk. When buying fresh coconut, shake it to make sure it contains water; if there is no water it may mean the kernel is tough and dry. Fresh coconuts keep up to a week, though the ripe fruit will keep for a few weeks. The flesh can be grated and frozen for up to three months. Creamed coconut can be stored in a refrigerator for six months.

Coconut extracts are used in hair and skin products and also as a cooking medium in many parts of India. It is an essential oil for deep treatment Ayurvedic massages.

The coconut tree is also the only tree which is used in its entirety and nothing gets wasted.

Coriander; (*Coriander sativum*)

This pretty leafy herb is the most commonly used garnish in India, and adds a green touch to brown and red curries, vegetable preparations and other meat and seafood dishes. The seeds of the coriander plant are the spice.

The seeds are picked when ripe, dried, threshed and cleaned of debris such as twigs, small pebbles or tiny lumps of soil. The seeds are kept whole.

Coriander leaves are fragile, with pale green stems; they are used in cookery as well as the seeds. The flavours and aroma of each are completely different. The seeds have a sweet aroma when roasted, with a subtle hint of pine and pepper, while the leaves taste and smell fresh and fruity with a whiff of ginger. Whereas the seeds are best ground or crushed after being slow roasted, the leaves cannot be chopped and set aside as they will turn black or oxidise rather quickly. Very often people tend to discard the roots and stems of the green herb; this is wrong because the best flavours are entrenched inside the stems and roots. These must be well washed, or soaked in cold water until all the mud and sand is cleared, then washed drained, chopped and used. They can be used for chutneys, pastes, masalas and curries and for adding flavour to cooked food. The leaves also require washing, but care has to be taken to ensure that you do not chop these while still wet. The ideal scenario is to wash the entire bunch well when you first get it, then drain it well before placing it in the refrigerator. In many kitchens there is a string tied to a rack or window over the sink and the bunch is placed inverted on the string to allow for good drainage and also to keep it aired.

Small bunches of coriander tied with string or rubber bands are available and look like parsley. Coriander seeds and ground coriander are also available. When selecting fresh coriander it is important to check that there are no flowers in the bunch. This means that older shoots ready to fruit have been harvested so the flavour will not be so rich. Also look between the bunch for grass, rotten shoots, mushy paste on your fingers and a foul smell very unlike the bunch. Often simply spreading the shoots and smelling will tell you whether the bunch is fresh and clean or not.

Rich sources of vitamins A, B and C are all found in coriander. Coriander seeds are said to be diuretic, antibilious and carminative; they help lower the blood cholesterol. A blend of seeds infused in hot water, cooled and drunk is cooling and helps reduce fever. Asthma sufferers should use coriander sparingly. Coriander oil is used in perfumery. A cold coriander seed-infused pack can also be applied on the forehead when a person is suffering from high fever.

Coriander is suited to most Indian dishes, as a spice or herb in daily curries, meats, vegetables, soups, chutneys and cool drinks. Its volatile oil is used to flavour chocolate and liqueurs. Yoghurt-based salads and drinks like lassi and raita are sprinkled with coriander for a delicious spark. It is used commonly and extensively throughout the sub-continent.

Cumin; (Jeera); *Cuminum cyminum*

Cumin is sometimes confused with caraway seeds or black cumin. This gentle spice can be tasted in rich meat curries of northern Kashmir, the river fish preparations of Bengal, hot coconut curries of the south and the superb vegetarian dishes of Gujarat, as well as in fresh chutneys and well-matured pickles.

Cumin is grown widely throughout India, China, Iran, Indonesia, Japan, Morocco, Russia, Romania and Turkey. Cumin is a small slender seed and is part of the coriander family.

Cumin seeds vary in colour and range from a tobacco brown to sage green; they have ridges lengthways. These seeds are actually the fruits of the herb. Another variety of the cumin is black cumin, otherwise known as kala jeera. These seeds are dark brown to black and are smaller and finer than cumin. The smell of cumin is either loved or hated. It has a warm bitter taste, but black cumin is not as bitter in flavour.

Cumin can be bought whole as seeds, crushed coarsely or ground into a powder. Cumin is often mixed with coriander powder; this mixture is called dhana-jeera. The Parsees would add other ingredients to that to make the same kind of masala. A combination or blend of spices is used extensively and commonly in Indian cookery.

Hot cumin water is excellent for colds and fevers and is made by boiling a teaspoon of roasted seeds in three cups of water. Add some honey to soothe sore throats. It is also prescribed for indigestion, flatulent colic and biliousness. A little crushed cumin blended with honey makes an excellent, rather warming, settler.

Cumin oil is used to make perfumes. It is also used to manufacture soap. In India, for instance, cumin seeds are sometimes scattered between the folds of linen or wool to keep insects away.

Cumin is suited to almost any cuisine in the world. It is used in the cuisines of North American, in North African dishes like couscous, in Spanish stews and in the Middle East in kebabs. In India most curries have cumin added before the main ingredients. Roasted cumin powder can be used as a garnish sprinkled on top of yoghurts, salads or chaats to act as a dark contrast as well as for flavour. It is also used in spice blends such as tandoori masala, certain garam masalas and paanch phoron.

In short, cumin is one of the vital ingredients of sub-continental Indian cuisine and only a few out of the thousands of dishes are cooked without it.

Curry leaves; (Kadhi patta); *Murraya koenigii*

No curry is complete in southern India without the powerful-smelling curry leaves, which are synonymous with most other south Indian dishes. The use of curry leaves is not common in north Indian cuisine styles.

Curry leaves come from a tree that is native to India and Sri Lanka and thrives in tropical climates. Curry leaf is now also grown in Kenya and Tanzania and exported to the UK. This tree is widely grown and cheap. It grows to a reasonable height and is virtually self-pollinating during the monsoon when tiny shoots can be seen sprouting around the mother tree. These can then be removed and transplanted

The plant has a strong sweetish curry-like smell with dark green elongated leaves and a slightly bitter but pleasant taste. In Gujarat it is known as sweet neem as the leaves look very like neem, but neem is horrendously bitter, hence the name 'Mitho Limbdo' or sweet neem.

Curry leaves are available fresh or dried. Dried leaves are greyish-green and brittle. Buy fresh curry leaves that have a springy stalk and are unbruised. Since these do not keep well in the refrigerator for more than a week or so and you may need to keep them longer, strip the leaves off the stalks and freeze in a small airtight container. Use as desired. Alternatively, chop or shred the leaves very finely and distribute them in an ice tray, then fill the tray with water and set. Remove the cubes and keep in the freezer in a bag and use directly in curries. This prevents them from losing much of their colour and flavour.

Many of the cures of the Hindu Ayurvedic medicines rely on curry leaves. The stems and the leaves are used as a tonic, stimulant and carminative. They are made into a paste to treat bites. Fresh leaves are mixed with lemon juice and sugar for digestive disorders. The leaves, boiled in coconut oil, are massaged into the scalp to promote hair growth and help retain colour.

In Gujarat the herb is used to beautify vegetable delicacies. The leaves are also ground with coconut and spices to make superlative chutney, which is a good accompaniment to any meal. In southern India curry leaves are used to flavour meat, vegetables, lentils, breads and fish. Curry leaves are dropped into hot oil before adding the main ingredient or used to scent the oil that is poured on top of many dishes to add richness and flavour. In Kerala the leaves are also added to boiling curries without being fried or sizzled first to enhance flavours. This practice also applies to certain Goan curries and Parsee curries, in particular the light green curry.

Dry raw mango powder; Aamchoor; *Mangifera Indica*

The mango has always been and shall always be one of the most exotic and sought after fruits in the world. It is a native of India and boasts some great varieties among some hundred or so different breeds. Pakistan also has some superb mangoes and a common banter among friends on either side would often lead to which of us produces the better breeds. And then there is the remainder of the sub-continent offering some impressive varieties.

During the season of mango blossoms one is often blessed with the scent given off by flowering trees; this also determines the strength of the crop or the season itself. Barring unnatural or untimely attacks of dew or premature rain there is a good chance that the crop will be abundant.

(For those who do not know, dew and early rain will immediately destroy the crop.) Destruction of the crop is due to the immediate drop in temperature on the flowers or the fruit itself, resulting in rot.

In the first weeks of April a few varieties will emerge filling fruit stalls and beckoning the die-hard addicts. The scents around the vendors are powerful enough to make one want to dig deep inside one's pockets and buy the expensive first fruits of the season.

Mangoes like most other fruit start a deep green colour and when they are fully grown turn to the varied colours we know from golden pink, to a deep pinkish red to a golden yellow. Both smell and colour characterise the quality of the fruit.

Indian folklore dating back to Sanskrit poems and songs often refers to mango as the fruit of love, friendship and goodwill. Songs and poems describe lovers meeting below a flowering mango tree where the scents are believed to invoke romance.

Mangoes are extremely versatile and can be used in hot curries, pickles, chutneys, desserts, salads and of course as an exotic fruit. Then you have the Parsee-style seasonal lamb dish cooked with almost ripe mango in rich deep gravy. The fruit has several uses and applications whether in the raw stage, the ripe stage or the dried stage.

During festive periods mangoes are given as gifts to endorse friendship. Textiles bearing the traditional Indian style mango design are also an endorsement of the fruit's value.

Aamchur is quite simply dried raw mango powder. 'Aam' means mango and 'Chur' means powder. It is made with those varieties of mango that would not make good ripe fruit. Of the dozens of varieties there are several that are simply not good eaten as ripe fruit, and also wild mangoes, which are generally not cultivated but grow in forests or jungles (this also gives these mangoes their colloquial name 'Jungli' or wild). Normally these mangoes are fibrous and extremely hard, as well as having only little flesh that is very tart.

The unripe fruit is peeled then sliced thinly and sun dried. This is then either kept whole or powdered and sold as aamchur. The dried mango slices look like pieces of wood and have a shrivelled or a frayed appearance depending on the type of mango.

Powdered mango may look lumpy but these are soft lumps and will disintegrate when touched. The colour is hard to describe but would be a darker shade of beige. The taste is tangy and the sourness may differ between varieties. Mango powder stores well though it does not like very bright places. Clean, tightly lidded jars are best and for a good life ensure that wet or damp spoons are never immersed in the jar. In fact to prevent the powder from sudden death keep it away from moisture.

Fennel; (Saunf); *Foeniculum vulgare*

Fennel is a much-loved spice throughout India and in other parts of the world. But in no other country to which it is native is it used so extensively. The attraction for fennel starts at a very young age when school children are seen eating the fresh green stalks and seeds sold outside schools during break times.

Fennel is native to the Mediterranean but also grows in Argentina, Bulgaria, Denmark, Egypt, France, Germany, Great Britain, India, Italy, Japan, Romania, and the USA. It is the dried ripe fruit of a herb. The plant has tiny yellow flowers and flimsy leaves.

Fennel seeds are small long cylindricals, have fine longitudinal ridges and are brilliant green when fresh. When they are dried for storage they change to a dull greenish yellow. The seeds have a warm, sweet concentrated flavour, which turns mellow and bitter on roasting.

Fennel is available as dried, ground seeds or fresh on stalks. Look for fennel seeds that are evenly greenish-yellow, and avoid bags that have prickles. Dry roasted fennel stores best.

Fennel is used to aid digestion; it is one of the safest medicines for colic in babies. Some infants are fed fennel water daily, especially in India, to fight colic pain. It also stimulates the appetite and relieves flatulence. Fennel aids in relieving wheezing, asthma and catarrh. Infused with water, it can be used as an eye bath. Indians either chew paan or make a digestive combination known as 'mukhwas' after a rich spicy meal; fennel is one of the main elements.

Fennel can be used whole or powdered with lamb, potatoes, chutneys and pickles; it adds richness to meat gravies and golden crisp brittles known as 'chikki', and fennel-flavoured syrup can also make a refreshing drink. School children and adults alike eat little candied or sugared fennel droplets formed around one seed and sold in a multitude of colours. They are also popular in France.

Fenugreek; (Methi); *Trigonella foenum-graecum*

There are certain foods and customs used in India and other countries for special occasions such as weddings, funerals and festivals, and with medical or religious significance. Fenugreek is associated with childbirth.

Fenugreek is very easy to grow in a mild climate. It has a thin oval leaf and slender pods that contain 20 seeds each. Enthusiasts and diabetics eat the leaves as a vegetable in India. Fenugreek is grown in Argentina, Egypt, France, the Mediterranean and all over India.

Fenugreek is a hard oblong tawny seed about 3 mm (¹⁄₈ in) in length; there is a diagonal groove across one side. The seeds smell of curry. Fenugreek is one of the most powerful and bitter of all Indian spices. Cooking the seeds subdues the bitter taste, but overuse can destroy a perfectly good dish.

Fenugreek seeds are available whole, crushed or powdered. 'Quasuri', or Kasuri methi as it is better known, are the dried leaves which are sold in packs, either whole or powdered. Kasuri methi is used to flavour meats, vegetables and onion-based curries. It should be stored in tightly closed dry jars, away from heat and light, where seeds will keep for six months and leaves for four months. So prized were the leaves from Quasur, now in Pakistan, that it has given its name to the word for dried leaves. Their flavour is best released when slow roasted before being crumbled and used.

Fenugreek contains steroidal substances called diosgenin, which are used in the production of sex hormones and oral contraceptives. The seeds are eaten to relieve flatulence, diarrhoea, chronic coughs and diabetes. The seeds also encourage lactation; they are crushed and given to cows and to lactating mothers (cooked with bulgur) to increase their milk supply. Fenugreek is also used in hair tonics. The powdered seeds give a yellow dye.

Fenugreek is an essential ingredient in the manufacture of curry powder and is used extensively in southern Indian breads, batters, chutneys and lentils. The leaves are eaten in a number of different ways. The seeds are also used extensively in Bengali cuisine.

Garlic; (Lahsun); *Allinm sativum*

Garlic is a hardy perennial herb of the onion family. It has small white flowers and flat leaves. Fully grown garlic bulbs are dug from the earth, the soil shaken off the leaves and tied together. These are then dried for three to four days in the shade, and the leaves are then removed.

The garlic bulbs are onion shaped and surrounded by a white pinkish covering and inside are half-moon-shaped cloves in a pinkish or white

papery covering. Garlic has an unmistakable aroma. Its flavour is much more pungent than onion.

Dried bulbs are the most familiar, but the fresh green herb is also available, in winter. Garlic can also be bought in flakes, powder and in oil form. When buying garlic look for plump, firm bulbs that are brightly coloured and unbroken. Old garlic sometimes has blackish-green fungus in the folds. They can be stored in an airy dry place at room temperature. Strings of garlic are also available and these can be hung and will keep for several weeks before drying up inside. Older garlic is easier to peel, chop and cook.

Doctors believe that garlic oil capsules can help control high cholesterol and high blood pressure and aid digestion. They also help with rheumatism, cancerous growths and whooping cough. Garlic is good for treating skin complaints. Rub a garlic clove on stys. Garlic has also been used to treat bronchial congestion, asthma, leprosy and worms. Though the ancient Indians knew of this and it is still practised in India today, new research in the USA has found garlic to be hugely helpful in healing or treating acute arthritis. However, it was a 15-year-old Indian student who helped develop the product, which is expected to change the treatment for the future.

Garlic is used all over the world. In India it is used in marinades, chutneys and pickles, curries, barbecued meats and vegetable dishes and many preparations. Garlic and ginger complement each other. Garlic can be eaten raw or cooked.

Mustard; (Rai); *Brassica nigra/ Brassica juncea/Sinapsius alba/ Brassica hirta*

Mustard is widely used in Indian cuisine across the entire sub-continent. In temples it is used to anoint the deities. It is believed to create a peaceful personality, sharpen intelligence and calm the mind.

Mustard comes in three main types: brown, white and black. The plant produces an attractive bright yellow flower and grows in India, Argentina, Chile, Denmark, Great Britain, Japan and the USA. The mustard leaves and flowers are very bitter and, therefore, in several parts of India mustard is sown on the periphery of fields growing valuable crops to discourage wild animals from destroying the crops. In the region where I spent a few years of my childhood this was common to protect opium crops. This is officially grown opium for pharmaceutical use and the bulbs, which cause hallucinations and light-headedness, are much sought after by several animals and birds.

The mustard spice comes from the seeds of the plant in thin longish pods. White mustard seeds are pale tan in colour. Black mustard seeds are the largest of the three varieties, though these too come in two sizes.

Mustard can be obtained as powder, paste, whole seeds, or split skinned seeds. An Indian would normally prefer to use the smaller seeds when cooking due to their more pronounced flavour.

Mustard oil is also used extensively in regional Indian cookery especially in the Punjab and Bengal. In south India it is virtually a must in many of its multifaceted vegetarian cooking styles.

Mustard is also used for medicinal and other practices. For arthritic pain, warm mustard oil is an excellent liniment. Mustard oil massaged into the scalp is thought to aid hair growth. Traditional Keralan Ayurvedic therapeutic head and body massages use mustard oil in a precise manner. Mustard oil is also believed to ward off evil.

Mustard is an excellent preservative and split seeds, which look like tiny lentils, are used in the making of traditional pickles. Mustard not only helps in the taste and texture but also in the maturing of traditional seasonal pickles. In Bengal mustard seeds are crushed to a paste for use in marinades and curries. In southern India mustard seeds are used in sizzling or baghar for vegetable preparations, curries, etc., along with other spices. Sizzling or tempering is a simple method of heating oil until it is very hot, dropping in the seeds and cooking them until they pop and crackle but not allowing them to burn.

When fried, sizzling mustard seeds give off a nutty aroma which for many including myself instantly stimulates an appetite for the food. However, it can quite easily go awry and one needs to be careful not to allow the seeds to burn as that will destroy the flavour totally and make everything bitter. Mustard seeds are generally followed by other ingredients such as curry leaves, cumin or onions, etc. These should be added in quick succession so that the heat of the oil may be reduced rapidly, thereby preventing burning.

Nutmeg/Mace; (Jaiphal/Javitri); *Myristical fragrans*

Nutmeg is widely cultivated in Sri Lanka, the West Indies and India. It grows on an evergreen tree, 10–12 m (30–36 ft) tall, with dark leaves and apricot-like fruit, which splits open when ripe and exposes the nutmeg within.

Mace is the red lace-like matter enclosing the hard kernel, inside which is the nutmeg. The mace or aril changes its colour to pale yellowish orange, once carefully peeled off, pressed flat and dried. The kernel dries in its shell and is removed once dried.

In India, nutmeg is also sold still in its outer shell, which has a glossy dark colour and is egg shaped.

Nutmegs are oval in shape with a dusty brown exterior and a rough rather crinkly appearance. Dried mace is yellowish-red; the lacy blades are normally brittle depending on the origin and the effort that goes into the process. Nutmeg and mace have some similarity in flavour, though the two are not replaceable by one or the other and are distinct.

Nutmeg tends to taste bitter sweet, while mace tastes bitter. The aroma of both is perfumed, sweet and distinctive, though nutmeg is the better known taste and flavour of the two and is definitely a king among spices.

Mace is available whole as aril, cut into flakes or ground in powder. Nutmeg is available whole or in powdered form, but the powder loses its flavour quickly. Since nutmeg is also quite oily it cannot be ground into a powder without blending it with something else that will prevent it from becoming sticky. Mace keeps well in its ground form but is not popularly used like this.

In India nutmeg is used in a paste form for external applications and in powdered form, blended with water, for skin complaints such as ringworm and eczema. It is also used to cure digestive disorders, insomnia and rheumatism and in the production of toothpaste, candles and perfumes.

In Malaysia the pectin agent derived from the ripe fruit is used in jellies and jam. Both spices are used to enhance meats, rice and desserts in India. Nutmeg is often sprinkled on creamy milk desserts. It is more commonly used within the cuisines of the Parsee and Muslim communities though, and in other countries both are added to cheese dishes, soups, sauces and vegetables, desserts, pies etc.

Onion; (Piyaz); *Allium cepa*

Onions are one of the oldest cultivated vegetables and are now cultivated practically all over the world. The onion bulb grows underground. After they have been dug from the earth, they are left to dry until the skin is brittle. There are different varieties of onions: they range from large to small, pink or purple, round to oval and even egg shaped, to what are also known as shallots. India also grows white onions and these are one of the most widely eaten vegetables. Onions are the basis for most forms of Indian cuisine styles and are very widely used except in the Jain community.

Onions contain essential oils and organic sulphides, which give them a peculiar, sulphurous smell. This smell is released when the tissue of the raw onion is cut. The taste of the raw onion is quite pungent with a hint of sweetness. When cooked they have a sweet aroma and fairly sweet taste. Owing to their richness onions cannot be sliced and set aside for use later as they turn bad very rapidly, giving off a rather strong smell.

Moreover, if onions are improperly cooked in curries, gravies and any other food products they will bring about the rapid deterioration of the end product.

Onions are available dried, powdered, flaked, crisp fried and, of course, fresh. Fresh onions are available all year round.

Onions have a high iron content and are used for treating anaemia (they are high in minerals and vitamins). They also help reduce blood cholesterol and so are recommended for people with heart complaints. Onions have a diuretic property and are often used to relieve catarrh in the bronchial tubes. In the hot regions of India onions are believed to prevent sunstroke attacks when placed beneath the hat or cap, by absorbing the heat.

Onions are used in every kind of Indian cookery either to thicken, colour, flavour or accompany a dish, or to garnish. They can be ground to make a paste as a base for curries, boiled or fried until brown as a garnish, or sliced for salads. They enhance the flavours of tomatoes, ginger, garlic and meats, vegetables and potatoes. In some parts of India a raw onion eaten with thick chapatti and some pickle could be the staple for a farmer's lunch while tilling the fields. Most Indians can be seen eating either raw sliced or coarse cut pieces with their meal and are not conscious of any bad breath which often results.

Pepper; (KalliMirch); *Piper nigrum/ Piper longum*

The main producers of pepper are Brazil, Indonesia, Malaysia and India. Pepper is the fruit of a vine with white flowers and large leaves. However, it was India and the peppercorn that led to the global race for acquiring spices and contributed to a great deal of world history. Indeed it was the Arabs who first began to trade with India and introduced the spice to the Europeans and that led to the explorations of 'Spice Routes'.

The flowers lead to small berries, which are a deep green when unripe and very firm. These then become red, then, once they have been sun dried for several days, become the black spice that we are familiar with. There are several different varieties and more than 24 varieties alone are grown in south India.

When the fruits are yellowish-red in spring they are ready for harvest. The whole sprig, full of the berries, is picked and the berries dried whole until black. White peppercorns are simply black berries that are softened in water, separated from the outer skin and dried until a light coffee colour.

White peppercorns are smooth and creamy, whereas fresh peppercorns look like plump little green berries. Generally the most widely used pepper is round, black, wrinkled and hard. The taste of pepper is quite hot and spicy. Green pepper has a mild flavour that is fresh and aromatic, whereas the white is sharper and less pungent than the black.

Dried black peppercorns are used whole, crushed or powdered. Green peppercorns should be plump and are available fresh, dried, pickled in vinegar and bottled in brine. White peppercorns are sold whole or powdered. So-called pink peppercorns are actually berries from an entirely different plant and known as Echinus molle.

Ground pepper loses its flavour quickly and should not be purchased in large quantities. Fresh green peppercorns, which can add a little extra exotic touch to a sauce, should be stored in a refrigerator. The best way to keep them is wrapped loosely in a paper towel in the refrigerator. Regular peppercorns, i.e. white or black, should be stored in clean dry jars though if not frequently used, they should be stored in the refrigerator also. Previously used jars are perfectly acceptable to use but ensure that they are thoroughly dry and void of strong aromas of other foods.

Black pepper is believed to relieve colds, amnesia, flatulence and even impotency, as well as being a stimulant, a digestive and a diuretic. An application of crushed pepper is used as an external application for toothache and muscular pains. The oils are used in perfumery and flavouring. Unfortunately this spice, which rocked the world, does not possess any nutritional value.

Pepper is used in every type of regional Indian cookery, more in some areas and less in others. It gives flavour not only to lentils in the south but also to steamed rice dumplings and pancakes, fish in the east and, particularly along with its other strong relative – mustard meat in the north and vegetables in the west.

Green pepper is used in pickling and canning due to its preservative qualities. Several spice blends use pepper as a key ingredient, such as garam masala, not forgetting the all too famous Chettinad Masala from Tamil Nadu, the prime regions being around Madras (now once again known as Chennai). The all too famous 'Devilled Sauce' adopted in Western cuisine, also known as 'Sauce Diable', originated here within Chettiyar cuisine.

Pomegranate seeds; (Anardana); *Punica granatum*

The pomegranate tree bears fruits that are glossy red to pink in colour, in different sizes but always crowned by a calyx. The fruit is packed tightly with angular seeds, and these are semi-transparent red to pink. The seeds are coated with very little flesh even in the best of qualities and it is these seeds that are eaten whole with the juicy flesh. When ripe the seeds and the flesh are separated from the rind by hand by breaking them off, then drying for 10–15 days to get the tart, sticky seeds, which are thereafter known as 'Anardana'.

Historically the pomegranate is considered the fruit of plenty and in the Zoroastrian religion it is believed to be the fruit of eternity and fertility. The best pomegranates still come from Iran and Afghanistan.

Anardana therefore consists of the dried seeds with the flesh of the pomegranate. Anardana is reddish-brown to almost deep purple, sticky and naturally hard. Due to the dried fleshy residue on the seeds they tend to form into clumps when whole and not powdered. When powdered the texture is more like that of cheap quality dried tealeaves. Anardana has a dry taste and a sweetish sour smell.

It is readily available as whole seeds or powder, though anardana is used sparingly as it imparts a tart flavour and excess use brings about a rather unsavoury gritty texture.

The medicinal benefits of the skin and rind of the fruit are put to good use by sun drying it first, then powdering and mixing the powder with honey as a cure for diarrhoea and dysentery. Pomegranate juice is rich in iron and vitamins and is a natural face mask for oily skin. The seeds are also good in soothing stomach ache.

Punjabi cookery relies on anardana for flavouring pulses like chickpeas. In north India anardana adds relish to chutneys, curries, vegetables and lentils, as well as being used as garnish.

Rock salt; (Kala namak); *Sodium chloride*

Rock salt, better known in the sub-continent of India as 'Kala namak', is mined in the Gangetic plains in central India. The rock in its crystalline form ranges from translucent amber and deep brown to grey brown and has smooth irregular shaped surfaces.

When powdered, rock salt is fine and smoke grey or brown in colour. It can have an unpleasant smell rather like pickled eggs if kept covered and suddenly opened. The taste may be less powerful than common salt, but it is different and difficult to explain.

When sold as a powder, rock salt is ready for use, but is not as flavourful as the crystals. Both crystals of rock salt and powder are available in Indian shops, though the use of rock salt is not necessarily common throughout the sub-continent.

During the summer months it is quite common to see street vendors selling various types of chaats. Fastest selling among these is a fruit chaat sprinkled with rock salt. These chaats are nothing but simple fruit salads seasoned with rock salt to aid in preventing dehydration. Pineapple, various types of melon, banana are some of the popular fruits used.

Rock salt is a cure for flatulence and heartburn. It is also recommended for people with high blood pressure on a low salt diet, as it does not increase sodium content in the blood like ordinary salt. Rock salt is considered a very good antidote to dehydration in extreme dry heat, and spiked on top of lemonade.

Rock salt is also an important ingredient in several natural remedies and is commonly used in Ayurvedic medicine.

Saffron/Asafran/Zaffran; (Kesar); *Crocus sativus*

No matter what name it is known by, mention saffron and almost at once the words exotic, rich, expensive, romantic, rare and many more may come to mind.

This golden spice has suggested a romantic richness and rarity through the ages. Its vibrant colour and exhilarating bouquet make saffron worth its weight in gold in India. It is said that the Romans scented the streets with saffron oil before Nero entered.

Saffron is known to have grown wild in Persia and Asia Minor. Today Spain and India are the only major producers of the spice, though the Iranian variety is probably the very best in quality and richness. Saffron is grown in Kashmir and Kishtwar in Jammu and is the dried stigma of the crocus sativus bulb. The stigmas are delicately taken out of the flower and dried in the sun.

Fine orange-golden threads make up the saffron; fresh saffron is usually glossy and bright; exposing saffron to air and light reduces it to being brittle and dull. The best place to store saffron is once again in the refrigerator but it must be tightly sealed so that it does not absorb other aromas and flavours.

Lesser quality saffron is often available ground into deep orange powder, or sold as loosely entwined threads of dark orange. The best quality has individual stigmas and can be pinched and picked up individually. You will need very small quantities of the best saffron, which is highly fragrant and rich in colour. Always store saffron away from light. Its scarcity makes it the most expensive spice. A cheaper form of saffron is safflower, with thicker strands than saffron, which will not flavour the food but turn the food yellow.

Saffron can be given for urinary disorders, skin and menstrual problems as well as flatulent colic and curing fevers. It is also believed to be a powerful aphrodisiac and is used in the preparation of several sweets and drinks, which are considered to stimulate libido.

Saffron enhances sweet as well as savoury food. It complements rice, chicken and milk desserts. Soak in a small amount of warm milk or water

then add with the liquid to the dish to add richness and aroma. It is also used in drinks particularly the rich milky 'Falooda', a speciality of both the Muslims and the Parsees of India.

Star anise; (Anasphal); *Illicium verum*

This is indeed one of the most beautiful of all spices available to us and is actually used more frequently in China than in India. It does, however, form an integral part of most Garam masalas and the Parsees cannot do without it in their Dhaansaak Pulao.

Star anise is native to tropical and sub-tropical eastern Asia and is grown mainly in southern China and Vietnam. Star anise is the fruit of a tree of the magnolia family.

When dried, star anise has a mahogany colour and eight hollow, hard boat-shaped petals, which form the star. Each point of the star contains a bead-like shiny oval seed. Even though the spice is similar in some ways to the flavour of aniseed they are not related. The sweet taste of star anise is, however, more distinct.

In most countries it is available ground or broken into pieces, though in India it is preferred and normally sold whole.

Star anise is soothing to the stomach, relieves flatulence and is an essential flavouring in cough mixtures and several cough lozenges. When chewed it freshens the breath and aids digestion. The essential oils of the star anise contain anethole, which is used in flavouring confectionery such as chewing gum, as well as in liqueurs and pharmaceutical preparations such as cough syrups mentioned above.

One or two of the carpals of star anise greatly improve the flavour of Chinese roast chicken. Some Chinese tea also uses star anise. In India it is mainly used in certain meat curries and in rice dishes like biryani and Dhaansaak rice. It is also a vital ingredient in the famous Goan Xacutti and the Maharashtrian version, known as Shagutti.

Turmeric; (Haldi); *Curcuma longa*

Turmeric is at the very heart of almost every type of cuisine from the sub-continent of India as well as one of the most traditional and versatile spices in every part of India. Turmeric is used copiously in a multitude of Indian dishes varying from starters and snacks to lentils, meats and vegetables.

Turmeric is a member of the ginger family and grows best in tropical climates. India is the world's largest producer and exporter, it consumes 92 per cent of its produce and 8 per cent is exported to approximately 64 countries. Some other countries producing turmeric are China, Haiti, Jamaica, Japan, Malaysia, Peru, Sri Lanka and Vietnam. Turmeric is the root of an herbaceous plant. It has large fragrant leaves similar to

pandana leaves, which are used when making certain religious ceremonial Indian sweets. However, cured root of turmeric has the aroma, properties and colour necessary for cooking. The curing is only carried out commercially and is quite a difficult process if tried in the domestic environment. I have been unsuccessful on quite a few occasions, simply because the skill did not exist.

Fresh turmeric looks rather dull and is a deceitful camouflage of its actual beauty. A beautiful golden-yellow root lies within a rather hard harsh brown skin. This root is mainly exported in its dried form. The most widely available form of turmeric is a colourful golden yellow powder. Turmeric has an earthy, sensual fragrance; on its own it has a musky, dry taste. Turmeric is not recommended when cooking green leafy vegetables as they will turn grey and often acquire a bitter taste. The high content of iron in these vegetables clashes with the strong properties of the dried root.

Turmeric is available as a powder or as a dried root that can be powdered at home in a mortar and pestle with some difficulty. The powder (spice) should be stored in a dry jar and consumed within four months, or it may lose its liveliness. If a household does not use as much as we Indians would use, the best thing to do would be to keep the jar in the refrigerator. The root itself, if purchased in its dried form, will keep longer if well kept. Care needs to be taken when using turmeric, it stains hands, surrounding areas, work surfaces and clothes quite quickly if carelessly handled. It is one of the few spice stains that is extremely difficult to wash away.

An antiseptic cream for minor burns and wounds is made with turmeric. To make a sore throat balm it is boiled in milk and taken before going to bed, or at regular intervals during the day if time permits. This relieves an irritating dry cough and helps to release catarrh and phlegm. It also helps to purify the blood and soothe inflamed sinuses. It is used in water to cleanse the skin and makes an ideal face mask when mixed with milk for an oily skin or cream for dry skin. Turmeric can also be used as a dye.

Turmeric has been used as a poultice for sprains and even fractures and has been known to have a soothing effect on painful arthritis. Very recently an extract has been achieved that will herald a new treatment for acute arthritis.

Virtually every Indian meat, lentil and vegetable (except green) dish uses turmeric. It is added to food for its taste or thickening agent, as well as its colour. If it is added to the dish before the main ingredients it imparts a deep colour and a strong taste. Added after the main ingredients it lends a subtle flavour and a pale yellow colour. It is extensively used in pickling due to its excellent preservative qualities. The leaves of the turmeric plant can be used to wrap food in, like fish or sweets before steaming. The leaves may also be added to flavour ghee. These leaves smell rich and sweet.

Marinating meats, fish and poultry with turmeric will destroy the bacteria present on the surface, particularly in a tropical climate such as India. This enables the meat to last longer without fear of rapid contamination.

SIMPLICITY AT THE VERY HEART OF IT

KISS is a word I simply cannot forget, either when concocting a new dish, when planning a menu or whenever I feel the urge to over create. K for keep, I for it, S for simple and S for stupid. These were the words used by a famous American chef friend who unfortunately died in a plane crash but his words keep ringing again and again, and how true they are.

Today the world is embracing simplicity in cooking and customers are quite happy to eat and relish a dish that is quite simply garnished but well prepared with the flavours not getting confused or being overpowered with something else.

Even when cooking, raw materials should be treated with the greatest of respect and not destroyed by over zealous and over crowded preparation, where the product is neither identifiable nor enjoyed because the flavours have been lost. Over garnishing, on the other hand, also changes the dish completely and gives it a confused and complicated flavour.

Indian food in the rural world of India or in the homes of our vast sub-continent is simply that – wholesome, clean, simple, tasty and nutritious.

There are traditional dishes that are complicated and time consuming. However, these are mostly celebratory rather than daily food. Time-consuming food is prepared when guests have been invited or if there is a celebration in the family or for the Sunday meal. Most food prepared with lots of effort and time is normally heavy and not necessarily bearing health in mind. But then this is food for sheer indulgence and at such times taste and pleasure overrule health, cost and more often than not menu and food balance. Food prepared simply need not be in any way less in creative talent, or in its amalgamation of distinct aromas and flavours to food painstakingly prepared over a prolonged period of time using an array of raw materials.

USING NATURE'S BOUNTY TO ENHANCE AND CREATE SEASONALITY

Unlike in the Western world, the cuisines of the sub-continent of India still largely depend upon the different seasons of the year and fresh produce availability. Naturally there is the huge plethora of techniques for preserving/pickling/drying, etc., of foods that need to be eaten out of season.

Many fruits can be available in large cities throughout the year due to advanced refrigeration but by and large everything across the length and breadth of the sub-continent is seasonally prepared.

This naturally brings change and excitement in the household and women are seen making selections of various new products that come in the market and following age-old traditions and recipes handed down from mother to daughter.

What a family eats and what is cooked is also significant of changes in the weather, traditional and religious calendar events and local availability.

Harvest plays a pivotal role and there is joy and celebration around nature's bounty and naturally a bountiful harvest. A myriad different preparations of freshly harvested grain of varying types are cooked and eaten to celebrate the harvests. Creativity is at its peak during this period and there is enjoyment all around during and after the hard day's toil.

In the households maximum effort is made to harness the fresh produce and the best of the sub-continent's cuisines come to the fore. Recipes that will not be prepared until the next year's season are enjoyed and relished like there is no tomorrow. Depending on where you grew up, you may have vivid memories of the wonders of eating such delicacies and days of delicious feasting: eating freshly roasted young harvested wheat, millet, chickpeas, maize, often with freshly made jaggery (soft raw cane sugar).

Certain vegetables and grains are only cooked and enjoyed at certain times and very often women will not buy products in the market if they are actually out of season. There is, of course, so much to look forward to in this very rich and bountiful sub-continent that one is spoilt for choice and there is a continuous supply of fresh seasonal produce. The list is never ending and one simply cannot go on. So much is the dependence on seasonality that some food products become synonymous with certain times of the year and people will not indulge in them even if they are available.

EVOLUTIONS: CLIMATIC IMPLICATION ON PREPARED FOODS

The effect of climate may not always be so relevant in today's modern Westernised society, but it is very much a hugely important part of day to day living and eating healthily.

One must realise that the art of preservation and cooking techniques has evolved over hundreds of years of trial and error. It is believed that where the educated elders perhaps could not defeat nature's own cycle of degeneration and putrification of meats, etc., as a natural process, they initiated the ban of such meats from consumption as a religious taboo. Pork, for instance, is such an example. Historically, the pig was kept purely as a waste gobbler for argument's sake. It consumed food debris and other waste as it was supposed to do and thereby all sorts of bacteria and infections too. The animal itself became hugely resilient and immune to various bacteria and infections but the meat it produced became a carrier. This meat when improperly prepared and poorly cooked became a huge health hazard.

This was naturally pronounced by the fact that the tropical climes where it was initially reared were unsuitable for keeping cooked meat and bad hygiene practices and therefore the best way to prevent the people from eating the animal itself was to make it a religious taboo. The same applies to several marine species, which have a rapid rate of putrification if improperly cooked or stored.

The techniques for preserving meats and vegetables have also evolved from man's need to eat his favourite foods out of season, or historically, to preserve simply for the sake of sustenance during harsh non-agricultural months. A natural process of drying left over or excess fish, as well as the need to eat fish when the seas are too rough to harvest from, must have taught preserving or drying fish and other seafood. Salting, pickling, spicing, and preserving in oil or brine have evolved through centuries of trial and error and the need for different textures and tastes.

Climate no doubt plays a vital role in all preserved foods. Hot humid climates call for different means of preservation as chances of bacterial infestation for rapid multiplication of bacteria are greatly increased due to the temperatures. Colder climates will tolerate easier or less intense methods of preservation. Often the climate itself acts as a preservative, for example at the two poles or in Inuit and Eskimo territories where the meat does not spoil due to extreme cold temperatures. The best example of this is the 'Bacalhão' (pronounced 'Bakalihao'), which is dried cod. In Iceland this is cold dried and in places such as Portugal and Spain the fish

is sun dried; two geographically separate regions practising different methods of drying or salting the same type of fish.

Take a simple item such as a packet of crisps or biscuits. In the UK you could open a packet and leave it open for a while without either product becoming soft and stale. In Mumbai or Goa or most parts of India these would become soft in less than an hour. Why? It's quite simply the weather and climate that dictates this.

To accommodate the climate and the impact it has on food and ingredients, people learn different techniques that are appropriate to help with the preservation of food so that it is not harmful when consumed. Hence, the reason for traditional meat dishes being fatty or oily – the fat layer on the top of the food was simply to create an air barrier to prevent bacteria from attacking. This, however, is not true of actual Indian cuisine or cooking. Oil is a precious commodity and therefore it is also wrong to assume that all Indian food is greasy. Some cooks and chefs find it easier to immerse chopped or sliced onions, which are the main base for most gravies, in excessive oil so as not to let them burn whilst cooking. This is an easier way to cook but not the best and the wisest, and definitely not representative of real Indian cooking.

Oil is still used extensively as a preservative for pickles, though it is not uncommon to use salt, vinegar or other acidic preservatives. Meat pickles in particular, such as those made with beef, venison or wild boar, prawns and other fish which are first salted and then pickled, mostly use oil as an extended preservative. The same applies in several other parts of the world, especially in tropical climes.

Creativity in every sense of the word when applied to culinary genius oozes evidence in the myriad products that line numerous shelves in supermarkets, shops and delis, local or imported from the far corners of the globe.

FRESHNESS AND ITS IMPORTANCE

Everyone always claims that the key to creating the best dishes when cooking is the raw material itself. This is not space science or a philosopher's quote, and it is the very basics of cooking. One has only to try cooking with stale or poor quality raw materials and it will soon be very clear which is superior. When the same food is prepared with fresh and superior quality raw materials the two appearances, textures and tastes are poles apart. The very best restaurants also naturally create the very best food simply because the chefs always only buy the very best ingredients.

This is naturally more expensive but is the corresponding reflective fame and popularity of the establishment enough for one to understand why?

Thus we know and understand that so far as it is possible to adhere to, we should use the freshest and best raw materials available to us. Nowadays the world over is realising the importance of organically and locally produced food and many are simply going back to the very basics preached and practised by our forefathers.

However, it is not always possible to obtain the freshest ingredients throughout the year or when we often need them most. This is where preserved, treated, frozen, chilled, sun dried, marinated alternative produce is used. Of course one has to learn to use them effectively for the best results. Using preserved and/or chilled/frozen raw materials cannot be the same as using fresh but if used well and intelligently the results can be quite rewarding.

One has to realise that many frequent diners can often tell the difference quite easily and the person using the raw materials needs to better his or her skill to create a product that is not only acceptable but also appreciated and enjoyed.

Man has therefore extended his skills and creativity to enhance the life of various products that cannot be made available due to seasonality or simply being from a different geographical region. This is so we can expand the horizons of those who create food for the many millions who may experience products from across the globe often not native to their part of the world.

The technologically and scientifically challenged create and invent equipment and techniques that transport, preserve, serve and make available products, sometimes beyond our wildest imaginations. The ever-demanding and hungry world is forever looking for new products to work with from distant lands and for those that they may otherwise only have obtained in their individual seasons. This, however, leads the creators of the food within the various cuisines of the world to get enthused and experiment and work with raw materials which are alien to their local cuisines.

Today in the UK almost all the vegetables and raw materials from throughout the Indian sub-continent are made available. One simply has to know where to find them. Each community within this diaspora is eager to create and bring to their dining tables food that they know of from their homelands and making this possible are the various importers who source these for them.

In Kenya, for example, the Indians grow those vegetables that their community demand in the UK and export them to a demanding public. Climatically Kenya is akin to India and almost all the vegetables that many need can be grown and exported. For example, the simple curry leaf that the Gujarati, Keralan, Tamil, Maharashtrian and other central and southern Indian communities need for their cooking is grown

extensively in Kenya and imported into the UK. Indians love the tiny yet slim okra and this is also imported from Kenya. Likewise there are several other products that are imported. In the UK this now applies not only to Indian, but also to Thai, Chinese, Malaysian, Indonesian, Vietnamese and Turkish foods etc. You name it, the UK's got it. I simply cannot name them all.

I have noticed we often get certain raw materials, especially some spices, of better quality here than in our own country, since only the best gets exported.

This has led to the UK today being at the very centre of the world's finest cuisines and some of the best restaurants of any cuisine in the world are found not surprisingly in the UK. Often the leading chefs of the UK today are in the forefront of creativity and ingenuity and it is not surprising that this is so.

So much is at our disposal that I often get giddy from over excitement at the wealth of raw materials that I want to simply play with and create with and only time bars me from doing so. Every so often when I visit the markets I get carried away like a small child who has seen or been presented with the toys of his or her dreams and often end up buying things I may not even use before their time is up.

This richness and variety that the UK now enjoys extends our horizons and makes us all the more aware of the diversity that our world has to offer. It makes us more creative and experimental. It makes all of us more discerning and by experimenting, we acquire a taste for more exotic and complex flavours.

This could not have been dreamt of even in the wildest imaginings of our forefathers but science and constantly improving and modernising technology have helped us to perhaps understand the world a little better, besides learning more about the foods and habits of other cultures from across the universe.

Fresh, preserved and frozen and chilled foods such as meats, seafood, vegetables and fruits, etc., are flown across the world in specially designed aircraft holds and containers to be received in a perfect state hundreds and thousands of miles away. The Japanese in their quest for fresh live seafood, for example, developed a finely tuned science of injecting just the perfect amount of liquid nitrogen into the brains of lobsters from the USA. This process numbs the brain, putting the lobster into a virtual yet harmless coma, thereby needing less oxygen to breathe as well as preventing stress and fatigue. Across the Pacific in Tsukiji market in Tokyo, increasing their temperature revives the lobsters and, allowing the nitrogen to dissipate, the lobsters are now flapping about and alert as they were when they left the US coast.

This is another example of how we have become more creative with the huge wealth of raw materials at our disposal, using the myriad of

ingredients that we have never cooked or worked with before. It not uncommon to see previously unknown names of dishes not native to the country or the surrounding regions on the menus of restaurants and hotels where the chefs have taken time to work out finely tailored recipes to satisfy an ever-increasing public demand.

FAMILY HEIRLOOMS

The sub-continent of India is rather a strange place in so far as its culinary heritage goes. In European and other cuisines of the world the changes in styles of the same food may differ slightly from region to region; in India this may change drastically and even change within a few miles. So much is the variation sometimes that the same product cooked and called by the same name could be totally different from its namesake in another region.

Food habits, cooking styles, recipes, methods and blends change from house to house and most definitely within the same community even. How often do we see the veritable potato, almost the whole of the country's staple vegetable, cooked in a million different ways? So much is the variation that recipes are difficult even to log or may lead to volumes for just one simple dish. An Indian woman or chef will instantly dispute one recipe as not being the right one as theirs is different and the way they were taught and brought up to prepare that dish was different. Both are right, however, and both have the same intense affection for each variation.

Most recipes and methods often go unlogged and sometimes great recipes are lost. It is the pride and honour of each new bride to come to her new home fully trained and well versed in the skills of domestic cooking. Therefore much is passed on from mother to daughter; often

whether out of a lack of interest or with only sons in the family some recipe heirlooms get lost as they are seldom if ever documented.

Some families treat their recipes as heirlooms and it is with great reverence that a family's culinary secrets are maintained and the dishes spoken of in social circles.

So secretive are some that they will never divulge the secrets of their valuable combinations or special blends or just the recipe itself. Most preparations do have an overlapping commonality, but there are always some differences and this is one major reason why certain recipes cannot be stereotyped or treated as common. A simple potato bhaji, for instance, may sound straightforward and easy,

but look deeper into it and in the various regions you will uncover 100 different preparations for the same dish.

Perhaps this is one reason why in the realm of Indian cookery authors, it was the women who first became known as food writers. Books were cheaply printed in paperback in monochrome and were created more like textbooks rather than recipe books. This was simply because no money was put into books, the authors were unknown women though excellent cooks in their own right, and quite simply every household had their own culinary styles and skills and books were not so popular.

It was easy to look at 20 different books, pick out the same name for a dish and discover that none of the recipes compared like for like. This goes on to prove the sheer diversity in the cooking. It was the advent of the working woman that prompted authors and publishers to go for the more glamorous books to attract the discerning and the adventurous cook. Women in the household were curious to learn the different cultures of the sub-continent and its multitude of cuisine styles, and cookery books began to gain popularity. The increase in non-vegetarian diners also led to the need to learn to cook different foods, meats, etc.

People moving from region to region for work or business often absorbed a bit of the local culture or style and adopted other forms of cooking into their day-to-day menu. This also helped to add further diversity to the style of cooking and dishes learnt or adapted became a part of the family's style of cooking and dining.

Yet it is impossible to understand Indian cuisine as a whole or in its entirety or for that matter for any individual to claim total authority on the sub-continent of India and its multifaceted cuisines. The depth, the intricacies, the variations and the complexities of each region make that a rare probability. Perhaps one reason why families are so protective or possessive with their own recipes and styles is a fear of their individuality being tainted or lost.

For instance, several of the spice combinations I use today in my day-to-day preparations are from combinations from my mother-in-law's family as well as those made by my grandmother and one other great aunt. Her mother as well as her mother-in-law's family influenced my mother's combinations. Yet I know that I have lost innumerable traditional dishes and will never know them. It is sad that some dishes that are part and parcel of the community's classical cuisine structure will be lost forever due to modern living and demands on time and other constraints. Sadly, my being in the UK will make it more difficult to approach elderly women who knew the basics of some of the food of our forefathers.

Some heirlooms are lost, some are not, some will go astray naturally through the process of migration and modernisation and sadly future members of a family may never know the intricacies of the cuisine of their very own family. In our own household, for instance, we are guilty of not cooking much traditional food and our children may not learn to eat the food we ate as children and enjoyed so much.

But even today in thousands of households throughout the sub-continent there are those dishes handed down from mother to daughter that have been going for centuries and it is good to see that this still exists. Family heirlooms need not necessarily be wealth in monetary terms but in the culinary styles of their heritage. It would easily take a chef like me a few hundred years to understand the diverse culinary arts of the sub-continent.

MENU PLANNING AND BALANCING

Menu planning is a term commonly known to all and most certainly a very crucial part of our eating habits and health too. We all speak of a well-balanced menu, but what would that mean to each one of us?

For one thing 'balancing' means that the menu flows into each course without the need for repetition. It means that the menu has to be designed in such a way that the food cooked and presented is not overwhelming either to the senses or to the body physically.

It means that the creator of the menu and the food knows and understands the intricacies of the food being prepared. It means the creator understands the nutritional value of the food and also realises that overlapping flavours, over spicing, for instance, or flavouring or colouring or dominance of any one flavour, will destroy the food completely.

These are general and understood by all good chefs. It is also one of the things we all learn in catering schools, but do not always practise. What does it mean to Indian cuisine? Is it also practised in the domestic domain?

Balancing is very important in a cuisine that could swing in the wrong direction totally and cause all sorts of complications for the family. For instance, the women in the household will never cook two pulses at any one meal. Pulses, being highly flatulent, can in excess cause indigestion and acidity. Therefore if a lentil is prepared for the main course, care should be taken to ensure that ingredients such as chickpeas, beans, etc., are omitted in the starters. Too much fat is taboo and so there is always only one or at best two fried items and these may be eaten to begin the meal, with some condiment such as chutney or a pickle or a dip. Vegetables and meats are carefully planned so that they compliment one another instead of opposing each other in their make up and properties.

The mainstay of diets across several communities of the sub-continent is rice, though even this has to be well planned. Depending on the contents of the rest of the meal a woman in the household or the chef decides what preparation will go best with the food so that not only is the preparation healthy but the diners are satiated and satisfied.

One therefore must take great pains to see that the menu is reflective of all these properties. Often the balancing flavours go in contradictory

fashion. If, for instance, you have a rather hot or powerful starter, then the main course has to be easier on the palate, such as a medium spiced curry with rice or some thinner version of a lentil with some accompaniment, which can lend to the total experience.

This no doubt comes with more experience, but so long as one looks at the menu before presenting it or producing the food and tries to understand the physical make up and composition of the food, there is no reason why even a novice cannot find the right balance.

Masalas and Soups

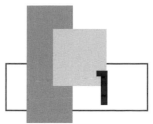

1

WHAT IS A MASALA?

A masala is a combination of spices, condiments and herbs, puréed, blended or mixed together to form a basis for any preparation. In short if you were to mix two or three ingredients such as ginger, garlic and cumin it would become a masala. If there is no specific recipe or methodology to follow and the blend is entirely your own, you have created your own masala.

In Indian cooking we make several different kinds of masalas for several different gravies, curries and items.

If you were to say the word 'Masaledar' it would mean full of masala. In this case a preparation might have all fresh ingredients such as green chillies, coriander, ginger, garlic and maybe cumin and other whole spices such as cinnamon, cardamom and cloves. In India a chicken tikka masala does not exist as it is seen and known of in the UK. If I was in India and you were to ask me for a chicken tikka masala, I would cook it with a masala exactly like I mentioned earlier in this paragraph, dry and tasty, but with the inclusion of chopped tomatoes and some garam masala.

Garam Masala

Chefs Notes

Quite simply this translates as hot masala.

- A garam masala is purely used for its flavouring properties and last minute taste giving in most cases. It is not a masala with which you can cook to make gravy, a sauce or a curry. It consists of whole spices such as cinnamon, cardamom, cloves, peppercorns, cumin, black cardamoms, nutmeg, mace, star anise and in some instances coriander seeds and a mix match of others.

- Most chefs have their very own recipe, which they guard intensely but in every instance the spices have to be roasted slowly in a slow oven or on top of one, or in a frying pan until they are crisp and dry. This is then powdered and stored in airtight jars away from direct light for use as required.

Measurements	Ingredients
1	Nutmeg, crushed coarsely
10–12	Green cardamom
10–12	Cloves
2–4 5 cm pieces	Cinnamon
2 level tbsp	Cumin
2–3	Black cardamom
3–4 flowers	Mace
2–3	Star anise
6–8	Black peppercorns
4–5	Bay leaves, crushed

- Use an equal quantity of all with the exception of peppercorns, nutmeg and star anise as a quarter. A little extra cumin may be used for quantity.

- To make garam masala for your home, I recommend you make just enough to fill a small jar. Garam masala will deteriorate over a period of time, but for best results keep the jar in the refrigerator.

Method

1. Roast all the ingredients gently as described in the Chef's Notes and pound to a fine powder. Alternatively, grind in a small grinder or coffee grinder and store in an airtight container.

   Use as desired but never use too much.

2. Garam masala is primarily a flavouring and should be used as one, to assist in making the dish prepared better. It is not good generally with fish and vegetable dishes.

You will often see the term masala used in this book. It simply refers to the items required for grinding, puréeing or blending as required by each individual recipe.

Fresh chutney, for example green chutney, is also a masala. You can eat this in its raw state as it does not need to be cooked. The chutney acts as a condiment to assist in completing or enhancing a product. This does not mean that the chutney cannot be used as a base for a curry, it can and that lends to its versatility. An example of this would be the green coconut chutney. If well puréed and smooth, this could make a good green curry.

Places such as the sub-continent of India, Malaysia, Thailand, Indonesia, Philippines, Myanmar and many others all use masalas in one form or another for their very own regional and classical cuisines.

The term masala is Indian and may therefore not apply to all the above but it is the methodology and the traditions behind it that dominate various cuisines. Many of these cuisines no doubt have had some Indian influence in their cultures, Buddhism and Hinduism being the prime reasons for the crossover of cultures.

In Thai cuisine, for instance, we see the very wide and similar use of masalas just as in Indian regional cuisines and this has a direct reflection on the heritage of both religious cultures.

Malaysia and Singapore too have a reasonably large south Indian population and this has influenced some of the cooking styles. In the West Indies or in Mauritius it is common to see the word masala used with chappaties and parathas. This once again is the domicile Indian population who over the years have influenced the local cuisine.

It is therefore important to realise that there may be hundreds of different masalas varying in composition, heat levels, flavours, textures and so on. Each region in the sub-continent, for instance, would have several masalas to boast of even though there may be one hugely popular dish for which the region may be known.

Chaat Masala

Chef's Notes

- This masala has been discussed at various times in the book. It also comes under the chaat section on snacks.

- This is a powder and a recipe on the composition may help you to understand the composition. However, it is easiest to buy the ready mixes.

Method

1. Place the cloves, cardamom, cinnamon, snipped red chillies, peppercorns and coriander seeds in a frying pan and roast very gently until lightly changed in colour and crisp.

2. Do not keep the heat high as it will sear the spices and they will burn thereby destroying the masala.

3. Powder all the spices and blend with the salt and the mango powder (aamchur).

4. Taste and use as desired.

5. Place in a airtight container for use when required.

6. This will last up to six months in a decent container.

7. Finely ground pomegranate seeds can be substituted for dry mango powder, though it will give a slightly different texture.

Measurements	Ingredients
4–6	Cloves
6–8	Cardamom
5 cm piece	Cinnamon or cassia
3–4	Red chillies (large)
8–10	Black peppercorns
1½ heaped tbsp	Coriander seeds
1–2 tsp powdered	Rock salt (Indian)
100 g	Dry mango powder

Chicken Masala for Biryani

Chef's Notes

- Normally for this type of biryani a 1:1 ratio of rice to meat is necessary, therefore approximately ½ kg of rice should be boiled until almost cooked but not fully.

- When boiling the rice add a few bay leaves to the water for flavour.

- When finishing the biryani there are two options. One is to blend the meat with the gravy and rice and allow it to cook a bit longer until cooked.

- The original method is to arrange alternate layers of the rice and the chicken and then to bake in a slow oven for one to two hours at least.

- As this may not be possible in bulk cooking the first method is more appropriate.

- Care of course has to be taken to ensure that blending is done carefully.

Measurements	Ingredients
500 g	Sunflower or rapeseed oil
50 g	Cinnamon
25 g	Green cardamom
20 g	Black cardamom
10 g	Cloves
5 g or 10 leaves	Bay leaf
10 g	Mace
10 kg	Onions (sliced)
50 g	Salt
100 g	Coriander (chopped)
100 g	Fresh mint
14 kg	Chicken (diced)

Method

1. Heat the oil and add the whole spices.

2. When swollen and browning add the sliced onions.

3. When brown add the puréed red chilli, ginger and garlic (purée 1), sauté for a few minutes and add the puréed yoghurt, tomato and brown onions (purée 2). Cook slowly until the gravy is rich looking and thick.

4. Check seasoning, add the fresh coriander and mint, simmer for 10 to 15 minutes and then add the chicken pieces. Cook until chicken is half done and remove to cool. (See Chef's Notes.)

Purée 1	Ingredients
150 g	Red chillies
150 g	Fresh ginger
150 g	Garlic
In as little water as possible	
Purée 2	Ingredients
3 kg	Yoghurt
5 kg	Tomato (chopped)
2 kg	Brown onions

Chôkelo Masalo

Chef's Notes

- This masala is cooked and used in many different ways as desired. It is Parsee in origin and can be used with vegetables, fish and poultry as well as meat and seafood.

- This masala can be used right away with poultry, fish and seafood. You may like to sauté the meat separately and add it to the masala, season with salt, add a touch of lime juice and some freshly chopped coriander.

- If using this masala at a later time you may wish to heat the masala and follow the process above. It tastes best with prawns or chicken though it is very versatile and you will see the colour, texture and taste change with every type of meat that you use.

- It is ideal to use with courgettes, French beans, other marrow, pumpkin, squash, fresh Swiss chard, spinach, okra and so on. It is not the best masala for potatoes but goes extremely well with cooking apples or the famous British Johnagold apples.

- A touch of lime and chopped fresh coriander gives it that extra oomph which I like very much.

Measurements	Ingredients
30–40 g or a 5–7.5 cm piece	Ginger
6–8 cloves	Garlic
3 tbsp	Sunflower oil
5 cm piece	Cinnamon or cassia
2	Whole red chilli (snipped and seeded)
500 g	Onions (finely chopped/minced)
½ tsp	Ground turmeric
¾ tsp	Ground red chilli
1 tsp	Ground cumin
1 tbsp	Ground coriander
250 g	Tomato (diced with seeds and pulp)
As desired, can be avoided if it were cooked again.	Salt

Method

1. Wash and scrape the ginger. Put in a small grinder/liquidiser with the garlic and purée to a fine paste. A little water or oil may be added to help make the paste, though avoid making it watery.

2. Heat the oil in a casserole or saucepan until it forms a haze, but do not make it too hot.

3. Add the cinnamon or cassia bark and the red chilli and fry until the red chilli is darkened but not blackened.

4. Add the chopped onion and sauté on a medium heat until it is pale brown in colour. Stir regularly and do not allow it to stick to the bottom. Also do not raise the heat, as due to the small amount of oil used the onion will burn rapidly.

5. Blend the turmeric, chilli powder, cumin and coriander powders with a little water in a cup until it is the consistency of single cream. (This prevents the spices from burning or singeing and giving off a bitter taste.)

6. Add to the pan and sauté gently until the spices are cooked. This is possible when the oil begins to get released at the edges of the pan.

7. As soon as that happens add the tomato and simmer gently for 15–20 minutes. Your basic masala is now ready to be used immediately or chilled for use at a later time.

Curry Masala

Chef's Notes

- This masala is primarily used for fish and shellfish. It is Goan in origin but with a few regional variations, simply because it is not possible to do several masalas that may have a few basic variations. It is no doubt a great masala and is very versatile.

- Whole grated coconut can also be used. This is the norm in India but it is possible to get a good texture with either coconut cream powder or coconut cream liquid. You will need a litre of water to grind the spices down really well and smooth.

- If Kashmiri chilli is not available look for a larger type of dry red chilli.

- Tamarind pulp can be extracted if ready-made pulp is not available. To extract the pulp you will need to form a ball with the tamarind approximately the size of a tennis ball. Break it up into a bowl and pour approximately one teacup of boiling water and allow it to soak for at least 40–60 minutes. Squeeze out the pulp and strain before use.

- The cinnamon is optional and is not always necessary. However, when using strong shellfish such as crabs or mussels it is a pleasant addition.

- Sautéing the masala is not always a must. It can also be added and then thinned down to cook. However, sautéing gives it a richer taste.

- If sautéing the masala then cook until it is dehydrated by more than half.

- Remember that the masala will stick so ensure continuous stirring and scraping of the bottom.

- Curry leaves are available quite commonly in the UK today.

Method

1. In a blender or food processor purée the chillies, coriander seeds, cumin, garlic, ginger, turmeric and coconut to a fine smooth paste with 1 litre water.

2. Heat the oil in a casserole then sizzle the cinnamon/cassia and fry for 1 minute.

3. Add the sliced onion and green chilli and sauté until the onions are soft and pale.

4. As soon as the onions are ready add the masala and sauté for a few minutes. Stir continually to prevent sticking.

5. Add the remaining water, the cokum (broken into quarters), the tamarind pulp and the curry leaves and bring to the boil. (There is no English name for cokum though in India it is often referred to as butternut berries.)

6. Add salt to your desired taste and the tomato and simmer for 10–15 minutes at least.

7. Remove and chill or get ready to cook your choice of meat in the curry.

8. For seafood or shellfish either quick pan fry the fish or shellfish and then add to the curry or add them in directly. If using shellfish such as crab it is better to sauté them.

9. Tomato is optional and you may add these entirely at your discretion.

Measurements	Ingredients
15–20 g or 5–6	Dry Kashmiri chilli
1 or 2	Green chilli (slit and seeded)
20 g (2 tbsp)	Coriander seeds
1 tsp	Cumin seeds
20 g (4–6 flakes)	Garlic
5–10 g (12 mm piece)	Ginger
1 level tsp	Turmeric
500 g tin or powder	Coconut
2 litres	Water
2 tbsp	Sunflower or rapeseed oil
5 cm piece	Cinnamon or cassia
1 medium	Onion (sliced)
3–4	Cokum/kokum (soft)
2 tbsp thick pulp. Ready made is OK	Tamarind
6–8	Curry leaves
As desired	Salt
1 medium	Tomatoes (large dice)

East Indian Curry Masala

Chef's Notes

- This quantity will make 8–10 portions.

- The East Indian community of the West Coast of India is mostly Roman Catholic. Converted to Christianity they still carry with them certain customary masalas and spice blends, which also make their cuisine unique.

- In Mumbai there is a tiny village that has remained untouched for centuries. Though I have not had the pleasure I believe there is a traditional East Indian restaurant there too.

- This, like most sub-continental masalas, would be ground on a stone and the smoothness of the grind is definitely better. However, if you use a good blender you will get a reasonably good result though you may have to add more water than desired.

- To use this masala you will have to sauté it again in a little oil until cooked before adding any meat. Coconut extract will need to be added to the curry when finishing the dish.

Method

1. Heat the oil in a large frying pan or wok until just hot.

2. Add the onions to the frying pan, stirring occasionally until soft. Do not allow them to burn; a pale colour is acceptable. Reduce the heat.

3. Add the garlic and sauté until pale.

4. Cool and blend all the ingredients and grind to a smooth paste.

Measurements	Ingredients
3–4 tbsp	Oil
1 large	Onion (thinly sliced)
3 cloves	Garlic
3 tbsp	Coriander seeds
½ tsp	Cumin seeds
¼ tsp	Fennel seeds
¼ tsp	Turmeric powder
3–4	Cloves
less than ¼ tsp	Fenugreek seeds
¼ tsp	Mustard seeds
10–12	Black peppercorns
¼–½ medium sized	Red pepper

Masala Scrambled Eggs (á la 'Hormuzd)

Chef's Notes

- This is a hot favourite with our kids, particularly the younger one, so much so that he introduced it to our neighbours who had never heard of a masala-scrambled egg. At 14 he has become an expert at making it and I have to admit he does a magnificent job with the consistency.

- This quantity will make 4 portions.

Method

1. Beat the eggs with the cream and add the coriander and salt and pepper to taste.

2. Melt the butter in a saucepan over a gentle flame and add the garlic and green chilli. Do not allow the garlic to discolour but let it become a very pale golden colour.

3. Sauté gently for 1–2 minutes then pour in the egg mixture.

4. Stir slowly and continuously on a low to medium flame until the egg begins to thicken.

5. Lower the heat and cook slowly stirring all the time until the egg has reached a soft clotted consistency. Do not overcook the egg.

Measurements	Ingredients
6–8	Free range or organic eggs
2 tbsp	Thin single cream (alternatively use full fat breakfast milk)
½–1 tbsp	Fresh coriander (chopped)
to taste	Salt/pepper
2 tbsp	Butter (softened)
2 cloves	Garlic (chopped)
1 small or half	Green chilli (finely minced)

6. Remember that the egg is the last thing to be cooked so prepare any bacon, sausages, toasts or bread before you start.

7. For best results pour out the egg into a dish and serve immediately.

Masala Ma Tatraveli Kaleji

Chef's Notes

*   Chicken livers have always been much liked by Indians and several preparations exist. This is a quick one and has a certain Parsee hint to it, though it could just as easily be influenced by Mumbai's Muslim cuisine. The same preparation can be applied to chicken hearts or a combination of both.

*   This method can be used for lamb and veal livers. When using meat livers dice them small so that they cook fast.

*   Liver can also be cut, cleaned and soaked in milk for a few hours before cooking. This often removes the smells associated with liver.

*   Unlike in the UK liver is treated as a delicacy in India and elsewhere it is enjoyed by several communities in various forms. This is just one such method but quite foolproof and guaranteed to please.

Method

1. Clean, wash and cut the chicken livers into halves or smaller.

2. Mix all the ingredients except the coriander, mint, salt and oil and rub into the livers.

3. Heat a heavy bottomed frying pan, add the oil, bring to smoking point and flash cook the livers for 4–5 minutes if you do not like them a bit pink. Do not over stir. The livers should be tossed with the pan or stirred gently with a wooden spatula, keeping the heat high at all times.

4. When cooked add the chopped coriander and mint, check the seasoning and serve.

5. A good mix of fresh mint and coriander makes the liver taste better and you may like to add an extra dash of lemon. My mother would add a very generous amount of both.

6. Serve with soft scrambled eggs and toast or with hot chappaties.

Measurements	Ingredients
250 g	Chicken livers
2.5 cm piece	Ginger (finely chopped or minced)
4–6 cloves	Garlic (finely chopped or minced)
1 large	Green chilli (finely minced)
1/4 tsp	Turmeric powder
1/2 tsp	Cumin powder
1/2 lemon	Lemon juice
2 tbsp	Oil
2 tbsp	Fresh coriander (chopped)
1 tbsp	Fresh mint (chopped)
As desired	Salt

Baffado Masala

Method

1. Roast the red chillies, peppercorns, cumin, cloves and cassia very gently in a frying pan until toasted and crisp.

2. Add the roasted masala to a blender with the ginger, garlic and turmeric, and purée to a fine paste by adding the palm vinegar. You may need to add some water if the paste becomes too thick, but add a little at a time and only as much as is required to allow the machine to grind.

3. Heat the oil in a casserole until a haze forms on the top then add the green chillies.

4. Allow to sizzle for half a minute or so and add the sliced onions. Sauté on a medium flame or heat until the onions turn light brown.

5. Add the puréed masala and sauté until the oil begins to be released again. When cooking the masala all the oil will be absorbed and the masala will stick on the bottom of the pan. The masala will be cooked when you see the oil released on the edges. Add a little water if necessary to deglaze the pan.

Measurements	Ingredients
75 g	Red chillies mix (regular and Kashmiri)
1 heaped tsp	Peppercorns
3 tbsp	Cumin
15	Cloves
30 g	Cinnamon or cassia
100 g	Ginger
150 g	Garlic
2 tsp	Turmeric
150–200 ml	Cider preferably or palm or plain vinegar
250 ml	Sunflower or rapeseed oil
12–15	Green chillies (washed and slit)
1½	Onions (central root stub removed and thinly sliced)
2 kg	Coconut cream
100 g	Salt

6. Now add the coconut cream and salt. Stir and mix well then bring to the boil. The masala will now start to bubble and splatter so be careful. Stir constantly for 5–6 minutes with a wooden spatula.

7. This masala will thicken and while this happens it will stick at the bottom, therefore it needs to be scraped continually at the bottom.

8. When some oil is visible on the top it means that the masala is now beginning to cook through.

9. Now either remove the masala, cool and store it to be used later or add more water or stock till you get the right consistency for a thick curry.

10. Add sautéed diced chicken or prawns, simmer, check seasoning and serve.

Tandoori Malai Masala

Chef's Notes

- This masala is one of the mildest marinades for chicken tikka. It can also be used for whey cheese (paneer), fish, large prawns, etc. It is, however, quite rich and has a tendency to burn more rapidly when cooked in a tandoor. It is not entirely suitable for barbeques or open griddle cooking. However, it is very good if the meat is grilled in the oven. Malai means cream and this is exactly how the meat turns out too, rich and creamy.

Method

1. Place all the ingredients in a blender and purée to a smooth paste. (You may use whole ginger and garlic and purée instead of paste if necessary.)

2. Stir regularly so that all the ingredients get puréed.

3. Marinade the chicken or meat of your choice with the paste and leave covered in the refrigerator for 6–8 hours. Part-boiled broccoli or cauliflower florets also make an interesting grill item with this marinade.

4. Char grill on skewers, broil in a hot oven or skewer and char grill in the tandoor. It will take 4–6 minutes for the chicken to cook.

5. However, do remember that this chicken colours very rapidly and can even burn so care and observation is the key. Also the masala will burn rapidly and turn bitter if over exposed.

Measurements	Ingredients
30 g	Cashew nuts
30 g	Ground almonds
3–4 pods	Green cardamon
1–2 blades	Mace
10 g	Ginger paste
10 g	Garlic paste
100 g	Greek yoghurt
100 ml	Double cream
40 g	Cheddar cheese
1 tsp	Lime juice
1 level tsp or less	Salt
4 tsp	Oil

6. If the marinade is to be used at a later time, put it in a sealable bowl and place it in the refrigerator. It is advisable to add a bit more oil. The masala will not keep for more than five to six days before turning rancid.

Patia No Masalo

Chef's Notes

- The 'Patia' or patio as we Parsees generally call it, is an out and out Parsee dish. Patia is usually eaten on an auspicious occasion or for a celebration. It is normally never complete as a dish without its two partners, namely boiled or steamed rice and lentils. This dish is served with prawns as Dhaan Daar Nay Kolmi No Patio, which means 'Dhaan' the rice, 'Daar' the puréed lentils, and 'Nay kolmi no patio' the prawn patia.

- Served with this would be some hot and sweet chutney, deep fried papads (pappadums) and thinly sliced or finely minced onion salad. Recipes are a plenty, methods are many and tastes differ from house to house or generation to generation. Many Parsee women may refute my recipe as their mothers taught them differently. However, I go by my taste buds and how I picked up things from various excellent cooks including my mother, aunts and chefs I met on my long culinary journey.

Method

1. Lightly roast the Red Masala ingredients in a frying pan over a very low flame until all the ingredients become crisp.

2. Purée in a blender or grinder with cane or malt vinegar. Though cane vinegar is the right product it is not available across the globe and malt vinegar may be substituted. If storing this masala for future use then also use some oil, which acts as a preservative and prevents the masala from drying out.

3. Heat the oil in a 2–3 litre saucepan and add the curry leaves.

4. Once the spluttering stops add the aubergine dices and fry until dark brown. Stir frequently so that the dice are coloured on all sides.

5. Tilt the saucepan in one direction and allow the oil to drain well before removing the diced aubergine from the pan.

6. Let as much oil as possible drain from the aubergine then remove them into a strainer and allow them to drain further. This oil will be used again at the frying/sautéing stages.

7. Repeat the process for the red pumpkin dices then mix the two fried dices, which will also have the curry leaves in them.

8. Return the oil to the stove and add the onions and sauté until they are a deep golden brown.

9. Next add 2 heaped tbsp red masala purée and sauté well, stirring and scraping frequently from the bottom to prevent sticking.

10. Continue to cook until the absorbed oil is released back from the masala. This will be visible in a ring around the bulk of the masala and bubbling will slowly reduce.

Measurements	Ingredients
4–6 tbsp	Sunflower oil
10–12	Curry leaves
150 g	Aubergine (baingan) (diced)
150 g	Red pumpkin (diced)
500 g	Onions (chopped)
250 g	Tomato (chopped)
Approx. 500 ml	Water
200 g	Tamarind paste
150–200 g	Jaggery (raw cane sugar sold in bricks or little cones)

Red Masala	Ingredients
4–5 large	Red chillies (dry) (if in India use Kashmiri chillies)
1 tsp	Cumin seeds
2 tsp	Coriander seeds
5 cm piece	Ginger
5–6 cloves	Garlic
5 cm piece	Cassia (break into smaller pieces before roasting)
3–4	Cloves
3–4	Black peppercorns
3–4	Green cardamom
Cane vinegar	As required for puréeing

11. Once the masala is cooked add the tomatoes and water and keep simmering until the tomatoes are totally mashed and cooked.

12. Keep the pan covered during this process. Stir from time to time to prevent sticking at the bottom.

13. Once the tomatoes are blended in, add the tamarind paste and the jaggery. To make the tamarind paste soak the whole tamarind in a cup of boiling water and set aside for an hour or so. Squeeze the tamarind in your palm to extract the pulp. Pass it through a strainer and press with a wooden spoon to try to squeeze out as much pulp as possible.

14. Check the seasoning and add the aubergine and pumpkin dices.

15. If cooking prawns, allow the masala to simmer for a couple of minutes and then add the cleaned/washed and chilled prawns. (Prawns are best kept mixed with a little turmeric.)

16. Check for seasoning once again. The patia should be a bit sweet/sour and hot. Some like it hotter and this can be achieved by increasing the number of red chillies in the masala. When the patia is eaten with the bland daar and rice, that is when it stands out best.

Peri-Peri Masala

Although this masala, whose name actually represents a dish in itself, has Portuguese African routes it is the classic Goan red masala. It is one of the most versatile masalas in Goan cooking. It is equally useful with seafood as it is with other white meats including pork. It is not commonly used with red meats. It is most definitely a king among masalas and has proved its worth a million times over.

Method

1. Scrape and wash the ginger. Peel the garlic and slice both coarsely.

2. Break up the red chillies into pieces (remember to try to select the larger varieties as the small ones can be treacherous).

3. Place all the ingredients in a bowl deep enough to hold everything.

4. Pour over approximately 200–300 ml vinegar, cover tightly and set aside for at least 3–4 hours. Overnight is better. Occasional remixing is recommended to allow for all the ingredients to soak up.

5. Grind the masala either in an electric grinder or use a mortar and pestle. Make a smooth fine paste.

Measurements	Ingredients
150 g	Root ginger
150g	Garlic
100 g	Red chillies
1½ tbsp	Coriander seeds
2 tsp	Cumin seeds
2 5cm pieces	Cinnamon
5–6	Peppercorns
As required	Palm vinegar or cider

6. If using a blender you may need more vinegar, therefore add only a little at a time so as not to make the paste watery. (Once stored the paste will automatically thicken as it dehydrates.)

7. Some oil when puréeing is also recommended if you aim to store the masala rather than use it immediately. The oil will prevent it from drying out and caking up.

Continued

8. This paste will keep indefinitely in the refrigerator if kept in a jar. Avoid using a metallic lid unless it has a good plastic lining. An old-fashioned glass jar with a rubber ring is the best.

9. After using what you need wipe the edges of the jar clean with a dry kitchen towel or tissue. Then pour a spoon of oil over the top or blend some in as suggested above. This will prevent it from oxidising too rapidly and drying out.

10. If it does look or go dry, add a little vinegar to revive it from time to time. Ensure that you wipe the sides clean with a tissue each time the level drops.

11. This masala will appear from time to time in the book therefore use as directed.

Green Chutney

Also a Masala for Fish or Chicken

• See also page 241 for an alternative recipe.

Method

1. Clean and wash the coriander and the mint well. Use the stalks and the top of the roots but wash well and remove any sand. The best way for this is to soak in cold water, agitate a bit to loosen the sand or soil and then lift the stalks off. If you pour into a colander or drain, the sand will remain at the bottom.

2. Scrape the ginger and cut coarsely.

3. Put all the ingredients in a blender or liquidiser, and purée to a fine paste, adding a little water at a time if needed to keep the blades of the machine cutting. Do not over water and make the masala thin.

4. It is better to scrape the sides with a plastic spatula and mix the contents of the grinding jug each time, than to allow the masala to thin.

Measurements	Ingredients
250 g	Fresh coriander
100 g	Fresh mint
30 g	Fresh ginger
20 g	Green chillies
30 g	Garlic
20 g	Coriander seeds
10 g	Cumin
30 g	Tamarind paste
30 g	Salt
100 g	Sugar
100 ml	Fresh lime juice

5. If using this as a masala for marinating and pan frying fish, for instance, or chicken, do not add the sugar.

6. Add salt as desired. Remember that you may also salt the meat for marinating and therefore use wisely.

7. If this is used as a chutney you can use it exactly as it is or temper it or sizzle it for a deeper flavour and to make it last longer. This depends on the use and the accompaniment. Below is a simple sizzling recipe for the chutney.

Method

1. Heat the oil in a small frying pan or a very small saucepan, whichever allows the oil to be 1–2 mm deep.

2. Once hot and hazy add the mustard seeds and cover with a lid or mesh to allow them to crackle but not jump out of the pan.

3. Reduce the heat and as soon as the sputtering has lessened add the lentils, curry leaves, red chilli and cumin.

4. Stir gently with a wooden spoon or spatula until the lentil changes colour and you get a lovely nutty aroma.

Measurements	Ingredients
2 tbsp	Sunflower/ rapeseed oil
1 level tsp	Black mustard seeds
1 tsp	White urad lentil
6–8	Curry leaves (snipped)
1 large	Dry red chilli (snipped)
½ tsp	Cumin seeds
A decent pinch	Asafoetida (hing)

5. Add the asafoetida and almost straight away pour and add the 'tadka' sizzling directly into the chutney.

6. Stir well and set aside for use.

Hot Madras Curry Powder

Chef's Notes

- Perhaps this is not the most appropriate powder to be in a cookery book for Indian cuisine, as most traditional kitchens would not be using it much. However, it has several uses and is also hugely popular across the UK, which makes it a useful contender.

- Normally Madras curry powder would also have three other types of lentils as well as some unpolished rice. Since it is easier to grind split yellow peas and they give a good colour as well as being readily available we will have them as the only lentil in this masala.

Method

1. Snip the red chillies and roast them gently in a frying pan or a warm oven. The chillies need to be roasted and ground separately from the other ingredients.

2. Roast the remaining ingredients either in the pan or in the oven. Often the oven is a better environment for roasting spices, etc., since the atmosphere is controlled as well as the fact that the spices do not singe and burn if you do not either stir well or keep a constant heat.

3. Once roasted grind all the ingredients except the chillies to a fine powder.

Measurements	Ingredients
250 g	Dry red chillies
400 g	Coriander seeds
25 g	Cumin seeds
1 tsp	Black mustard seeds
¼ tsp	Fenugreek seeds
20 g	Black peppercorns
A pinch	Asafoetida
½ tsp	Turmeric
8–10	Curry leaves
150 g	Split yellow peas

4. Blend the powdered chillies into the powder and pass everything through a fine sieve

5. If there is a lot of residue grind the leftover coarse powder again and then pass through the sieve again until you have a good fine powder.

6. Mix well and store in an airtight container. This masala keeps very well for up to a year but it must not be left open and exposed to direct light. Use as desired.

Saambaar Powder/Masala

Chef's Notes

•   Saambaar is the lentil accompaniment to many south Indian snacks or midday meals. Saambaar can also be eaten on its own as a soup if you like, poured over rice as a lentil. The masala is used to flavour the lentil but it is useful to season vegetarian dishes and other lentils. If making a vegetable stew, for instance, add some Saambaar masala for good flavour. The Parsees make a similar powder for their Dhaansaak and only spell and pronounce it differently – Saambhaar.

Method

1. Dry roast the spices and lentils, except the red chillies in a slow frying pan or skillet.

2. Stir regularly to prevent discolouring or scorching them. Once the ingredients are done remove and cool.

3. Now slow roast the chillies in oil in the same frying pan or skillet. To do this, wipe the skillet with a paper towel to pick up any spice residue and add oil in the centre.

4. Heat the pan on a low heat and try to distribute as much of the oil around the pan as possible.

5. Add the chillies and with a flat wooden spoon stir them around to give them an even heat all round. The chillies must not be allowed to discolour, therefore temperature is very important.

Measurements	Ingredients
100 g	Toor Daal
8 tbsp	Coriander seeds
100 g	Channa Daal (Split yellow peas)
1 tbsp	Peppercorns
4 tsp	Fenugreek seeds
2 tbsp	Mustard seeds
1 tbsp	Turmeric
18–20	Whole red chillies (snipped in large pieces)
1 tbsp	Oil

6. Red chillies are particularly sensitive to heat and will scorch in an instant. Roast them for 5–6 minutes on a slow to medium heat and then switch off the heat but leave them in the pan. The heat will further roast them and also make them crisp.

7. Once cool blend the ingredients together and powder in a coffee grinder or the small attachment with your blender.

8. This powder will keep for months in the refrigerator.

9. Use as desired.

Maelecha Kari

Malayan Poussin Curry Parsee Style

Chef's Notes

- Just how this dish got into Parsee cuisine is a mystery, although at one stage several Parsee businessmen went to Malaysia, Singapore and China to trade and set up businesses. This recipe has most definitely been adapted to suit Parsee tastes and perhaps designed to impress local businessmen when being entertained in the house. The combinations are unique as it quite simply represents both cultures – the lemon grass and the cucumber or marrow for the Oriental culture and the whole spices for the Parsee element in the dish.

- In the traditional Parsee style the lemon grass was not ground but added whole and then removed once the chicken was ready to serve.

- Outside India lemon grass leaves are not sold but for a more pronounced flavour you can grind the lemon grass stalk.

- The curry may also be prepared on its own as a plain curry and then used with the meat of your choice. However, preferred are poultry and seafood.

- Dudhee is a kind of gourd or marrow. Sponge gourd can be substituted.

Method

1. Deseed the marrow or cucumbers and dice into small pieces. Immerse in water and set aside.

2. Clean the poussin and cut into small pieces.

3. Either grate the coconut and remove the milk or squeeze out the milk from the ready grated coconut. Alternatively use approximately 250–300 ml coconut cream.

4. Grind the salt, onions, kesar, chilli powder, ginger, garlic, lemon grass, cloves, cardamon and cinnamon to a fine paste in a grinder or on a stone.

5. Sauté this masala in the ghee in a deep saucepan until browned.

6. Add the poussin and sauté for 4–5 minutes, then add the cucumber or dudhee and the coconut milk and bring gently to the boil, stirring regularly so that the coconut milk does not curdle.

7. Remove when chicken is cooked.

Measurements	Ingredients
6 small cucumbers or 1 medium dudhee	Marrow or cucumber
1	Poussin
1 whole or ½ kg	Coconut (cleaned and grated)
1 tbsp	Salt
400 g	Onions
2½ g	Kesar (saffron)
1 tsp	Chilli powder
10 g	Ginger
2–3 cloves	Garlic
2 leaves	Lemon grass
4	Cloves
4	Cardamom
5 cm piece	Cinnamon
125 g	Ghee

Paanch Phoran

Chef's notes

- This combination of whole spices is extensively used in Bengal, which is the reason for its popularity in various Indian restaurants in the UK. Paanch Phoran or 'Phodan' as it may also be referred to is more often used in vegetable preparations rather than in meats. It is a simple composition but it packs a lot of flavour. However, care needs to be taken when using it as too much will destroy every other flavour, besides making the food bitter.

Measurements	Ingredients
100 g	Fennel seeds
50 g	Cumin seeds
100 g	Mustard seeds
15–20 g	Fenugreek seeds
50 g	Nigella

- Remember the balance of ingredients is vital, however, the two most critical components are the nigella and fenugreek and these should never be allowed to be in excess.

- Cumin and fennel are tolerable and will not overly flavour the food or destroy the flavours totally.

Method

1. Mix all the ingredients together well, put in a jar and keep for use as desired.

2. This combination is always sizzled or tempered first in hot oil before use and therefore roasting is not required.

Rasam

A Rasam is a light lentil-based soup popular across south India. There are several Rasams though the one common feature is the use of lentil as a base. There are Tomato Rasams, the straightforward Daal Rasam, Lime Rasam, Tamarind Rasam and so on. So as not to give too many recipes around one basic soup, I suggest you use your own imagination once you have acquired the skills to make a simple Rasam as shown below. Rasams are light and nutritious and very refreshing. The heat levels vary from place to place and they can be eaten as a meal with boiled rice added.

Method

1. Wash the lentils and boil them in the water with salt and turmeric until cooked thoroughly and soft.

2. Remove any scum that floats to the top, keeping the liquid clear.

Measurements	Ingredients
50 g	Split pink lentil
2 litres (approx.)	Water
1 tsp plus to taste	Salt
½ tsp	Turmeric powder
1 tsp	Tamarind paste

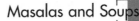

3. In a frying pan roast the spices for the masala gently and then pound or grind to a powder in a grinder.

4. Whisk the lentils to break them up or to purée them, then beat in the powdered masala and bring the liquid up to a simmer.

5. In a small frying pan add the oil for the sizzling. When the oil forms a haze and is hot add the mustard seeds till they stop crackling, then immediately lower the heat, add the red chilli and curry leaves and in a few seconds add this to the simmering Rasam.

6. To clear the pan you can add some soup to the pan, which will help to collect all the residue of mustard seeds or curry leaves and add it into the pot.

7. Next stir in the tamarind paste until it dissolves. Taste and serve.

8. For variations you can add some tomatoes at the beginning and crush them with the lentils or add some lime juice and reduce the tamarind a little only to prevent over souring.

Masala	Ingredients
2–3 large	Whole red chilli
1 tsp	Coriander seeds
½ tsp	Cumin seeds
4–5	Peppercorns
A decent pinch	Asafoetida
1 clove	Garlic
A few	Fenugreek seeds

Measurements	For sizzling/tempering
1½ tbsp	Sunflower oil
1 tsp	Mustard seeds
1 large	Red chilli (seeded and snipped)
8–10	Curry leaves (shredded)

9. Chopped fresh coriander may be added at the end for a different flavour as well.

10. Rasam may be garnished with rice, and tomato Rasam may also be served with a dollop of thick yoghurt.

Shorba è Subz

Springtime vegetable broth

Chef's Notes

• There are numerous quick and easy vegetable soups to prepare and recipes and styles will vary from household to household. However, much depends largely upon the local availability and produce. This is an easy and quick recipe involving fresh lemon grass or 'Hari chai ki Patti' as it is affectionately known, meaning green tea leaves, 'Subza' or holy basil and 'Pudina' or fresh spearmint leaves. The result is an intoxicating blend of flavours and aromas, enough to titillate even the most stubborn of palates. I would, however, urge the adventurous to use their own imaginations regarding use of ingredients. For argument's sake let's call this the Indian Tom Yam.

Method

1. Wash, clean, and prepare all vegetables. Bring the water to boil, add the sugar (optional) and salt and boil the peas until half done.

Measurements	Ingredients
1 litre	Water
1 tsp	Sugar (optional)
As desired	Salt
50–60 g	Fresh green peas
1 tbsp	Sunflower oil
1 tsp	Minced ginger
1/2 tsp	Minced garlic
2–3	Spring onions (thinly shredded)
50 g	Squash or marrow (peeled and sliced thinly approx. 12 mm wide and 20 mm long)
1 medium or 100–150 g	Carrots (shredded)
5–6	Runner beans (finely sliced). Slender French Beans can also be used
6–8	Gucchi mushrooms (or any other mushroom. Gucchi is what the French call Morelles and they are very expensive)
8–10 if in the Indian sub-continent: If not, use a couple of layers from one shoot cut into 5 cm pieces	Lemon grass blades
1 heaped tsp if thick otherwise adjust to your taste	Tamarind pulp
10–12 leaves	Tulsi or Subza (Holy Basil)
1 heaped tsp	Fresh coriander stalks (chopped and washed well)
5–6 leaves	Mint, finely shredded

2. Strain the stock into another casserole or pot and reserve. Cool the peas under cold running water so as not to discolour.

3. If necessary wash the pot in which the peas were boiled and return to the cooker.

4. Add the oil and heat until just hot enough to sauté the ginger and garlic without discolouring either.

5. Once both are pale in colour add the spring onions until just about sweated.

6. Now pour in the light green pea stock and bring to the boil.

7. As soon as it boils lower the heat so that it reduces to a slow boil and add the remaining ingredients except the basil and coriander.

8. Cook for a few minutes and then add the peas, the basil, shredded mint and coriander. Turn off heat and cover for 1–2 minutes for the flavours to infuse.

9. Taste the seasoning and serve hot after removing and discarding the lemon grass.

10. Alternatively add some boiled rice to the soup or even some rice vermicelli.

Pepper Water

Chef's Notes

- This is the classical south Indian soup although it is not commonly used or served in hotels and restaurants.

- Like most Indian food this is designed to have some medicinal implication. The spice combination, the use of garlic and the peppercorns, all make this a very useful soup when a person is feeling low, has a bad cold or flu and is designed for general well being. It is easy to prepare once you get the general hang of Indian cooking and the practice of roasting and grinding spices etc.

- This is the Hindu version of the classical 'Mullagtanni', meaning 'mullug', pepper, and 'tanni', water. The Anglo-Indian version is slightly different and can also differ from region to region. The anglicised 'Mulligatawny' has, however, become more famous.

Soup	Ingredients
1 litre	Water
¼ tsp	Cumin seeds
1 tbsp	Coriander seeds
6–8	Peppercorns
¼ tsp	Mustard seeds
A decent pinch	Asafoetida
6–8 cloves	Garlic
4–6	Shallots/Madras red onion (peeled and cut coarsely)
2 medium	Tomato (cut coarsely)
1 tbsp	Tamarind pulp
As desired	Salt

Method

1. Bring to the boil alll the soup ingredients and simmer for 10–15 minutes.

2. Purée and strain.

3. Heat the oil in a small frying pan and add the chilli, curry leaves and onion.

4. Sauté until the onions are lightly browned and add this to the soup.

5. Simmer for a few minutes and serve.

For sizzling/tempering	Ingredients
1½ tbsp	Oil
1–2 large	Red chilli
12–15 leaves (snipped)	Curry patta
1 small	Onion (sliced)

Sopa de Câmarao

Chef's Notes

- Prawn and potato soup flavoured with garlic. This soup is part of the Portuguese legacy on Goan cuisine. It is light and enjoyable and also allows the cook to make variations and adaptations to suit.

Measurements	Ingredients
500 g	Potatoes
500 g	Prawns (shell on)
6 cloves	Garlic
100 g	Butter
50 ml	Olive oil
1 medium	Onion (sliced)
1 litre	Stock or water
2 slender	Spring onions (very finely chopped)
To drizzle	Cream
To garnish	Parsley or coriander (chopped)
As accompaniment	Crisp melba type toast

Method

1. Peel, wash and roughly slice the potato.

2. Clean the prawns and save the shells. Wash the shells in running water and wash away any residual membranes, etc.

3. Dice the prawns into tiny pieces and place them in the refrigerator.

4. Peel and chop the garlic.

5. In a saucepan or small pot deep enough to hold ten portions of soup add the butter and olive oil and place over a medium flame until the fat begins to foam.

6. Add the garlic and sauté until pale. Do not let the garlic brown or discolour.

7. Add the sliced onion and continue sautéing until onions turn pale.

8. Add the prawn shells and sauté until well roasted and red, stirring all the time with a wooden spatula.

9. When the shells turn crisp add the potatoes, sauté for 1–2 minutes or until the moisture dries up a bit.

10. Add either a litre of stock or water. Retained rice water or vegetable stock can also be used. If using stock it is preferable to use chicken stock rather than seafood stock as the flavours will get confused and over pronounced.

11. Bring slowly to the boil and simmer until the potatoes are thoroughly cooked.

12. You may find that there is less liquid; in that case add more liquid. Often the age of the potato determines the absorption and more liquid may be required. However, it is best to add more liquid once the soup has been puréed, when you can judge the consistency better.

13. Purée the contents in a blender and strain to remove any gritty prawn shell fragments. If you prefer, remove the shells before puréeing.

14. Put the soup back on the cooker, check the seasoning and bring slowly to the boil. Simmer and add the prawns and spring onions, though the shells do impart a very good flavour.

15. Simmer for 1–2 minutes, check seasoning again and serve drizzled with cream and chopped parsley or coriander.

16. Serve with crisp toast or even a crusty roll.

17. A sprinkling of fresh crushed pepper gives this dish an added flavour.

18. Beaten egg may also be blended in at the very last simmering. This is traditional for Sopa de Câmarao and gives the soup a better body and texture. Do not over beat the egg but simply blend the yolk and white well. Too much beating will make the soup froth and you will have scrambled egg floating on the top.

Solkadhi/Sola Chi Kodi/Solkodi

Chef's Notes

• These three names for very much the same product represent the word 'curry' in every sense in their colloquial terms. However, the term 'soup' does not exist in Indian cuisine and therefore soup-like dishes are often referred to as 'Daals', 'Kodi', 'Kadhi' or 'Rasam' but these are mostly drunk and/or served as accompaniments to meals. They can be poured over rice and some can be eaten hot and some cold so they do not always conform to the description of a soup. This one, however, is made with cokum (kokum). Cokum is known to be very cooling and has several medicinal properties. It makes an excellent accompaniment to hot food. This recipe is part Goan, part Maharashtrian.

Method

1. Heat the water, bring to a boil and pour over the cokum in a bowl. Leave until cool.

2. When cool squeeze as much as possible out of the cokum into the water or, better still, whiz in a blender until the cokum is totally puréed.

3. Add the garlic paste to the blender and purée until fine.

4. Strain the cokum and garlic liquid into the coconut milk.

5. Season and taste. The taste will be a bit tart or sour but refreshing.

Measurements	Ingredients
500 ml	Water
6–8	Kokum/Cokum
1 tbsp	Garlic paste (fresh only)
500 ml (thinned with 200 ml water)	Coconut milk
As desired	Salt
2 tbsp	Fresh coriander (finely chopped)

6. Add the coriander, mix well and set aside for about an hour before drinking.

7. This is served cold. It can also be taken poured over rice, especially if someone has an upset stomach.

8. You can use either freshly grated coconut or frozen grated coconut, in which case you need to pour water into the coconut and purée it in the blender too. The liquid will have to be strained well as you do not want tiny bits of coconut in this. The appearance is that of a thin milk shake and the colour has a deep rose tint to it.

Gos No Soup

Lamb Broth Parsee Style

Chef's Notes

- Whereas there is no set tradition of soup drinking in the Parsee community, some soups are still made and more often than not these would be meat based. A combination of diced offal such as kidneys, liver, spleen and lungs also make a superb broth. These broths are great during the winter months and also act in providing strength during convalescence or when a person is suffering from a cold or flu. A final dash of crushed fresh pepper makes the soup more enjoyable.

Measurements	Ingredients
250 g on the bone	Lamb shoulder
2.5 cm piece	Ginger
4 cloves	Garlic
¼ tsp	Cumin seeds
1 tsp	Coriander seeds
¼ tsp	Turmeric
1–2 tbsp	Sunflower oil
1 medium	Onion (diced small)
1 litre	Water
1 medium	Carrot (diced)
1 medium	Potato (diced)
1 tbsp	Fresh coriander (finely chopped)
1 tsp	Lime juice
As desired	Crushed peppercorns
As desired	Salt

Method

1. Clean the lamb and cut the meat into tiny dice approximately 12 mm square.

2. Have the bones cut by the butcher into small pieces or simply break them into pieces. Wash the bones and drain well. Watch out for splinters.

3. Purée the ginger, garlic, cumin, coriander seeds and the turmeric in a small grinder/liquidiser with very little water to form a smooth paste.

4. Heat the oil in a casserole and add the bones, stirring occasionally to allow them to brown well.

5. Once the bones are adequately browned add the diced meat and sauté well on a high flame.

6. As soon as the liquid dries up add the onions and a little water to deglaze the pan.

7. Scrape the pan to remove all residues from the base and sauté the onions for 1–2 minutes.

8. Add the paste and sauté for a few minutes on low heat until you see bits of oil being released, which indicates that the masala is cooked. If at any stage the contents stick to the bottom of the pan add a little water to release the burnt residue.

9. Add the water and bring to the boil.

10. Lower the heat to a simmer and add the carrot and potatoes when the lamb is at least half cooked.

11. Cook until the lamb and vegetables are cooked.

12. Remove the bones and season the soup.

13. If serving immediately add the fresh chopped coriander, lime juice and crushed peppercorns. Taste and serve.

14. If serving later reserve the peppercorns, coriander and lime juice. This must always be added just before serving.

15. Also if serving later do not add the potatoes and carrot until the lamb is well cooked, and then cook them for only a few minutes until the potato dice are firm but not cooked fully. The vegetables will eventually cook in the latent heat of the soup and not discolour totally.

16. Serve with slices of thick toast or hot chappaties.

17. The same recipe may be applied when making a giblet soup.

18. If you get a lot of fat on the top of the soup, skim this off, as it is an irritant when drinking. Some lamb will produce more fat and this may need to be removed. A tip is to chill the soup, then remove the caked fat from the top, then reheat and serve.

Kaeri Nu Pannu

Chef's Notes

- As unusual as it may sound this particular soup is a digestive and is created specially for the ripe mango season when the heat is at its peak and the body needs to be cooled down. It is a great way to utilise one product to make two separate items. 'Kaeri nu Pannu' is made using the skin of squeezed ripe mangoes and the seeds or kernels with yoghurt and a few spices. It is very Gujarati in its origins and the delicate spicing is reminiscent of this culture. The Gujarati community makes great use of everything in season and can boast of some of the best vegetarian cuisine in the world.

- Since you will have to squeeze the juice of the mangoes to make this soup you may consider using it for a dessert, a lovely milkshake or even a home-made ice-cream. Or best, simply eat it with some hot fried poories or crisply fried flour tortillas.

- Remember to wash the fruit well from the outside before attempting to extract the juice. Also ensure that any sticky gum on the surface by the stem is removed.

Measurements	Ingredients
6–8 turned over	Ripe mango skins
6–8	Mango kernels or seeds
Water	1 litre
20 g (½ tbsp approx.)	Butter or ghee
½ tsp	Cumin seeds (coarsely crushed)
8–10	Curry leaves (snipped)
Asafoetida	A decent pinch
100–150 g	Yoghurt (organic live culture is best)
½ tsp	Powdered ginger
1–2 tsp	Sugar
As desired	Salt
4 leaves	Mint (finely shredded)

- The Indian Alphonso mango is the very best for this but other sub-continental Indian varieties are also very good. The South American/African and other mangoes will not work well as they lack the body, the flavour and the taste.

Method

1. Remove the pulp separately and keep depositing the skins and the seeds in a large bowl or casserole.

2. Add a litre of hot (not boiling or very hot) water to the skins and kernels and rub the water in. Try to loosen the remaining pulp clinging to the seeds and skins.

3. Soak for at least 1 hour so that more dissolves and the flavour builds up, then strain the liquid and reserve.

4. Add the butter or ghee to a casserole and heat. Do not let it burn if it is butter.

5. Add the crushed cumin seeds and sauté for a minute or so until it turns a deeper colour.

6. Add the curry leaves and asafoetida and after a few seconds the strained mango water and bring to a boil. Upon boiling bring it down to a simmer.

7. Beat the yoghurt with the ginger powder, sugar and salt and gradually whisk it into the simmering liquid. Increase the heat again to bring it back to the boil for about 20 minutes.

8. Serve hot. To make it more flavourful add a few leaves of finely shredded mint at the last minute.

Mulligatawny Soup/Mullugtanni Soup/ Mullugutwany Soup

Chef's Notes

• This soup has become by far the best known of all soups coming out of India. The recipes for this soup get very complicated as well and confusing. The hotels of India all have their own variations and it is not uncommon to see chefs arguing about whose recipe is best. What I have here is a combination of what we know to be soup prepared by us and since it is not a recipe that can be proclaimed as the only one, this one is open to imagination. The soup in India is not considered Indian as a rule because its origins have also been confused; it was created in India, however, but has too many Western influences.

• The word 'mullugtanni' actually means pepper water. In this chapter (page 21) we have also included a recipe for the classical pepper water.

Method

1. Wash the lentils well.

2. Heat the butter (preferred) or oil in a casserole and add cassia or cinnamon and after a few seconds the onions.

3. Sauté until the onions turn pale then add the ginger, garlic, lentils, tomatoes, potatoes, carrots, curry leaves and Madras curry powder and sauté for 4–5 minutes.

4. Now add the stock of your choice or water and some salt and bring gradually to the boil. Do not boil too briskly as it will begin to scum on the top. Any scum formed must be removed carefully.

5. As soon as it reaches the boil turn the heat down and simmer until the lentils are thoroughly cooked.

6. Cool briefly and liquidise the contents to a fine purée.

7. Wash the pan and add the puréed contents to it.

8. Gradually whisk in the coconut milk and return to the cooker.

9. Dilute if too thick but keep stirring as the coconut milk needs to be well mixed in and should not split.

10. Check seasoning and add the white pepper.

11. When it reaches the boil, add the rice, the chicken or lamb or even diced vegetables if you like, the lime juice and the chopped coriander.

12. If adding raw chicken remember that you may have to simmer for longer to allow the chicken to cook. If doing this add the rice soon after the chicken is cooked.

13. Taste and serve.

Measurements	Ingredients
20 g (or 2 tbsp)	Masoor or pink lentils
20 g (or 2 tbsp)	Toor or yellow lentils
100 g	Butter or oil
5 cm piece	Cassia or cinnamon
1 small	Onion (sliced)
2.5 cm piece	Ginger (sliced)
4–6 cloves	Garlic (sliced)
200 gms	Tomatoes (cut coarsely)
100 gms	Potatoes (sliced thick)
1 small	Carrot (sliced thick)
10–12	Curry leaves
40 g (see page 15)	Madras curry powder
1–1½ litre	Lamb, chicken or vegetable stock or water
200 g	Coconut milk
A pinch or two	White pepper powder
For garnish	Boiled rice
4–6 tbsp for garnish	Chicken or lamb (diced) (pre-cooked if lamb and or using the stock)
½ lime	Lime juice
1 heaped tbsp	Fresh coriander (chopped)
As desired	Salt

Môr

Chef's Notes

- Across south India this cold yoghurt (buttermilk) meal accompaniment (pronounced 'moore') differs in its style and recipe, though the principle remains the same. It is meant to enhance and aid better digestion and must be taken cold. It is easy to prepare. The Hindus and Keralan Syrian Christians both have their own unique styles. Here we will stick to the Hindu version. I am classifying it as a soup because it is one if had on a hot summer's day either with the meal or before or after. This is very much like other South East Asian cultures, where a soup need not necessarily indicate the beginning of a meal. Buttermilk is available ready made these days. However, thinned low fat yoghurt, of the consistency of a milk shake, will also suffice. Buttermilk is simply the milky water derived from churned full fat yoghurt or cream after the butter is removed.

Measurements	Ingredients
¼ tsp	Cumin seeds
¼ tsp	Fennel seeds
¼ tsp	Black peppercorns
1500 ml	Buttermilk
1 small	Onion (finely minced)
1 medium	Green chilli (seeded and very finely minced)
4–6 leaves	Fresh mint (finely shredded)
1 tbsp	Fresh coriander (finely chopped)
1 tsp or as desired	Salt

Method

1. Place the cumin, fennel and peppercorns in a small frying pan and roast them very gently on a slow heat. Take extreme care not to burn them. Roast only until the aromas come wafting through.

2. Powder them in a mortar or in a coffee grinder.

3. In a large bowl mix or whisk in all the ingredients together and season.

4. Chill well and serve in small glasses or cups.

5. A ¼ tsp turmeric powder may also be added to taste. This is good for the overall effect but does alter the flavour a bit.

Chaats and Starters

2

'Chaat' quite simply means lick in Hindi, Gujarati and a few other Indian languages. Chaats are basically finger foods or light salads that are eaten cold and vary at different times of the year.

Chaats are simple to make and use very few ingredients, unless you are going in for something complicated.

The normal chaat masala consists of three main ingredients. These are: dry mango powder known as 'aamchur'; black salt or 'kaala namak' as it is known in Hindi. This is a form of rock salt. It is deep purple in colour when in its rock form and is also used in medicinal applications, though largely as a digestive; and Jeera or cumin powder.

Other ingredients are added through taste and can often vary, though red chilli powder is the most common. Your best bet is to buy the ready made packets, which give you these products balanced and packed conveniently.

The only difference is when purchasing certain varieties, which can sometimes be a bit hot so please check before using, or ask the shop-keeper or learn from experience. Chaat masala is also very useful when cooking several dry vegetable preparations.

Aloo Chaat

Chef's Notes

- The best known of Indian chaats is very simple to make.

Method

1. Place all the ingredients in a bowl and toss lightly until well blended with the masala. Taste and add more masala if needed.

2. Serve as it is or with beaten yoghurt and some crisp small poories (see page 226) if serving it as a starter.

3. One must remember that chaat masala should be added only at the very end. Never blend the masala and keep the salad for later use.

Measurements	Ingredients
1 large or 2 medium	Boiled potatoes (diced small)
1 small	Onion (finely minced)
1 medium	Green chilli (finely minced)
1 tbsp	Fresh coriander (chopped)
1	Tomato (chopped) (use plum type to avoid liquids)
1 tsp or more as desired	Chaat masala (see pages 3–4)

Variations

- You may like to add some fruit to it such as diced apple, banana or melon.

- Take crispy poories or deep fry flour tortillas cut into small pieces, crush lightly and blend into the chaat just before serving.

Channa Chaat

Method

1. Use boiled chickpeas instead of potatoes and proceed as per the method for Aloo Chaat or blend both. Crush the chickpeas a little with a fork before blending.

Cashew Nut Chaat

Method

1. Use roasted cashew nuts and proceed as per the method for Aloo Chaat. You may take as many as you like or take half cashew and half potatoes. If you like fresh mint then a few leaves snipped into tiny bits and added will make a pleasant change.

To make your own roasted cashew nuts

Method

1. Take the cashew nuts and put them in a steel or glass bowl.
2. Pour over boiling water and allow them to soak for 1–2 minutes. Drain and allow them to dry in the strainer.
3. For every 250 g cashew nuts take 2 tsp oil and rub it in.
4. Sprinkle as much salt as you would need, approximately 1 tsp, and mix well.
5. Place on a baking tray and roast in a moderate oven for 30–40 minutes or until well done. 120–140°C is best.
6. Stir at regular intervals and do not allow them to brown too much. If this happens switch off the oven, remove the cashew nuts for a while and, when the oven cools a little put them back until they are crisp.
7. Under normal circumstances if the cashew nuts have not discoloured, switch off the oven and allow cooling.
8. You can store these cashew nuts in an airtight jar for up to a month.
9. Add a little sprinkling of red chilli powder for some zing and a great flavour. Use as desired or serve plain as a snack.

Fruit Chaats

In India fruit chaats are very popular in summer. They do not need onions, tomatoes, etc.

It is basically diced fruits tossed with the chaat masala (see pages 3–4) and served, sometimes with chopped coriander and definitely fresh mint leaves, otherwise eaten immediately.

Fruits such as bananas, apples, melons, pomegranate, oranges, pears, peaches and nectarines will all make good chaats.

Hara Moong Aur Anar Ki Salaat

Green sprouted moong beans and pomegranate salad

Method

1. Soak the green moong beans in water overnight. Then drain and fold them into a kitchen cloth. Dampen the cloth and set it aside in the warmth of your kitchen. Keep the cloth wet at all times. The best way to do this is to place the cloth in a small flat small colander or a strainer, then place the moong beans in the cloth and fold the edges over. Keep well wet and place the colander or strainer over a bowl. Over watering is not necessary, just keep the cloth well dampened. In 2–3 days you should have sprouts just big enough for the salad. Alternatively you can buy these ready sprouted.

Measurements	Ingredients
100 g	Green moong beans
See page 30	Aloo chaat
1–2	Pomegranates

2. Take the sprouts and blend them with all the ingredients for the aloo chaat (see page 30).

3. Clean and deseed one to two pomegranates, depending on the size.

4. Mix the seeds into the salad and serve.

5. You could also add some boiled corn kernels; approximately 3–4 heaped tbsp will do the trick.

6. Serve this chaat in a slit toasted pitta with some soft cheese. Paneer and feta also make a good combination.

7. Remember chaats are mostly cold and not normally served hot as done in the UK.

8. A cold chicken tikka chaat or a prawn chaat with lettuce and the rest of the ingredients also make excellent accompaniments to meals, served as starters or with drinks.

Important

- A chaat is a last-minute put together item. However, you can keep all your mise-en-place ready provided you do not add the chaat masala. The rock salt and dry mango powder in the masala have an uncanny way of making the salad smell putrid if kept in contact with the fruit and vegetables' natural acids.

- Even though the chaat itself is not spoilt, the odour is off putting. Therefore it is always best to keep everything separate and then blend at the very end.

Chaat Milavut

Chef's Notes

- Call it a salad or call it a snack – it is supposed to be finger lickingly good either way.

Measurements	Ingredients
150–250 g	Potato (boiled, peeled and small diced)
½–1 medium	Onion (finely minced)
1 medium	Tomato (seeded and diced)
1–2 (depending on your tolerance)	Green chillies (finely minced)
1 tbsp	Coriander (finely chopped)
Some plain tortilla chips	
Bombay mix	
Crispy water biscuits or crackers	
Anything else you have that is crisp but not sweet	
1 tsp	Chaat masala powder
¼	Lime (juice only)
1 tbsp	Tamarind chutney
1 tbsp	Fresh green chutney (see page 241)
100 g	Greek yoghurt

Method

1. You will need a large bowl for mixing and something for dishing out.

2. This chaat is made by putting all the ingredients in a bowl and mixing well.

3. Crush the biscuits and other larger bits before you blend everything and serve.

Akoori

Chef's Notes

- Akoori is a Parsee speciality and like several other preparations it was painstakingly created, perhaps centuries ago. I would like to address a point here that could be very useful and which I personally find very effective (my mother may not agree).

- The akoori mix without the egg can be kept covered in your refrigerator for months. You can then use it as you wish with one egg or two or more. Just add the fresh coriander when you finish the preparation. The mix also makes an excellent omelette.

33

Method

1. For the very best slicing results, especially when browning, always select an oval or egg-shaped smaller onion.

2. Peel the onion at both ends and core it. Slice over the longer side of the onion i.e. the two tips should be opposite to you horizontally. After slicing always break up the onion slices gently between your fingers, so that you have fine shreds rather than slices.

3. Heat the oil and brown the sliced onions to get a lovely golden colour. Remember not to overheat the oil and to stir continuously.

4. When pale golden, drain and keep on a paper towel to dry. Onions brown automatically with heat in them, therefore they should not be removed when actually brown but a shade lighter.

5. Place half the oil back into the pan and reheat gently. Add the ginger, garlic and green chillies and sauté until the garlic is golden in colour. Once again do not overheat the oil and, if there are many onion particles present, do strain and then use.

6. Reduce the heat and add the masalas, i.e. all the powders, and continue to cook gently for 1–2 minutes.

7. Add the tomatoes, stir for a minute and then add the onions again.

8. At this stage you may add the sultanas. The Parsees of Bharooch in Gujerat love it this way.

9. Now add the vinegar, lime or lemon juice, salt and sugar. Cook for 1–2 minutes until the liquid evaporates and oil is seen re-emerging at the bottom.

Measurements	Ingredients
2 medium	Onions (sliced)
6 tbsp (reusable)	Sunflower oil
1 small piece, roughly 2 cm	Fresh ginger
4 cloves	Garlic
1 medium	Green chillies (finely minced)
¾ level tsp	Cumin powder
1 tsp	Coriander powder
A large pinch	Turmeric powder
½ tsp	Red chilli powder
1 medium	Tomato (seeded and diced small)
1 tbsp	Golden sultanas (optional)
1 tsp	Malt vinegar
½ tsp	Lime or lemon juice (preferably lime)
1 tsp	White sugar
1 tbsp (use a bit more if your conscience allows you)	Butter
2 tbsp	Single cream
6 large	Organic free range eggs
1–2 tbsp	Fresh coriander (chopped)

10. Remove from the heat and drain off as much oil as you can. Collect the oil, as it is good for use in other cooking.

11. Add the butter, cream and eggs and beat them in the mixture.

12. If using the mixture hot then beat the eggs in a separate bowl, add the cream and then pour into the pan with the hot mixture, stirring continuously.

13. Cook the scrambled egg on a very low heat, stirring continuously to achieve a creamy texture.

14. When you reach the desired consistency add the fresh coriander and check the seasoning again.

15. Serve with toast, on toast or with hot pain rustique.

Aloo Paneer Aur Channa Pakora

Chef's Note

- An interesting little snack item, which is ideal for a starter, a midday snack or an afternoon tea session.

- Feta or Haloumi cheeses may also be substituted if you cannot get paneer. Remember though that Haloumi tends to melt so one needs to be careful when frying. Other cheeses that give a good flavour are strong Cheddar or Red Leicester.

- Crushed roasted coriander seeds also can be added for added flavour as well as crushed peppercorns.

- This quantity should make 40–50 small dumplings.

Method

1. Crush together in a food processor the potato, Paneer, channa daal, ginger, garlic and mint until it has the consistency of coarse breadcrumbs.

2. Wash, dry and finely shred the palak leaves.

3. Into the crushed ingredients mix the onion, coriander, green chilli, cumin powder, lime juice and chaat masala.

4. Check the right consistency by adding the besan, until you get very soft dough.

5. Lastly add the shredded spinach leaves and mix them in gently.

6. Form into little dollops and deep fry one or two first and check the seasoning.

7. Fry the rest a few at a time so as not to cool the oil too rapidly, until golden brown.

8. Serve with fresh tomato or green chutney.

Measurements	Ingredients
200 g	Potato (peeled and boiled)
100 g	Paneer
100 g	Channa daal (soaked)
12 mm piece	Ginger
3 cloves	Garlic
10 leaves	Fresh mint
15–20 leaves	Palak (fresh and young)
1 small	Red onion (minced)
1 level tbsp	Fresh coriander (chopped)
1 small	Green chilli (finely minced)
$\frac{1}{2}$ tsp	Cumin powder
1 tsp	Lime juice
$\frac{1}{2}$ teaspoon	Chaat masala (pages 3–4 and available in Indian stores)
As required	Besan
As desired	Salt

Aloo Rajmah Aur Cheese Ki Tikki

Chef's Notes

- These tikkis are good to fry and set aside drained over a kitchen towel for later use.

- They can be made a day in advance and chilled. Reheating can be done in an oven.

- Microwave reheating is possible but not recommended for reasons of colour and appearance.

- They can be covered in breadcrumbs or rolled in semolina.

- Serve with fresh green coriander and mint chutney or good ol' tomato ketchup.

Measurements	Ingredients
100 g	Red kidney beans (uncooked)
250 g	Potato
150 g	Onions (finely chopped)
3–4 medium cloves	Garlic
5 cm piece	Ginger
2 medium	Green chillies
To shallow fry	Sunflower oil
1 tbsp	Fresh coriander (chopped)
	Salt
1 tsp	Fresh mint (shredded)
150 g	Cheddar (grated)
250 g approx.	Cornflour

Method

1. Soak the red kidney beans (rajmah) overnight in cold water, or for a few hours at least.

2. Boil in enough water with some salt until absolutely soft. Once on the boil simmer until cooked but remember to skim off the scum that keeps coming to the top.

3. Peel and thickly slice the potatoes. Boil in just enough water that the slices are covered.

4. Boil until soft, drain and return to the pan.

5. Put the pan back on medium heat and with a flat wooden spatula scrape and cook the potato until dry. there will be some sticking at the bottom and continuous scraping is necessary to prevent burning. (You can save the water and use it for making a soup or to thin a curry)

6. Once completely dry and almost mashed, remove the potatoes into a flat wide tray, bowl or dish and spread out to cool.

7. Drain the boiled beans and retain the water if you like to use it. Lightly rinse the beans in a strainer or colander to remove the scum and starchy coating on them. Do not over wash.

8. Once well drained and dry, blend the kidney beans with the potato and mash coarsely with a fork or a masher. You do not need to make it very fine.

9. Sauté the onions, garlic, ginger and chilli in very little oil and add to the potato and kidney beans mix. Blend in the coriander, salt and mint. Mix well and form into a large dough ball.

10. Divide into 5–cm diameter balls and set aside. Divide the cheese so that each ball gets the same amount of cheese.

11. Take a ball and flatten it in the palm of one hand until it is approximately 12 mm thick, then place a portion of cheese in the middle.

12. Fold the edges in to cover the cheese completely without the edges breaking.

13. Form into a ball, smooth the edges thoroughly and close any breaks you may see.

14. Make up the rest into similar balls.

15. Once all the balls are prepared flatten each to make a cake or patty – round, oblong, oval or diamond shaped, as you desire.

16. Apply cornflour on each side and dust off any excess.

17. Shallow fry one side then flip over to do the other until golden brown. The oil should be hot but not smoking hot.

18. These can also be shallow fried on a griddle. A chappati tawa or griddle is best for this as they are very gently tapered in the centre for a little oil to collect. However, when frying on a griddle the top and bottom will be very beautifully coloured but the sides will not.

19. If using the shallow frying method remember, do not place too many at one time in the oil. This will result in rapid cooling of the oil and it may make the tikkis disintegrate or break up. Besides they will absorb too much oil and will not get a good colour.

20. The moment the oil begins to foam you know that you have added one too many to the pan, or the oil has gone cold.

Baadal Jaam

Chef's Notes

- This dish consists of deep-fried or pan grilled aubergine slices topped with a tomato sauce and a tangy yoghurt dressing. The word 'Baadal' means clouds and 'Jaam' means fruit, in short 'Fruits of the Clouds'.

Method

1. Clean, wash, wipe and slice the aubergines into roundels approximately 6 mm thick.

2. Pan fry in a thick-bottomed fry pan using very little oil, but allowing each side to brown well before turning over. They may be deep fried but get a bit soggy and absorb a great deal more oil.

3. Drain well on a kitchen towel then arrange without overlapping on a baking tray.

Measurements	Ingredients
2 long or medium broad ones	Aubergines
5–6 tbsp or as required (a soft aubergine will absorb more oil)	Oil
½ kg (or a medium can of chopped plum tomatoes)	Tomatoes
One medium	Onion
4–5 large cloves	Garlic
2.5 cm piece	Ginger
½ tsp	Red chilli powder
½ kg	Yoghurt (use Greek style or very thick yoghurt)
¼ teaspoon	Cinnamon powder
½ tbsp	Fresh coriander (finely chopped)
1 tsp	Lemon juice
To sprinkle	Chaat masala (available from Indian stores)
1 tsp	Quasuri methi (crumbled) (dried fenugreek)
To taste	Salt

4. Give the tomatoes a quick whirl in a blender to chop them roughly. If using canned, drain and mash them coarsely with a potato masher but fine enough to make a thick spreadable sauce.

5. Peel and finely mince the onion.

6. Finely chop the garlic or pass through a garlic press. Scrape and finely chop the ginger. The ginger and garlic can be minced together in a blender but if the quantity is less use a mortar and pestle or just finely mince with a knife.

7. Sauté the onions in the same pan, adding the rest of the oil. If required add 1 tbsp fresh oil.

8. Sauté till light brown then add the ginger and garlic and continue till golden brown.

9. Add the chilli powder, tomatoes and salt and cook till it reaches a thick consistency. Check for seasoning.

10. To make the topping put the thick yoghurt in a bowl and whisk until smooth. Add 1–2 tbsp milk if required to get a thick pouring consistency.

11. Sprinkle the cinnamon powder over and whisk it in.

12. Add the coriander to the yoghurt with the lemon juice and check the seasoning.

13. Sprinkle chaat masala on the fried slices of aubergine, as you would crush pepper.

14. Some Quasuri methi may be added for that extra bit of flavour to the sauce. The word Quasuri comes from a town in Pakistan, which is known to produce the best fenugreek. The name has now become synonymous when using dried crumbled slow roasted fenugreek.

15. Spoon the sauce equally on all the aubergine slices.

16. Cover with foil and bake in a preheated oven at 140°C/275°F for 5–10 minutes.

17. Transfer the slices onto a serving platter and top with dollops of the dressing.

18. Alternatively place the slices overlapping on a oven proof platter, spread the tomato sauce over, bake and then serve in the platter with the yoghurt dollops on the top or covered all the way. You can sprinkle some deep-fried egg noodles on top or 'Sev', which is Indian chickpea vermicelli available in Indian sweet shops. You can even top it with chewda, which is known in the UK as Bombay Mix.

Baked Corn à la Todiwala Family

Chef's Notes

- This is by no means an Indian cuisine dish, as one might imagine. However, it is one that is very popular in our home and is an example of East meets West of sorts. A few boiled cauliflower florets add that extra flavour.

Measurements	Ingredients
250 g	Corn kernels
150 g	Cauliflower florets
1 heaped tbsp	Butter
2 heaped tbsp	Refined flour
250 ml	Milk (cold)
1 medium	Capsicum (green pepper) (chopped)
As desired	Salt
As desired	Crushed black pepper
2	Eggs
Few sprigs	Fresh coriander (chopped)
1 medium	Green chilli
50–100 g	Cheddar (Grated)

Method

1. Boil the corn kernels if fresh in just enough water until tender and drain. Retain the water.

2. If adding cauliflower cook the small florets in the same water. Add more water if required, but always use just enough to cover the vegetable when cooking.

3. Melt the butter in a thick-bottomed pan. Add the flour and cook slowly without discoloration, stirring all the time.

4. Remove the pan from the heat and whisk the milk in a little at a time to get a smooth texture. Cold milk helps to prevent lumps from forming in hot roux.

5. When all the milk has been added and the batter is smooth, return to the heat and cook till the sauce is thick. Remove. If the sauce becomes too thick add some of the reserved vegetable stock until you have the desired consistency.

6. Add the capsicum and simmer for 1–2 minutes only.

7. Add the salt and pepper and check the seasoning.

8. Separate the eggs into two bowls but keep the larger bowl for the whites.

9. Beat the yolks and add a little sauce to them, beating continuously, then pour into the remaining sauce and beat it in.

10. Remember if you pour the yolks directly into the hot sauce you may cook them and the consistency of the sauce will be spoilt.

11. Mix in the corn and cauliflower florets, the coriander and the green chilli. Blend a little so that the flavours get released in the sauce.

12. Taste again and season if necessary.

13. Beat the whites of the eggs till stiff and fold them into the now ready mix.

14. Pour into a greased pie dish, sprinkle the cheese on top and bake at 140–150°C (300–400°F) for about 30 minutes, or until nice and golden on top and well set.

Besan No Poro

Chef's Notes

• This simple masala omelette is made with besan (chickpea flour) and eggs but can also be made using only chickpea flour. It was traditionally created to save on the expense of eggs. However, with today's huge health problems this one could be quite fashionable with less cholesterol and egg protein.

• The following quantities will make 2–3 flat omelettes.

• These omelettes can also be eaten with several vegetable preparations instead of bread or chappaties. They are great stale as well.

• Can also be had in a sandwich with some slices of tomato and cucumber inter-layered.

Method

1. Sieve the besan into a deep bowl and add enough water to make a smooth paste.

2. Break the eggs in and beat the mixture.

3. Add all the other ingredients except the oil and chutney and mix well.

4. Taste and season as desired.

Measurements	Ingredients
4–5 tbsp	Besan
2	Eggs
1 medium	Onion (chopped)
1 medium	Tomato (plum tomato preferred) (chopped)
1 large	Green chilli (chopped)
1 tbsp	Coriander (chopped)
½ tsp	Cumin powder
¼ tsp	Turmeric
½ tsp	Chilli powder
1 tsp	Lemon juice
To taste	Salt
As required	Oil
As required	Hot and sweet chutney (mango is best)

5. The batter should be the consistency of a pancake mixture, no doubt you will have a bit of chopped ingredients inside but the thickness is important. If the batter is too thick the omelette will be heavy, as it will not spread well in the pan.

6. Heat the oil in a thick-bottomed fry pan or a non-stick pan and proceed as you would for a flat omelette.

7. Swirl the batter around until the entire bottom is covered.

8. Let one side cook until golden brown on the bottom, flip over and cook the other side.

9. Make as many as you can. This depends on the thickness you want and the size of the pan you use.

10. They make an ideal accompaniment and can be eaten with plain pickle or hot and sweet chutneys, which are the best and which the Parsees enjoy most.

11. Another way is to chop the chutney into tiny pieces and then spread this on the flat omelette, roll the omelette and eat as a roll.

Bhujelo Poro/Baked Spicy Omelette

Chef's Notes

- This omelette, a Parsee speciality originating from Gujerat, is a great one to be eaten as soon as it is baked. Whatever you wish to eat with it – toast, hot soft bread or croissants – should be kept ready. For breakfast a really fruity jelly is ideal. The Parsee would have an extra dollop of butter and I would recommend this to anyone who can forget their diet for a day.

- This quantity will serve three to four people for a snack.

Measurements	Ingredients
2 slender	Green chillies
6–8 sprigs	Fresh coriander
2 cloves	Garlic
12 mm piece	Fresh ginger
½ tsp	Cumin
¼ tsp	Salt
Pinch	Turmeric
Masala	Ingredients
4	Egg whites
4	Egg yolks
1 tsp	Plain flour
2 tsp	Sunflower oil
	Butter

Method

1. Preheat the oven to gas mark 7/210°C.

2. Grind the masala ingredients into a fine paste using a pestle and mortar. If using a blender use a little water.

3. Beat the egg whites until very stiff and fluffy.

4. Gently fold in the yolks, then the flour and the ground masala.

5. Heat a large (25 cm/10 in) non-stick oven-proof baking pan and add the oil until it heats to a haze, smoking point but not too hot.

6. Add the mixture, put a dollop of butter on the top and after a few seconds place the pan in the oven.

7. Make sure all the ingredients are well distributed as well as the butter on the top.

8. Bake until the omelette is golden brown on the top, cooked and light and fluffy.

9. To check whether it is cooked, insert a clean knife into the centre of the omelette and see if it comes out clean.

10. Eat the omelette with soft bread or toast and some sweet chutney. A good hot well-buttered pain rustique is the best.

Hot Channa Pakora

Chef's Notes

- A quick, easy snack once the mise-en-place is ready. Several variations of this can be made and one needs to use one's imagination and create more out of one base.

Method

1. Soak the Kabula Channa (white chickpeas) overnight, then boil until soft. If using tinned chickpeas, drain and set aside. You can retain the liquid and use it for the batter but often this may result in rapid colouring. However, it also makes a delicious soup.

2. Gently roast the dried spices and either crush them to a coarse powder in a mortar and pestle or in a small coffee grinder. The texture should be that of coarsely ground peppercorns.

3. Place all the ingredients in a large bowl and mix well.

4. Break the chickpeas or crush them a bit in the mix so that they will adhere better to the batter.

5. Mix well to form a wet yet thick batter, just thick enough for little dollops to be dropped into hot oil. Add a little of the chickpea liquid if it is too dry.

6. Add some freshly chopped coriander or some shredded curry leaves for additional flavour.

Measurements	Ingredients
250 g	Kabuli Channa (white chickpeas) or
500 g	Chickpeas (tinned)
3 slender	Spring onions (finely chopped)
1 tsp	Ginger (finely minced)
2 medium	Green chilli (seeded and finely minced)
1 tbsp	Sesame seeds (hulled)
1/2	Lime (juice only)
As desired	Salt
150 g	Chickpea flour
100 g	Rice flour
100 g	Semolina (coarse)
For deep frying	Sunflower oil
Dried spices	**Ingredients**
1 tbsp	Coriander seeds
1 tsp	Cumin seeds
1/2 tsp	Lovage or carom
8–10	Peppercorns
1 or 2 large	Dried red chilli

7. Taste prior to frying, then fry one piece and taste before frying the remainder.

8. Heat the oil well but not too hot and fry the pakoras in small dollops. Check that the centre is cooked and not gooey when done. If the oil is too hot they will brown too rapidly and not cook through. If the oil is not hot enough they will absorb too much oil and be unhealthy as well as looking and tasting bad.

9. These can be quite easily reheated in hot oil prior to serving. You can even half cook them, drain them well and either store in the fridge or keep on a kitchen towel and refry them after a couple of hours.

10. These will keep in the refrigerator in an airtight container for up to three days to be refried and served with tangy fresh minty chutney or tamarind and date chutney.

Chicken Samosa

Chef's Notes

- A samosa is simply a pastry with a variety of fillings, shaped into a triangle and deep-fried. Samosas vary across the length and breadth of the sub-continent and it is not uncommon for people from the North, particularly the Punjab, to dislike the samosas from the south. Some will even say that those are not samosas. As well as every community having differing styles, there is a difference between Muslim and Hindu styles.

- If making lamb samosa, use lamb mince instead of chicken.

- The quantity given will make approximately 30 samosas.

Method

1. Open the ready made pastry pack. Remember to keep a damp cloth ready to cover the pastry as you work on the individual samosas.

2. Take a side plate and use it as a guide to cut the whole pack of pastry into a round disc using a sharp thin-tipped knife. The trimmings can be cut into small pieces, deep-fried and either eaten as they are or mixed in a chaat.

3. Now cut the pastry in half and keep one pile on top of the other.

Measurements	Ingredients
1 pack of small sheets	Spring roll pastry (Singaporean or Malaysian is best)
As required for sealing	Plain white flour
1 kg	Chicken mince
50 g	Ginger/garlic paste
50 g	Fresh mint
4–6 leaves (fresh) or 10 (dry)	Curry leaves
15 g	Green chilli
300 g	Onions
500 g	Green peas
10 g	Garam masala powder
½ tsp	Turmeric
1 tsp	Chilli powder
2 tsp	Curry powder
1 heaped tsp	Cumin (whole)
1 heaped tsp then to taste	Salt

4. Peel the pastry taking two sheets at a time. One sheet is too thin for this and will not make a good samosa.

5. Cover the pastry with the damp cloth while you get your *cold* mince and a tablespoon ready.

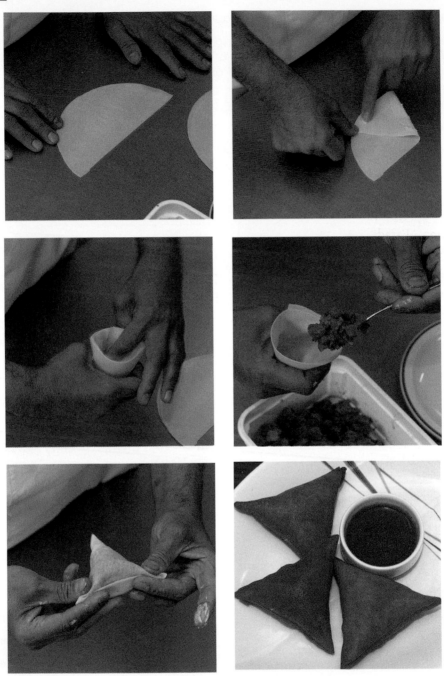

6. You will also need a sealant. A thick paste made from the plain flour mixed with a little water until it is the thickness of porridge will provide this.

7. Now take one edge of the half round pastry, fold it over in a triangle to the centre and apply some paste to stick the edge.

8. Then fold the other edge over to form the cone of an isoceles triangle, making sure the lower tip is fully sealed and does not display a hole.

9. Fill the cone until approximately 2 cm from the top.

10. Then fold one edge in over the filling, apply the paste and fold the other edge over.

11. Rub your fingers over the top a few times until you are sure the samosa is well sealed.

12. When all the samosas are complete fry in hot oil and enjoy with fresh green chutney.

Chicken Temptation

Chef's Notes

- A restaurant known as Paradise in Bombay in the 1960s first introduced this preparation. Paradise is still serving this item. Ours is different and uses diced roast chicken blended with fresh herbs, stuffed in a bread slice and batter fried.

- This quantity will make 4–6 temptations.

Method

1. Heat the butter gently in a pan and lightly sweat the onions until they are soft.

2. Add the ginger, garlic and green chilli and sauté for 1 minute.

3. Add the diced chicken then toss for a minute or so until heated through.

4. Blend in the coriander and remove from the heat.

5. Mix in the mustard and add more to suit your taste.

6. Cool and keep ready for making the temptations.

7. To make the batter beat a little water into the egg in a bowl then gradually mix in the two flours sieved together until the batter is smooth with the consistency of single cream. Add more water as desired.

8. Once the batter is ready, cover it and allow it to sit for a few minutes.

Measurements	Ingredients
1 tbsp	Butter
250 g	Onions (finely chopped)
5 cm piece	Fresh ginger (finely chopped)
4–5 cloves	Garlic (finely chopped)
1–2 medium	Green chilli (finely chopped)
1 kg	Roasted chicken (boned and diced small after roasting (with skin))
1 tbsp	Fresh coriander (chopped)
1 heaped tsp	English mustard (coarse)
To deep fry	Oil
Batter	**Ingredients**
As desired	Water
1	Egg
2 tbsp	Besan/chickpea flour
4 tbsp	Plain flour
1 tsp	Mustard paste

9. Take a slice of white bread (thin preferred) and trim the top crusty side. Put a spoonful of the chicken mixture in the middle. Fold the edges over in a triangular shape and press the sides in to seal.

10. Dip each triangle in the batter and fry in hot deep oil until nice and golden.

11. Serve cut into two and opened with green chutney, garlic mayonnaise or spiced tomato ketchup.

Curried Vegetable Puffs

Chef's Notes

- In Mumbai in particular the curried lamb puff is the more popular and much-liked snack item. Introduced by the Parsee, East Indian and Goan communities, it quickly became the best option for a midday appetiser. A vegetarian option is also desirable. Diced vegetables are tossed with spices and cohered with finely chopped tomatoes and cooked until dry. The filling is then stuffed between two layers of flaky or puff pastry and baked.

- Sold in delis across the city it has now moved from a predominantly non-vegetarian snack to a range offering various fillings.

Measurements	Ingredients
500 g	Diced vegetables (a combination of carrot, peas, French beans, potato, and fresh spinach is ideal)
3 tbsp	Sunflower oil
50 g	Garlic (finely minced)
50 g	Ginger (finely minced)
2 large	Green chilli (finely minced)
200 g	Minced onions
5 g	Turmeric
20 g	Coriander powder
15 g	Cumin powder
10 g	Red chilli powder
200 g	Tomato (minced)
1 tsp	Lime juice
1 tsp	Sugar
2 heaped tbsp	Fresh coriander (chopped)
24–30, 7.5 cm squares	Puff pastry sheets
1	Egg (beaten, for brushing)
As desired	Salt

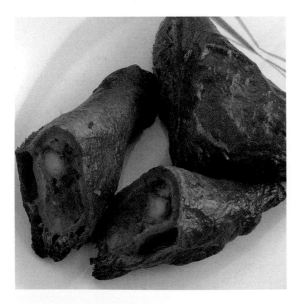

Method

1. Blanch the vegetables in only as much water as is desired and set aside. Do not over cook and ensure that the colour is not lost. (Upon baking they will cook further.)

2. If using fresh spinach just flash blanch, cool quickly and squeeze out any moisture, then chop and set aside. The spinach will be blended only towards the end.

3. Heat the oil in a large frying pan or a casserole deep enough to accept all the vegetables when added in.

4. Sauté the ginger, garlic and green chilli.

5. When the garlic begins to change colour add the minced onions and sauté until the onions turn a pale brown.

6. Mix the turmeric, coriander, cumin and chilli powders in a cup with just enough water to make a paste of pouring consistency and add to the pan.

7. Add a little more water to the cup to release residue and keep for later additions. Once you add the spices remember the base will begin to stick.

8. However it is essential to see that the spices cook thoroughly and to achieve this without spoiling it is best to add a little water to release the spices at the base as well as prevent them from burning and turning the dish bitter.

9. When oil is seen being released at the base of the pan it shows that the spices are cooked.

10. Add the tomatoes and cook until the liquid is almost dry.

11. At this stage add the vegetables, the lime juice and sugar. Lastly add the chopped spinach.

12. Cook for 1–2 minutes and check the seasoning. Add the coriander and remove. Cool in a strainer to remove any moisture and unwanted oil.

13. To use the filling take a puff pastry sheet and roll it out in a rectangle to approximately 3 mm thick.

14. Cut the sheet into 7.5–8 cm squares and brush with the beaten egg.

15. Place a spoonful of the mixture in the centre of each square, brush the edges with egg and fold over either in the shape of a triangle or a rectangle.

16. Lay on greased or non-stick trays and place in the chiller or deep freezer to allow the pastry to settle and become firm.

17. Brush the tops with egg and bake in a hot oven at 180–200°C/gas mark 6. Takes approx. 10–12 minutes.

18. Remove and serve hot or warm. The puffs need no accompaniment but some may prefer to have tomato ketchup.

19. These will keep quite well and may be eaten after a day or two, as long as they are kept well covered in the refrigerator.

Currimbhoy Salad

Chef's Notes

- This was one of the most famous salads served at the Taj Mahal Hotel in Bombay at the time I worked there. I do believe that it was the most popular salad in the Taj Group of Hotels also during that period. It is simple and easy to prepare. The end result for all those liking a little zing is absolutely fabulous. It makes an excellent accompaniment to crumb-fried food or seafood fried in semolina. For the die-hard vegetarian you can skip the boiled egg and use a mayonnaise without eggs.

Measurements	Ingredients
250 g	Cos lettuce (or any large leafy lettuce)
2–3 cloves	Garlic (finely minced)
2 medium	Green chilli (very finely minced)
2 heaped tbsp	Fresh coriander (chopped)
4	Boiled eggs
200 g	Mayonnaise
½	Lime (juice only)
Small dices cut from four slices of thin sliced white bread, deep fried and well drained	Fried croutons
As desired after blending the mayonnaise	Salt

Method

1. Break the lettuce leaves into 2.5 cm pieces or smaller, wash and drain well.

2. Take the garlic, green chilli and coriander and add to a bowl big enough to take in all the combined ingredients.

3. Peel the boiled eggs and dice them up coarsely. The size of the dice should be approximately ½ cm. Keep these in another small bowl or on a small plate.

4. Now add the mayonnaise to the bowl with the garlic, chilli and coriander and blend well. Season with the salt and lime juice and taste again.

5. Add the diced eggs and lettuce leaves and mix well. Do not over mix as the lettuce with go limp very rapidly. Only start this process when you are ready to serve.

6. Add half the croutons while mixing and reserve the remaining for the final service.

7. Serve in a bowl or on a platter and sprinkle the remaining croutons on the top with some fresh chopped coriander if you like.

8. Unfortunately this salad does not keep well once mixed and therefore all preparation should be complete prior to blending.

Fofos De Arroz

Chef's Notes

- A simple rice and cheese croquette made from leftover boiled rice, or rice boiled and cooled for the occasion. Ideally thick par-boiled type rice or a risotto type is the best.

Method

1. Take the boiled rice, add a little salt and mash it a bit with your palms until it is soft enough to be shaped.

2. Combine the cheese with the coriander, chilli and paprika, mix well and taste.

3. Make even-sized balls with the rice and set aside.

4. Divide the cheese into as many even balls as the rice.

5. Flatten the rice ball on your palm until approximately 12 mm thick.

6. Place a ball of the cheese in the centre and fold the rice over carefully.

7. Make cylindrical or egg-shaped forms but ensure that there are no visible cracks then roll them lightly in the flour.

8. In another dish beat the eggs lightly until both white and egg are well mixed.

9. Dip each fofo in the egg and then crumb them.

10. Chill the fofos in the refrigerator for a couple of hours at least if possible. Chilling makes them firm and also helps the cheese not to overheat and expand, thereby cracking the fofos.

Measurements	Ingredients
As much as you may have	Boiled rice
1 heaped tsp per fofo	Cheese (grated)
1 tbsp	Fresh coriander (chopped)
1 chilli for 6–8 fofos, 7.5 × 2.5 cm	Green chilli (chopped)
$1/2$ tsp for the above	Paprika or chilli powder
3 tbsp for up to 8 fofos	Flour (plain or any)
2	Eggs
As needed	Breadcrumbs
A little to taste depending on the cheese	Salt
As needed to semi deep fry. Approximately 2cm depth in the fry pan	Oil

11. Heat the oil until almost smoking and fry when you need them. Do not over heat the oil.

12. You can keep fofos in the refrigerator overnight or few hours before service. Fry when you are ready. Only ensure that they are kept covered and that they have paper at the bottom.

13. In Goa these are rolled in semolina instead of breadcrumbs. This gives a lovely crunchy texture and is quite different.

14. Serve with a garlic and tomato chutney or an aioli type dip.

Frango Jirey Mirey

Chicken with Cumin and Black Pepper

Chef's Notes

- This is a Goan speciality and one much liked with drinks. It is a real tongue tingler. Jirey means cumin and Mirey for black peppercorns.

Method

1. Place the tamarind in a glass bowl and add the boiling water. Set aside for about 30 minutes.

2. Extract the pulp by passing through a strainer placed over a bowl. If using the ready made pulp then skip the above method.

3. Roast all the dry ingredients together in a slow fry pan until they change colour, approximately 6–10 minutes.

4. Stir continuously with a wooden spoon. Set aside for a few minutes to cool, so that the spices become crisp.

5. Transfer them to a blender and purée to a fine paste with the vinegar, oil and tamarind pulp.

6. Place the shredded chicken in a bowl and marinate with approximately 2–3 tbsp masala.

7. Taste and add more if you like but remember it can become hot. The rest can be put in a jar and stored in the refrigerator for future use. Just remember that each time you use it you must use a dry spoon and wipe the sides with a clean tissue after you finish, including any vapour on the inside of the lid.

8. Mix the masala well into the chicken and add salt to your taste and set aside for at least 30 minutes.

Measurements	Ingredients
200 g tamarind soaked in 200 ml boiling water or use ready made pulp	Tamarind pulp
1 tbsp	Cumin seeds (roasted)
1 level tsp	Black peppercorns
4–5 large	Red chilli (of medium strength)
5 cm piece	Ginger (scraped and cut roughly)
6–8 cloves	Garlic
3–4	Cloves
3–4	Cardamom
2.5 cm piece	Cassia or cinnamon
100 ml	Malt vinegar
100 ml	Sunflower oil
400 g net weight	Boneless chicken (shredded)
1 tbsp	Fresh coriander (chopped)
To taste	Salt

9. When cooking use a heavy bottomed fry pan or a wok. Heat the utensil well before adding any oil.

10. Add 2 tbsp oil and as soon as the oil is at smoking point add the chicken, toss it once or twice only and allow it to sauté briskly.

11. Do not stir too much as it will loose too much fluid.

12. Stir from time to time so that all sides are covered.

13. The chicken should not take more than 2–3 minutes to cook. When you think the chicken is done check the taste, sprinkle some fresh coriander and drizzle some lime juice if you like.

14. Check the salt and serve immediately.

Mumbai No Frankie

Chef's Notes

- One time Mumbai's best selling (non-vegetarian) street snack until overtaken by modern American junk food, this stuffed rolled chappati is still a favourite with many.

- Frankie can be eaten as the 'Frankie' or the meat can be separate and eaten with a main meal.

- Ginger/garlic paste is made by taking equal quantities of each and puréeing them in a blender with a little water or a little water and a little oil. It can be stored if made in excess and used for several preparations. The addition of oil prevents the paste from oxidising.

- To make your own red chilli paste, soak a handful of red chillies in a little water, until they become swollen and soft. Purée in a blender. Any extra can be stored in the refrigerator. If you snip the chillies first the result is easier. Storage must be in a tightly sealed jar.

- A little oil, ghea or butter is to be used for each chappati on the skillet or griddle. You will need to grease the skillet each time for each use. Also, make sure you wipe it clean with a kitchen towel and remove any residues.

Method

1. Clean wash and drain the lamb well in a colander.

2. Heat a casserole well, add the oil and brown the lamb until all the water dries out. Stir so that all sides get evenly browned.

3. Add the onions, the ginger/garlic paste, coriander powder, cumin and chilli paste.

4. Sauté until the onions and the masala start to brown and get a rich dark colour.

5. Keep scraping the bottom as you go along with a wooden flat spatula to prevent sticking and burning. Add a little water if you feel that the bottom is burning. The addition of water will also help to prevent the spices from burning as well as allowing a more even colouring and cooking.

6. Check the salt and add as desired.

7. Lower the heat and cover the pan.

8. When the lamb is more than half cooked add the yoghurt and tomatoes (puréed together first if preferred), cover and continue cooking.

9. You should get a very rich looking thick gravy.

10. When the lamb is cooked add the lemon juice, the mint and coriander, the garam masala, then cover and set aside. Later you may like to remove any excess oil floating on the top with a tablespoon and save it for future use in other lamb dishes.

11. To make the Frankie, heat a tawa or griddle pan to a medium heat.

12. Beat an egg well and add 1 tbsp water.

13. Add salt and if you like some chilli powder.

14. Coat the pan with oil or butter, heat one chappati or flour tortilla on the pan and pour a little egg on the top, enough to coat the tortilla. You may like to brush the egg instead though the Indians definitely prefer a thicker coating of egg. The omelette-like taste of the chapatti enhances the flavour of the Frankie.

15. As soon as you see the egg coagulating flip it over and coat the other side. Then flip again.

16. When both sides are golden brown remove on to a plate or board.

17. Place 1 tbsp lamb or more if required along one side of the 'baida roti' (egg roti), sprinkle with sliced onion, coriander and mint then roll and serve.

Measurements	Ingredients
500 g	Boneless lamb (diced very small 12 mm × 12 mm)
2 tbsp	Oil
2 medium	Onions (very finely chopped)
2 tbsp	Ginger/garlic paste (see page 135)
1 tbsp	Coriander powder
1 tsp	Cumin powder
1 tbsp	Red chilli paste
4–5 tbsp	Thick yoghurt
1–2	Tomato (chopped) (optional)
1 tbsp	Lemon juice
1 tbsp	Mint (chopped)
2 tbsp	Coriander (chopped)
1 tsp	Garam masala
To taste	Salt
Roll	**Ingredients**
1 for every 3 chappaties	Egg
	Oil, ghee or butter
	Flour tortillas or plain flour chappaties
1–2 for the above meat quantity	Onion (sliced)
1 tsp per egg	Coriander (chopped)
2–3	Mint leaves (snipped or coarsely chopped for each roll)
Pinch	Salt

Kaera Na Cutless

Chef's Notes

- This is quite a classical preparation in Parsee cuisine, though not practised much these days, due to the modernisation of daily life. These are simple yet tasty banana or plantain cakes, an ideal accompaniment to or as a starter to a meal.

Method

1. Boil the bananas without peeling in water with the turmeric and salt until soft. Drain and cool thoroughly before peeling.

2. Boil or steam the potatoes in their jackets, cool thoroughly and peel.

3. Gently roast the coriander seeds and cumin seeds until aromatic and slightly coloured. Do not use high heat or ignore while roasting.

4. Crush in a mortar and pestle to a coarse powder, ensuring that no whole bits remain.

5. Peel and mash the bananas with the boiled potato and blend in the remaining ingredients except the crumbing ingredients.

6. Work well to form a soft yet dryish dough.

7. Do not over work as the potato may get starchy.

8. Check seasoning.

9. Divide into even balls depending on the size you prefer.

10. Make oblong or round shapes, dust with the crumbing flour, dip in beaten egg and roll in breadcrumbs.

11. Coat well in this mixture before frying in hot oil.

12. Serve on a base of cassia bark-flavoured tomato gravy or even with a mayonnaise-based dip.

Measurements	Ingredients
6	Raw green bananas (raw plantains will also do)
1 tsp	Turmeric powder
3 medium	Potatoes (boiled in their jackets)
1½ tsp	Coriander seeds
1 tsp	Cumin seeds
2 medium	Onions (finely minced)
4–6 cloves	Garlic (finely minced)
2 medium	Green chilli (finely minced)
1 heaped tbsp	Ginger (finely minced)
1	Lime (juice only)
2 tbsp	Fresh coriander (chopped)
For frying	Oil
Crumbing	**Ingredients**
150 g	Flour
2–3	Eggs (beaten)
As required	Breadcrumbs

Khaman Dhokla

24 pieces

Chef's Notes

- This is a very popular snack item but is also eaten as part of a full Gujarati meal. They are steamed chickpea cake pieces, sizzled for added flavour. It will take a few attempts to get this right, however patience and analysing any shortfalls will help you gain the experience.

Method

Measurements	Ingredients
250 g	Split Bengal Gram (split yellow peas or split chickpeas)
2.5 cm	Ginger
2–3 medium	Green chillies
50 ml	Oil
As desired	Salt
Pinch	Asafoetida
½ tsp	Bicarbonate of soda
½ tsp	Mustard seeds
1 sprig (10–12 leaves)	Curry leaves
150–300 g	Grated coconut
1 tbsp	Coriander leaves (chopped)

1. Soak the split yellow peas overnight. The level of water should be approximately 2.5 cm over the lentils. Do not refrigerate but leave covered with a cloth outside.

2. Purée in blender or food processor, but not too fine.

3. Beat well with a circular motion to incorporate air, either with a wooden spoon or a whisk.

4. Leave covered with a cloth to ferment for approximately 5–6 hours depending on the weather.

5. Grind the ginger and green chillies together to a smooth paste. Use a mortar and pestle if you have one or a small stick blender attachment.

6. After the split pea mixture has fermented (it will rise a bit and smell fermented too) add 25 ml oil, the salt, asafoetida, ground green chillies and ginger and bicarbonate of soda mixed with little water. Beat again.

7. Grease an ovenproof pie dish about 5 cm deep with a little oil. Pour the mixture in to about 2.5 cm thickness.

8. Steam until done and remove. You will know it is done when a clean knife inserted comes out clean without any batter sticking to it.

9. If you do not have a steamer place the dish into a larger tray; pour boiling hot water up to half the level of the batter and place in a hot oven, approximately 150 to 200°C. Cover the dish with a foil to allow it to steam within.

10. Allow it to cool slightly, but run a knife along the edges to release the now steamed cake.

11. Cut into cubes in the dish but do not remove.

12. Heat the remaining oil to almost smoking point but not too hot, then add mustard seeds. As the seeds crackle, add the curry leaves and pour this evenly over the steamed 'Dhokla'.

13. Serve garnished with grated coconut and chopped coriander leaves.

14. Sometimes a tablespoon of buttermilk is also added to the batter for a more soured effect. This is much liked by the Indians.

Kira Wada

Chef's Notes

• This delectable crisp lentil cake or dumpling as it may be called, is quite easy to make and is a really interesting snack or starter. Serve with fresh coconut chutney or even some ketchup. Hailing from Kerala in south India it is an example of the myriad varieties of Indian snacks.

Method

1. Soak the channa daal (split yellow peas) for a few hours in cold water. If you can soak them overnight even better.

2. Once soft and well absorbed they are ready for the next step. To check this you can take a few soaked lentils and chew them. If you get a firm bite in the centre they need to be soaked a bit more. If on the other hand they are soft right through they are ready.

3. Place the lentils, onion, ginger piece (skinned or unskinned, if unskinned then well washed), green chilli and the coriander sprigs into a food processor and crush until the crushed bits of the mixture are the consistency of bulgur wheat or large grains of sugar.

4. Remove to a large bowl.

5. Finely shred the spinach and the curry leaves and sprinkle over the mixture.

Measurements	Ingredients
250 g	Channa daal (split yellow peas)
1 medium	Onion (cut into pieces)
5 cm piece	Ginger
1–2 medium	Green chilli
A few sprigs	Fresh coriander
100 g	Fresh spinach leaves
10–15	Curry leaves
1 tsp	Cumin seeds
10 g or as desired	Salt
Good pinch	Asafoetida
As required for deep frying	Oil to fry

6. Gently roast the cumin seeds in a small fry pan, cool and crush to a coarse powder.

7. Add the cumin, salt and asafoetida powder to the mixture now and mix in well.

8. You may need to almost knead the mixture but not too much as the onions may give off too much liquid and make the mix too soft.

9. Heat the oil until you see a haze over the top.

10. Make small balls of the mixture and flatten them between your palms so that you get a little cake, tapered at the ends and thin at the edges.

11. Fry these until golden brown and serve with the recommended chutney for best results.

12. The kira wada can be half fried and re-fried when required. However they can become a bit too dry and crisp and that makes them less enjoyable.

13. The other point to bear in mind is not to leave the mix too long after everything is blended otherwise it becomes too soft and that also destroys the texture.

Kaanda Bhajia

Onion Bhajia

Measurements	Ingredients
2 medium	Onions
2	Green chillies (finely minced)
1 level tsp	Chilli powder
2 tbsp	Coriander (chopped)
1 tsp	Cumin (crushed coarsely)
½ tsp	Ajwain (lovage) (crushed). Also known as thymol or carom seeds
½ tsp	Turmeric powder
½ teaspoon	Lemon juice
6–7 tbsp	Chickpea flour
½ tsp or as desired	Salt
To deep fry	Oil
Two tbsp	Water

Chef's Notes

- This is perhaps the most popular of all Indian snacks and the most commonly found throughout. In the UK it is also the most misunderstood and wrongly done. It is very simple to make and the results will astound you. The correct term is bhajia or bhajji, which simply means fritter.

- The bhajias you see in shops and supermarkets throughout UK do not always represent the bhajia we Indians know and what you make will be similar to those in an Indian home.

- This batter will give you approximately 20–30 small bhajias of the size required. They should not be the size of tennis balls.

Method

1. Slit the onions into half, remove the root stubs and slice them as thinly as you can.

2. Place in a deep bowl and add the green chillies, chilli powder, coriander, cumin, ajwain, turmeric and lemon juice.

3. Sieve the (besan) chickpea flour with the salt.

4. Heat the oil in a Karai-type container or any suitable pan to hold oil for deep-frying.

5. Mix the chickpea flour slowly into the onions and rub it in with your fingers, until the mix is firm and sticky.

6. Add the water and mix further for 1–2 minutes, check the salt and you are ready to fry.

7. Keep a strainer ready over a bowl for draining the bhajias when ready.

8. With your already messy fingers put small dollops of the batter into the oil to fry. Each bhajia should be no bigger than a small fritter, approximately 2.5 cm.

9. Do not keep the oil too hot. The fritter should fry slowly so that it gets crisp and golden. If the oil is too hot the bhajias will fry too fast and remain raw inside and gooey. If you then try to refry, they will burn, remain soggy and taste bitter.

10. On the other hand if you want to serve them later, you can half fry and remove them. Fry when you are ready in hot oil this time. If the oil is not hot when refrying, the bhajias will absorb too much fat.

11. Also do not put too many in the oil together when frying or else you will have soggy bhajias again.

12. Serve the bhajias with any of the green chutneys or the fresh tomato and garlic chutney.

Tantia Shingdana Ani Nishteachi Usli

Chef's Notes

- A simple salad from the Konkan coast of boiled egg, peanuts and seafood.

Method

1. Separate the egg yolks from the whites. Dice the whites and crumble the yolks with a fork.

2. Blend all the remaining ingredients and season to taste.

3. This salad also tastes good if blended with a little chopped fresh mint and dill.

4. Remember that tamarind pulp does not like soft lettuce leaves and even though the leaves will taste good they will wilt and spoil very quickly. Cos, little gem and frisée are some others you can use. Rocket does work but keep it towards the last of the blending.

Measurements	Ingredients
3–4	Eggs (hard boiled)
4–5 tbsp	Fresh grated coconut
1–2	Green chilli (finely chopped)
2 tbsp	Fresh coriander (chopped)
2 tbsp	Tamarind pulp
4–5 tbsp	Roasted peanuts (chopped)
2–3	Shallots (chopped)
1 medium	Tomatoes (chopped)
4–5 tbsp	Poached seafood (the blend of seafood used is entirely at your discretion, however a good blend gives a better flavour)
A few leaves	Lettuce (preferably use iceburg, cut into small squares. You can use other types of lettuce except soft leaved)

Roasting

3

This chapter is dedicated to various forms of cooking in the cuisine of the sub-continent and tries to cover the broad spectrum of styles in the heading. While it is virtually impossible to cover the sub-continent and all of its styles, we have tried to bring some classic dishes and hope that we can cover the essence of the styles to reflect these in other cuisines, cultures and styles.

ROASTING

Though roasting is not necessarily an Indian form of cooking as compared to Western cuisine, there are various styles that do have components of it in various forms. We can always relate to the 'Tandoor' as the classical Indian oven, the roots of which go back to Persia and the Mughuls' influence.

In some parts of Rajasthan, for instance, whole birds and joints of animals are roasted under hot sand with heat applied from top and bottom. In certain parts of Kutch in Gujerat local fishermen wrap whole cleaned, gutted and marinated freshly caught fish in palm leaves and bake them buried in the sand, on the beach. In some parts they simply gut and clean the fish and roll them in sand and then bake them. The resulting effect is that the scales and skin bond to the sand and when ready to eat this simply peels off leaving a beautiful and delicate fish dish.

Then there is the most popular of all Indian stuffed roasted chickens, 'Murgh Mussalum'. The recipe differs from every great chef young and old and each one is the very best in its own right.

Cooking spices on dry heat over a griddle is also referred to as roasting.

There is a style of cooking that is done entirely on a hot stone, again dry, and thus is also referred to as roasting.

Indian cuisine has always adapted in its various styles, some rudimentary, and some actually having evolved over centuries and becoming specialised cooking forms. Some styles of cooking involve cooking in pots with heat applied in the form of hot embers on both sides of the pot, i.e. the bottom as well as the top. The vessel, mostly made of copper plated or silvered, is sometimes half embedded into the ground to ensure that heat is trapped in and the cooking is guaranteed over a long period of time. This is often applied to slow cooking for items such as a 'Biryani', where the meat and rice are cooked together to perfection. 'Dum Pukht' is a term used to describe food cooked under pressure or in a sealed vessel.

Meat in the sub-continent is not bred for the table as a rule and most of the time the animals also have other uses, e.g. beasts of burden. Where goats and sheep are bred primarily for the table it is often the case that these animals are made to walk over long distances to pasture. This makes the meat tougher and more muscular than the meat you will find

in the Western world. The meat is definitely leaner but since it is muscular it often needs to be cooked on a slow heat until it becomes tender and succulent.

Since most of the sub-continent does not have the climate nor the facilities and amenities to hold meat by hanging until it is almost tenderised and the perfect balance between rigor mortis and readiness for cooking are achieved, meat is often cooked soon after it is slaughtered.

To achieve the best results from cooking meat that is muscular, often sinewy and exposed to the elements, which lead to rapid degeneration of the protein, methods and styles of cooking, and marinating have evolved. These styles not only produce excellent results, they also deliver safe, healthy and nutritious food.

The very well-known word 'Bhuna', pronounced 'Bhoona', is a blend of the words roasted and braised and could mean either. It is often confusing if one who does not know Indian forms of cooking hears the word used in the culinary context, but to an Indian chef or housewife it is absolutely clear and they would know in what context it is meant.

BRAISING

Braising is a common process and suits the meats of the sub-continent best. In Indian terminology the word braising may not be used or understood in its Western context, it is very much a day-to-day cooking affair in the household, in vegetarian cooking and most definitely in non-vegetarian cooking.

Braising not only gets some of the best cooking results, it allows the woman to go about her chores while the food is cooking very slowly.

Braising encourages the production of rich, flavourful, often dark and delicious gravies, which go extremely well with both rice and Indian breads.

Roganjosh, Bhuna and many others are fine examples of braising in the highest form.

STEWING

Stewing is not something new to Indian cuisine and is quite commonly used. All the different cuisine styles of the sub-continent contain some element of this style of cooking, whether it is vegetarian or non-vegetarian.

One of the best-known dishes of the Parsees, 'Dhaansaak' is basically a lamb stew incorporating two techniques, where first the lentils are stewed/boiled with vegetables and puréed. The lamb is then braised for a while with masala and then cooked very gently in the puréed lentils and vegetables until tender.

Muslim communities make similar food using a different blend of spicing, though the methodology can be common but not entirely similar.

Likewise there are several other preparations that are representative of the three styles, some incorporating one or more styles in one dish.

THE TANDOOR

The tandoor, originating from the Persian 'taftoon', is classified as an oven and even though the cooking is not done in a totally enclosed atmosphere it is a type of open oven; therefore we can refer tandoor dishes as roasting. They would of course also be referred to as chargrilling or charbroiling and the breads are naturally baked, though the style of baking bread is almost like that of a pizza with the exception that the bread is stuck to the sides or walls of the oven and not placed at the bottom.

For the sake of simplification we can use the tandoor as yet another form of roasting and baking, however the meats and other products marinated for the tandoor may also be cooked under a conventional griller or an oven if a tandoor is not available. The results, however, will vary.

The tandoor is a very versatile piece of equipment but anything cooked in it needs to be cut down into small bite-sized pieces. These cubes are known in simplified terms as 'Tikkas'. A Tikka in simple terms would therefore mean a cube. It is misinterpreted and misused as a term but in the tandoor one has to use bite-sized pieces simply because the meat/vegetable/fruit is cooked at an extremely high temperature and the heat is applied directly to the product to enable rapid cooking.

Where a brazier is used, as in the streets of the sub-continent, the skewers are smaller and the meats are diced and not cubed. This style of cutting into dice is known as 'Boti'. These are often kebabs, or as we would call them 'kavaabs', and would contain ingredients such as liver, kidney, spleen, lamb dice, sheep's udders and testicles, chicken and so on, even small minced meat kavaabs better know as 'Sheek Kavaab'. The word Sheek means skewer.

Therefore we hope simply to be able to put some more insight into Indian cooking when applied to these three forms or styles of cooking and where possible a suitable reference is made.

Gosht Pakavani Reet

How to Cook Simple Lamb

Chef's Notes

- This is the basic simple way to cook lamb in the Parsee household but it is no different to any if you simply wish to cook lamb. Besides the typical ginger/garlic paste there is no other spicing or flavouring. Ideas and suggestions are given and the rest is left for the cook to decide. This is a simple mode towards taking on greater challenges and it is something a first-time cook needs to do. It makes one appreciate the intricacies even in the most simplistic cooking, the flavours, tastes, textures and aromas which ensue.

- This recipe originally was used by Parsees in the olden days to train the young lady cook in the house, before she learnt greater skills and eventually independence in the kitchen.

- As a variation whole garam masala and snipped red chillies can be added.

- Chunks of part fried, parboiled potato and can be added when the lamb is just more than half cooked.

Method

1. Heat the ghee in a pan and sauté the onions until golden brown.

2. Add the ginger/garlic paste and sauté for 1–2 minutes.

3. Next sauté the cleaned and washed lamb until all the water has dried up.

4. Add the salt and enough water to cover the lamb then cook covered until the lamb is done. A rigid timing cannot be adopted because different lamb, and different cuts of lamb, will cook at different time spans.

Measurements	Ingredients
100 g	Ghee or sunflower oil
1 medium to large	Onions (chopped)
1 heaped tbsp	Ginger/garlic paste (see page 135)
500g	Lamb or goat's meat
10 g	Salt

Adrak Kay Punjey

Chef's Notes

- This would literally translate as 'palm or five fingers of ginger', however the fingers represent the bones of a small rack of lamb showing five bone tips marinated in a masala redolent of the flavours of ginger and chargrilled. A good quality meat is best for this as the cooking process has to be short and the more tender and juicier the meat the more the penetration of the spices for flavour tenderisation and taste.

Measurements	Ingredients
Approx. 200–250g each or 800–1000g combined weight	Rack of lamb sold as portions in supermarkets showing 4–5 bones on each
2 tsp	Salt
1 tbsp	Lemon juice
½ tsp	Ground turmeric
1 tsp	Cumin
4 pods	Cardamom
2.5 cm	Cinnamon/Cassia
7.5 cm	Ginger
4–5 cloves	Garlic
2 large	Green chillies
3–4	Cloves
4–5	Black peppercorns
200 g	Yoghurt greek style
1 tbsp	Coriander stalks (chopped)
2 tbsp	Sunflower oil

Method

1. Clean the chops and trim off some of the fat if needed. Otherwise ask your butcher to larder trim them for you.

2. Scour the fat part with a sharp knife in a set pattern and rub in some of the salt, lemon juice and turmeric and set aside.

3. Put the cumin, cardamom, cinnamon and cloves in a small frying pan and roast them gently on a slow flame or heat until they are aromatic and lightly coloured. Remember that you *must* not let them burn, therefore they will need constant agitating.

4. Put all the ingredients into your blender and make a fine paste. You may wish to break the cinnamon/cassia into small pieces, cut the ginger into pieces and break the chilli into bits before adding them to the machine.

5. Check the seasoning after adding the remaining salt and marinate the chops.

6. Coat them thoroughly in the masala by placing them in a tray just big enough to hold them. If you space them out too much you may not have enough marinade. The best thing would be to leave the chops marinating overnight, in a lidded container just large enough to hold them all and have them coated with the marinade.

7. Leave them out for a couple of hours at least before placing them covered in the refrigerator. If you leave them in your refrigerator for more than a day there is nothing to worry about. You can keep them in the marinade for up to three or four days so long as they are well covered.

8. Preheat your oven to approximately 200 to 220°C, gas mark 6 to 7.

9. Roast the chops on a lightly greased or non-stick tray or pan, fat side up, to the desired level of cooking.

10. Reduce the temperature of the oven to between 160 to 180°C, gas mark 3 to 4 once the chops are in the oven.

11. Remember that due to the marinade the chops will remain pink inside. This does not mean that they are raw. They should be pink rather than over cooked and discoloured.

12. Test them for yourself. The duration of cooking time will depend on the number of hours the chops have been marinated. For top quality chops you should try to keep them to a maximum medium level, for best results.

13. Turn them once or twice in the oven but not too much as that will result in overcooking some parts and an uneven result, as well as making the masala burn in the tray.

14. There are several ways in which to use the pan drippings, if you have any. One of the best is to slice two medium onions and sauté them in a little oil. Try not to use the lamb fat drippings, as the taste will become too strong. You may wish to skim and discard the fat or reuse it if you are happy with the flavours.

15. Add to the onions two chopped tomatoes, sauté for a while and add the pan juices.

16. In this you may wish to add chunks of parboiled potato and simmer till they are cooked, to serve as an accompaniment or just serve the gravy as it is.

17. Season at will but you will automatically get a good flavour. Sprinkle some chopped coriander and fresh mint at the very end if you have to complete the gravy.

18. These chops will also cook very well on the barbecue, which is exactly what they are for anyway.

19. In case you decide to grill or barbecue them, do not place them with all the marinade on. Scrape off a bit before placing on the fire. It is better to grill single chops rather than an entire rack at once.

20. Use the marinade for something else later or just make nice gravy from it.

Masala Nu Roast Gos

Chef's Notes

- This is a Parsee-style roasted joint of lamb. Once roasted the lamb may be sliced and served cold as a sandwich filler, served hot with the gravy shown below with boiled rice or a light cumin pulao. This style of marinating is quite typical but very adaptable and the simplicity of it all makes it suitable for most meats.

Method

1. Trim the leg of lamb to suit as for roasting.

2. Roast the cumin and coriander on a low heat until they change colour slightly and cool.

3. In a blender grind together the ginger, garlic and the roasted cumin and coriander to a fine paste with only as much water as is necessary to keep the condiments.

4. Peel the potatoes, remove any spots, wash and keep them soaked in water.

5. In a casserole big enough to take the leg of lamb add the oil and heat until a light haze forms on the surface.

6. Reduce the heat a little then add the leg of lamb.

7. Brown well on all sides until the meat is well sealed.

8. Remove the lamb from the casserole and add the whole spices.

9. Sauté for 1–2 minutes on a low heat until the cloves swell a bit, then deglaze the casserole with a little water to release the residue from the lamb stuck at the base.

10. Scrape with a wooden spatula until the base is scraped clean and add the onions.

11. Continue cooking until the liquid evaporates and the onions are now being sautéed.

12. Sauté until the onions are soft and add the ground masala.

13. Add some water to the container to release any stuck masala and add this to the pan too.

14. Continue cooking for 5–6 minutes and put the lamb joint back into the casserole.

15. Coat it well with the masala, check seasoning and add salt as desired.

16. Lower the heat a little, cover the pan tightly and continue cooking the lamb.

17. At this stage if your casserole is ovenproof put the covered casserole into the oven at approximately 150°C, gas mark 3.

18. After about 15 minutes remove from the oven, turn the meat and put it back into the oven.

19. If cooking on the cooker turn the meat after 10 minutes or so and also check to see that the contents are not burning at the base.

20. In either case if the contents dry out too much or the onions are burning, add some water or stock of you have any to loosen the contents at the bottom of the pan.

Measurements	Ingredients
1–1.25 kg	Leg of lamb (roast trimmed)
1 tsp	Cumin
1 tbsp	Coriander seeds
50 g	Ginger
50 g	Garlic
12 or so small	Potatoes
2–3 tbsp	Sunflower oil
2 2.5 cm pieces	Cinnamon or casia
3–4	Green cardamom
2–3	Cloves
3–4	Peppercorns
3 medium	Onions (chopped)
200 g	Tomato (chopped)
1 tsp and then as desired	Salt

21. In another 15 minutes or so the lamb should be approximately half cooked. At this stage add the tomatoes and the potatoes and if necessary some water or stock, cover and continue cooking for another 10–15 minutes.

22. If not using a thermometer the best way to test the lamb would be to notice the cooking process and the shrinkage accordingly.

23. When the lamb is almost cooked the muscles at the shin will have retracted and the lamb will itself feel soft to the touch.

24. If in doubt insert a thin skewer or a roasting fork and check to see if the fluid released is running clear.

25. When the lamb is done remove it onto a tray and also remove any gravy stuck to it. Remove the potatoes and set these aside.

26. Check the gravy and if necessary add enough liquid to have a pouring consistency.

27. Either serve the lamb sliced hot with the gravy and the potatoes or serve it later by slicing it when cold.

28. A little freshly chopped coriander adds a touch of magic to the gravy.

29. This is best served with chunks of deep-fried parboiled potato and steamed rice.

Bhuna Gosht

Braised Lamb North Indian Style

Chef's Notes

• This is perhaps the best-known lamb preparation, namewise across the globe. Several variations of the dish exist and, once again, due to the simplicity of the name itself one can easily call any like dish a 'Bhuna'. However, it is not only the throwing together of spices and condiments that can produce a classic. This recipe is a classic and if done well you will see what I mean.

Method

1. Clean the lamb well and remove sinews, gristle etc.

2. Blend all the marinade ingredients well in a bowl large enough to hold the lamb, preferably with a lid.

3. When the marinade is well blended, add the lamb, mix in well, clean the bowl edges with a piece of kitchen towel, cover and set aside for at least 2 hours. If you like leave it in the refrigerator overnight – 6–8 hours gives a better result.

Measurements	Ingredients
1 kg	Lamb leg (cut into 2.5cm cubes)
2 tbsp	Fresh coriander (chopped)
2 tbsp	Fresh mint (chopped)
To taste	Salt
Marinade	**Ingredients**
2 tbsp	Garlic paste
1 tbsp	Ginger paste
1 tsp	Turmeric powder
2 tsp	Red chilli powder
2 tsp	Cumin powder
2 tsp	Coriander powder
½	Lime (juice only)
150–200 g	Thick yoghurt (Greek style preferred)

Continued

4. Heat the oil in a deep casserole roughly 25 cm in diameter until a haze forms and the oil is quite hot. Add the sliced onions and sauté over a medium flame, stirring with a flat wooden spatula from time to time. Always remember that onions will brown from the outside therefore folding the sides into the centre will help to get an even colour.

5. Continue cooking until the onions are a deep golden brown. Do not allow over browning or blackening.

6. Reduce the flame to low. Remove the onions with a slotted spoon allowing as much oil as possible to drain off. Spread the onions onto a plate. Note that the latent heat will create a carry over cooking process, therefore the onions need to be spread out so that heat escapes and they do not burn.

7. Add the whole spices to the oil, which should not be very hot, and allow them to swell and brown a bit. Meanwhile remove the lamb from the marinade and separate as much as possible. Some will stick to the meat and that is quite OK.

8. Add the meat to the pan as soon as the spices change to a light brown colour and increase the flame to medium, or high if you can keep watch. Stir the lamb from time to time but do not allow it to stick at the bottom. If the marinade does burn at the bottom add a little water by the tablespoon to deglaze the pan.

9. When the meat is well browned add the water, cover the pan and simmer the meat.

10. Meanwhile, make the gravy. Place the tomatoes, browned onions, yoghurt and the remaining marinade in a blender and purée to a smooth paste.

11. Add this to the simmering lamb and mix in well, add salt to taste, cover and continue to cook.

12. When the lamb is almost done, continue cooking with the lid off on a low flame and allow the gravy to thicken. The gravy is ready when you see the oil released from the meat and the gravy almost leaves the sides.

13. Check seasoning, mix in the coriander and mint and serve with hot parathas or chappaties.

Tempering/sizzling	Ingredients
4 tbsp	Sunflower oil
450–500 g	Onions (thinly and evenly sliced after being slit into two and centre stub removed)
3 × 2.5 cm pieces	Cinnamon sticks (use cassia)
6	Cloves
6	Split green cardamom
3–4 large, broken in half	Whole red chilli
150–200 ml	Water
Gravy	**Ingredients**
250 g	Tomatoes (cut coarsely)
150 g	Onions (browned) (as shown below)
200 g	Yoghurt

Chora-ma-gos

Lamb Cooked with Black-eyed Beans or Cow Peas

Chef's Notes

- A preparation such as this immediately takes you to a combination of at least two cooking cultures. Cooking with pulses, grains, beans, etc. immediately refers to our Persian/Mughal heritage and is used more frequently by the Muslims and Parsees of India. The other spice combinations represent any other part of Indian, really. Parsees all over the Indian sub-continent make this dish but it can vary in combination. This version is what I grew up with and one our family enjoyed immensely. But then mum has always been an excellent cook.

- Do use good British mutton if you like the flavour. I would recommend, however, that you trim off some of the fat otherwise the flavours become too strong. This is a similar problem if cooking in India with older animals, be they goats or sheep.

Measurements	Ingredients
500 g	Mutton or lamb
250 g	Cowpeas (dry) (Black-eyed beans)
250 g	Onion
2.5 cm	Ginger
6–8 cloves	Garlic
½ tsp	Turmeric
1 tsp	Ground coriander
½ tsp	Ground cumin
3	Green chillies (chopped)
½ bunch	Coriander leaves
100 g	Cherry tomatoes
½ tsp	Crushed pepper
1 tbsp	Vinegar
To taste	Sugar (optional)
1 tsp	Salt
5 g	Chilli powder
1 tbsp	Sunflower oil
1½ litre (approx).	Water

Method

1. Wash the mutton/lamb and cut into 12–18 mm pieces.

2. Pick, wash and soak the cowpeas for at least 2–3 hours. (Picking the beans is not necessary in the UK as they come fully cleaned.)

3. Chop half of the onions and cut the rest into big dice.

4. Mix the mutton, peas and cut onions and boil in the water with some salt.

5. As soon as you get a brisk boil reduce the heat and bring the boil down a bit. Remove the scum as it comes to the top when boiling.

6. Sauté the chopped onion until golden in colour then add the ginger and garlic paste (puréed together), turmeric, coriander, cumin powder and chilli powder.

7. Add this mixture to the boiling pot and check seasoning.

8. Add the green chillies, coriander leaves and tomatoes; simmer on a slow flame until the meat and beans are fully cooked.

9. Then add the crushed pepper, vinegar and sugar and chilli powder and check the seasoning once again.

10. Serve hot with bread or chappaties; onion and cucumber could also be served with it. Rice is also a good accompaniment.

Chutt Patta Gosht

Chef's Notes

- The words 'Chutt Putta' mean something that is a bit hot and tongue tingling. This preparation is not classical in its origins but is made in several different ways. It has a bit of a punch but is quite delightful and full of flavour. It should be ideally served as a lamb accompaniment when there is other food on the table that is wet or in a gravy. This is the way many Indians would eat too. Often the hottest dish on the menu is dry and therefore acts as a condiment to the meal.

Measurements	Ingredients
500 g	Lamb (diced 1 cm × 1 cm)
100 ml	Sunflower oil
20–25	Curry leaves
1 tsp	Cumin (whole)
1 tbsp	Cumin (powdered)
1 tbsp	Coriander powder
1 heaped tbsp	Chilli (crushed or powdered)
1½ tbsp	Ginger/garlic paste
2 heaped tbsp	Tomato paste
200 g	Yoghurt
3 tbsp	Fresh mint (chopped)
4 tbsp	Fresh coriander (chopped)
1 heaped tsp	Garam masala powder
Salt	To taste

Method

1. Clean and wash the lamb and allow to drain well.

2. Heat the oil till a haze forms over it then add the curry leaves. As they finish crackling add the cumin seeds and in 5–10 seconds when the cumin turns brown but not blackened add the lamb.

3. Sauté the lamb and allow it almost to dry out and brown well.

4. When it begins to bubble towards the end and very little moisture remains, reduce the heat and add the powdered cumin, coriander and chilli powders.

5. Sauté for 1–2 minutes then add the ginger/garlic paste and a little water to release the spices and dried juices at the bottom of the pan.

6. After a further minute add the tomato paste and well beaten yoghurt and stir well.

7. Level out the contents in the pan, clean the sides with a spatula then cover and simmer slowly until lamb is cooked. Stir from time to time and repeat the cleaning process each time.

8. Add a little water if you find that the lamb is not yet tender but the contents are drying up then stir and continue cooking covered until lamb is tender.

9. When the lamb is tender open the pot, add the coriander and mint and cook for a further 5–6 minutes.

10. Add the garam masala and salt and cook for a minute further or until the gravy is really thick.

11. Check the seasoning.

12. If you find that there is a great deal of oil floating on top, remove it gently. For this you may have to tilt the pan and spoon out as much as you can in a small bowl and retain for future use. Oil will be released because of the lamb getting rendered. Also there is no gravy or onions to absorb the fat. Yoghurt also gives off its own fat.

13. Eat the lamb in hot chappaties with freshly sliced onions tossed with shredded tomatoes and green chilli.

Cyrus's Gos No Palav

Lamb Pulao

Chef's Notes

- Recipes for lamb pulaos vary and there are several with each person claiming that his or hers is the very best. This one has been time tested by me and I have tweaked and added to some old recipes and traditions and come up with a recipe which is more foolproof than many I have tried. Pulaos are not what one considers healthy eating and are always eaten at celebrations and festive occasions or when you wish to indulge occasionally.

- In the sub-continent top quality basmati is used for pulaos and biryanis. Like great wines basmati is graded by age and quality. Most households will store good rice in air tight containers and use it in rotation but never in the year it was produced. Older rice has a better aroma and if kept well ages like a good wine.

Measurements	Ingredients
500 g	Lamb
200 g	Greek yoghurt
To deep fry	Oil
500 g	Onions (very thinly sliced)

Method

1. Cut, clean, wash and drain the lamb. Blend in the yoghurt well, cover and place in the refrigerator overnight.

2. Wash the onions well in cold water and drain well. Remove as much water as you can before frying. If you have a salad spinner, use that. It is very effective.

3. Heat the oil and fry the onions, stirring regularly.

4. Remove into a colander when the onion is light brown. The carry over cooking and latent heat will make them deep golden when cooled.

5. To make the masala finely chop the ginger, garlic and green chilli and set aside.

6. Heat the oil and sizzle the whole spices including the red chilli. Do not overheat the oil otherwise the spices will burn.

7. As soon as the spices swell and brown (not burn) add the raw sliced onions and sauté until brown.

Masala	Ingredients
5 cm piece	Ginger
4–6 cloves	Garlic
2 large	Green chilli
100 g	Oil (from that left over after onions are fried)
10 g (2 cm piece)	Cinnamon or Cassia
4–5 pods	Cardamon
3–4	Cloves
2–3 large	Whole red chilli
500 g	Onions (very thinly sliced)
1 tsp	Cumin
2 tsp	Coriander powder
1 level tsp	Red chilli powder
½ tsp	Turmeric powder
300–400 ml	Water
As desired	Salt

8. Remove the fried onion and masala once the onions are browned but take care to squeeze out as much oil into the pan as possible.

9. Reheat the oil to smoking point and add the marinated meat. Do not agitate too much but allow the heat to build up so that the meat seals well and does not release all its fluids.

10. Continue sautéing until the liquid begins to dry up.

11. Once almost dry add the green chilli, ginger and garlic and sauté until you see the garlic change colour.

12. Blend the cumin, coriander, red chilli and turmeric powders in the water and add to the lamb.

13. Sauté for a couple of minutes until the liquid dries up again.

14. Check the lamb and add just enough water to almost dry up but leave a rich thick gravy when the lamb gets cooked. Add the sautéed brown onions mixed with the whole spices and mix well.

15. Cover with a tight lid and cook on a slow flame until the lamb is almost done. The lamb will not be ready until it is completely soft.

Rice for the Pulao

Method

1. In a large casserole or pot bring the water to the boil along wth the bay leaves, cardamom and salt.

2. Meanwhile wash the rice well in a bowl until the water runs clean then drain and set aside.

3. When the water is boiling add the rice and stir continuously for 1–2 minutes, maintaining the heat high.

Measurements	Ingredients
4–5 litres	Water
2	Bay leaves
4–5	Cardamom pods
1 level tbsp	Salt
500 g	Basmati rice

4. Boil for approximately 6–7 minutes or until the grains are just done but not soft or mushy. Keep the rice just slightly underdone for better results.

5. Drain and leave in the colander.

The Final Pulao

Method

1. Preheat the oven to between 180 and 200°C.

2. Boil the potatoes and cut them into quarters.

3. In a small saucepan or frying pan gently heat the saffron until it becomes crisp. Do not allow it to burn or singe. At no stage should you leave it unattended and let it discolour. Once crisp and emanating its aromas add the water and slowly heat to a simmer. Once simmering set it aside.

4. Put half the boiled rice in a bowl and mix in the saffron. Remove any leftover strands in the pan. You can add some rice to the pan to absorb any residues and thereby clean the pan out of any waste.

Measurements	Ingredients
3–4 medium	Potato (cut into chunks)
Good pinch	Saffron
³/₄ teacup	Water
2 tbsp	Butter (melted)
2–3 heaped tbsp	Fresh coriander
2 heaped tbsp	Fresh mint
2–3 medium	Tomatoes (quartered)
3–4	Eggs (boiled)
1	Lime (juice only)

5. Take an ovenproof pot with a tight-fitting lid, large enough to take both the lamb and the rice, and pour in the melted butter and coat the base.

6. Mix some of the previously fried brown onions in the plain boiled rice and spread it well at the botttom of the pan.

7. On this sprinkle half the coriander and mint and half the tomatoes and potatoes and spread these out.

8. Gently spread the lamb including all its gravy over the rice and scrape the pot clean with a spatula.

9. On top of the meat now sprinkle the remaining coriander, mint, tomatoes and potatoes.

10. Cut the eggs into half and place them yolk side up in between the potato and tomato, dotting them evenly.

11. Now cover evenly with the saffron rice.

12. Sprinkle the remaining brown onions (retain a spoonful if you wish to use them as a garnish later) and the lime juice over the rice.

13. Cover with the lid and place in the oven but not directly on the bottom. Keep one of the oven shelves below to allow air circulation and no direct heat to the base.

14. If the lid is not tight-fitting you can place some foil over the top of the pan and then place the lid over it to ensure that all the heat remains in the pot.

15. In India we would seal the pot with dough to make a perfect seal. You can do that too. It does not damage the pot and will break off once fully baked.

16. Keep the pulao in the oven for close to 1½ hours. After about 40 minutes or so reduce the heat to 120°C.

17. You do not need to look at the pulao or open the pan, just allow the steam inside the pot to cook the lamb and the rice fully. The heat builds up very slowly inside the pot, which is why a good 90–120 minutes' cooking time is essential.

18. When you are ready to serve open the pot and gently mix the rices with the lamb. Remove into large platters and serve with some sprinkled brown onions if you like. We do.

19. Serve the pulao with either a masala daal or some simple cucumber raita and fresh onion salad known as cachumber.

Dahi Nu Vindaloo

Vindaloo of Lamb with Yoghurt

Chef's Notes

- This one is no doubt of complete Parsee origin. I cannot shed light as to where within the Parsee diaspora this must have been created, but nevertheless it is reworked out of a very old recipe I found among the many treasured recipes of my maternal grandmother. Perhaps the Parsee added yoghurt to tone down the heat of the chilli as compared to the Goan vindaloo and made it more in keeping with richer Parsee tastes.

- It is essential to get large chillies since they are less hot and are very good for the colour, The Indian Kashmiri chilli is the best for this. Alternatively substitute with good whole paprika if you like.

Method

1. Cut the lamb into 2.5 cm pieces, removing all unwanted membranes and gristle, etc.

2. Grind the masala ingredients to a fine paste in a blender. (Do not add too much vinegar, add it a teaspoon at a time, until the paste gets really fine. There is yoghurt as well so the blender will not need much vinegar. Your paste should be thick not runny.)

3. Transfer the lamb to a glass or plastic bowl and add the masala as well as the fried onions. Add salt as required. Mix well, wipe the sides of the bowl with a tissue and set the lamb aside for a few hours where possible. Where time is of the essence at least an hour needs to be given.

4. Transfer to a casserole with a tight-fitting lid that will take all the ingredients to follow. Cover tightly and cook on a slow gentle heat. Stir regularly to avoid bottoming until the lamb is about three-quarters done.

5. Add the tomatoes and jaggery, simmer for a few minutes and add the potatoes and other vegetables if you wish. The carrots if being added are better added half done.

6. Check for seasoning and blend in some freshly chopped coriander prior to serving.

7. Serves with a garlic flavoured pulao or just some good crusty bread.

Measurements	Ingredients
500 g	Lamb (cleaned)
3 medium	Onions (chopped and fried golden, drained and set aside)
To taste	Salt
2 large	Beef tomatoes (chopped)
2 tsp	Jaggery (raw cane sugar)
225 g	Baby or new potatoes (peeled and if desired fry to a golden brown in the same oil, or half boil and fry)
	Green peas, diced carrots and beans can all be used to give a stewy effect and colour (optional)
2 tbsp	Fresh coriander (chopped)
Masala	Ingredients
8–9 large	Red chillies
1 tsp	Whole coriander
1 tsp	Whole cumin
1/4 tsp	Turmeric
5 cm	Fresh ginger
6–8 cloves	Garlic
250 g	Live yoghurt (I strongly recommend the Greek style yoghurt)
1	Lime (juice only)
As required	Cider vinegar

Dhaansaak

Chef's Notes

- The best known of great Parsee cooking. 'Dhaan' means rice and 'Saak' stands for the combination of lentils and lamb that go with it. In the Parsee household 'Dhaansaak' is the traditional Sunday roast. To a Parsee, Dhaansaak is always lamb unless someone in the family does not eat lamb or is a vegetarian. It is also not complete as a meal unless accompanied by Cachumbar or onion salad and deep-fried lamb kebabs. Cooking Dhaansaak is a painstaking affair but very simple and can be started the day before to enjoy the Sunday lunch, which is what we Parsees do. The end result can be a sheer achievement and if done well will go down as a masterpiece.

- The recipe is in three stages and each one can be used as an independent recipe as well. This will not only simplify things but make you understand how intricate and in-depth Indian cooking really is.

Dhaan the Pulao

Method

1. Heat the oil in a casserole and add the spices.

2. When well browned add the onions and sauté gently, stirring regularly until they are a deep brown.

3. Add the rice. (The rice should be washed and drained before being added. If using basmati in the UK you may not need to wash it.)

4. Sauté the rice for 5–6 minutes on a medium heat, turning regularly so that all the grains get evenly cooked.

5. Add hot water up to 2.5 cm above the level of the rice, stir for 1 minute, cover and allow to cook. Do not keep a high flame. Instead reduce the flame to a low so that the pulao cooks gently.

6. Check from time to time, stirring from the bottom up with a flat wooden spatula. If you need more water add it slowly, a little at a time.

Measurements	Ingredients
5 tbsp	Oil
1 2.5 cm piece	Cinnamon
3–4	Cardamom
3–4	Cloves
4–5	Star anise
2 medium	Onions (cut in half and finely sliced, centre root stub removed)
100 g (or 500 g per person)	Basmati rice
As required	Hot water
To taste (approx. 2 level tsp)	Salt

7. Your pulao should take approximately 15–20 minutes. When the grains are cooked, set aside but do not uncover the pot.

For garnish

Slice one or two onions as before and brown to a light golden. Drain and remove onto a paper towel to drain well. If well fried these will be crisp and should be sprinkled over the rice just before serving. You will also need chopped mint and chopped coriander.

The following are two recipes for two different masalas. One is to be added to the lentils and the other should be added as a flavouring at the end. Both can be prepared in larger quantities and kept for future use.

Keep the wet masala (1) in the refrigerator in an airtight jar and the dry masala (2) in an airtight jar in your larder.

Masala 1 for Cooking lamb

Method

1. Roast all the ingredients of the masala except the fresh coriander gently on a skillet or wok. Stir regularly. This will enable the spices to give off their flavour better.

2. When the chillies and the spices look roasted, in that they have changed colour but not discoloured, remove and transfer to the grinder with the fresh coriander.

3. Take a little water at a time and grind it to a fine paste in your blender.

Measurements	Ingredients
1 5 cm piece	Cinnamon
6	Cardamom
6–8	Cloves
2 tsp	Cumin (whole)
10	Peppercorns
1 heaped tbsp	Coriander seeds
8–10 large	Red chillies
3 2.5 cm pieces	Ginger (coarsely cut)
10–12 cloves	Garlic (coarsely cut)
30–50 g	Fresh coriander (use stalks as well)

Masala 2 for the final flavouring

Method

1. Follow the same method of roasting as before, cool and powder the masala in a grinder. This quantity is sufficient for the amount of Dhaansaak we are to make. However it is also a brilliant masala for last-minute meat dish flavouring and you can increase the quantities of the individual in equal proportions to make more.

Measurements	Ingredients
3–4	Cardamom
3–4	Cloves
2–3	Star anise
1 heaped tsp	Cumin
8–10	Peppercorns
2–3	Red chillies
2 tsp	Dry fenugreek

The Daal

Method

1. Wash the lentils and transfer to a large casserole. Add water up to 2.5 cm over the level of the lentils then add all the remaining ingredients and boil. Cook on a low flame once on the boil.

2. While cooking scrape the bottom regularly with a wooden spatula. When the lentils are fully cooked, purée the entire pot pourri, cover and set aside.

Measurements	Ingredients
100 g	Toover daal (toor)
50 g	Split chickpeas
50 g	Yellow mung bean
100 g	Pink lentils
1 small	Aubergine (cut into pieces)
100 g after skinning	Red pumpkin (diced)
2 tbsp	Fresh dill (coarsely cut)
1 leaf	Colcasia leaves (arbi) if available
50 g (if not available use 1 tbsp dry methi leaves)	Fresh methi leaves
To taste	Salt
1 tbsp concentrated, or 1 cup freshly made	Tamarind paste
100 g	Jaggery
2 tbsp	Coriander stalks (chopped without the root ends. To be well washed before adding.)
2 tbsp	Mint stalks (chopped without the root ends)

The Lamb

Method

1. Cut the lamb into decent sized pieces about 2 cm square. I prefer to use leg of lamb only but you may wish to use another cut. Bones should be used whereever possible in cooking for their flavour.

2. Heat the oil in a casserole and sauté the lamb on a high heat.

Measurements	Ingredients
500 g	Lamb
2–3 tbsp	Oil
150 ml	Water
As required	Salt

3. Once the lamb has sealed well and the meat is well coloured add masala 1 (the wet one.) Sauté until you see the oil escaping along the sides.

4. Add the water, check the salt, cover tightly and cook on a medium fire for approximately 20–25 minutes to cook well.

5. Do not overcook, but stir at regular intervals and add a little water at a time if required.

6. When ready and you have a nice thick rich gravy blend the lamb with the lentil purée.

7. Now blend in masala 2 (the dry one) and check seasoning. This is your 'saak'. You can serve this on its own with any kind of rice if you do not make the dhaansaak pulao. However, your Dhaansaak as a dish remains incomplete (see below). We Parsees call this 'Masala Ni Daar Ma Gos', meaning lamb in lentils cooked in masala.

8. Before serving sprinkle with chopped coriander and chopped mint and blend.

To serve Dhaansaak

Dhaansaak must be served as an entire meal.

- The daal and lamb
- The brown pulao (onion and garam masala) sprinkled with brown onions.
- The kebabs garnished or dotted on top of the pulao and cachumber. This is essential.

Method

1. Take a large onion and slice it finely. Mix in some chopped mint and coriander, one finely chopped medium green chilli, one small tomato seeded and shredded, salt and about 1 tsp vinegar. Mix well and serve as an accompaniment. You can also serve fried papads. When selecting papads for this you must have the lentil papads and not the Madras Pappadams.

Dhaniawala Gosht

Chef's Notes

- The explanation simply means 'lamb with coriander'. It is a simple preparation and is one of those items where you do not need a great deal of preparation if you have the basic ingredients. However, the end result is great and this lamb will appeal to all except to those who do not like the flavour of coriander and I know only a very few who don't.

Measurements	Ingredients
3–4	Red chilli (whole, cut into pieces)
2 × 2.5 cm pieces	Cinnamon stick
4–5 tbsp	Oil
500 g	Lamb (diced from leg of lamb)
3 medium	Onions (chopped)
1 heaped tbsp	Ginger (finely chopped, almost minced)
2 tbsp	Garlic (finely chopped)
1 tbsp	Cumin seeds roasted and crushed
2 tbsp	Coriander seeds roasted and crushed, not powdered
As required	Water or stock
To taste	Salt
4 medium or 1 can	Tomatoes (peeled and chopped)
3–4 tbsp	Fresh coriander (chopped)

Method

1 Roast the red chilli and cinnamon stick in a fry pan on a low heat. When they get lightly browned and give off their flavour, cool and crush in a mortar and pestle or in a small grinder. Remember not to make them too finely powdered but like the consistency of crushed peppercorns.

2. Clean the lamb of any gristle, sinews, etc. and set aside.

3. Heat the oil in a casserole until almost at smoking point and add the lamb. Allow to seal well and brown keeping the heat on high .

4. Add the red chillies and cinnamon and sauté for 1–2 minutes.

5. Add the onions and sauté with the lamb stirring constantly until the base of the pan is scraped clean. Add a little water at this stage to help clean the bottom. Sauté until the onions are opaque but not browned.

6. Add ginger, garlic, cumin and coriander, sauté for 2 minutes on medium heat, then either add water or some stock, enough just to cover the lamb. This means that the liquid should be just up to the level of the lamb. If not too confident add a little at a time but keep the pot covered.

7. Add salt and simmer until the lamb is half done.

8. At this stage if there is too much liquid, continue cooking with the pot uncovered until the liquid is thick.

9. Add the tomatoes and cook on a medium heat until the lamb is cooked and soft and the gravy is thick and not watery.

10. Before serving mix in the fresh coriander and check seasoning.

11. This can be served with plain steamed rice or bread.

Gos Ma Eeda Athwa Adlo

Lamb with Eggs or Shin

Chef's Notes

- This recipe is an old classic and a very traditional one at that. In a traditional Parsee home three basic masalas exist and these are Laal Murcha no Masalo, Dhana Jeera no Masalo and Aadu Lasan no Masalo. In order these are ginger garlic paste, coriander and cumin paste, red chilli with spices. Today times have changed and things have been simplified but there are still hundreds of refrigerators that will proudly display these all-time favourites. The masalas give the housewife tremendous flexibility and she can virtually create 100 different products by playing around with her masalas. The dish here is an example of the richness of the cuisine and the culture. The Parsees are primarily meat eaters but also love their potatoes and this becomes evident in many Parsee dishes.

- The recipe can be cooked with lamb shank instead of diced lamb and makes a very tasty dish. The kidneys, however, remain unchanged. The shank may be shredded and then re-added to the dish or left as a whole. Remember the best lamb for all of this type of high class cooking is organic bio-dynamic lamb. Across the sub-continent lamb is mostly naturally organic since no actual feed is given or pastures grown for grazing.

Measurements	Ingredients
500 g	Lamb (diced)
250 g	Kidneys
1 tbsp	Adu lasan no masalo (garlic ginger paste)
1 tbsp	Marcha no masalo (red chilli with spices)
To taste	Salt
5	Cloves
5	Cardamom
125 g	Ghee (use oil if you wish)
250 g	Sour yoghurt
3 heaped tbsp	Browned onions
Few strands	Saffron
5	Eggs (boiled)
100 ml (approx.)	Water

Method

1. Dice the lamb and kidneys into small pieces.

2. Wash, drain and mix in the two masalas with salt.

3. Crush the cardamom and cloves, fry in the ghee until light brown then add the lamb and kidneys.

4. Sauté for 5–6 minutes.

5. Add a little water and continue cooking.

6. Mix the yoghurt, browned onions and saffron and set aside for a while and then purée.

7. When the lamb is almost done and the liquid almost dry, add the yoghurt mix.

8. When the lamb is cooked, add the boiled eggs either whole or cut into halves.

9. Leave on a slow flame or heat for a few minutes.

10. You may like to add a few chunks of deep-fried potato for that extra touch.

11. One or two tbsp chopped coriander will enhance the flavours greatly.

Laal Murcha No Masalo

- This is a simple red masala with whole red chilli, coriander seeds and cumin seeds gently roasted and ground to a fine paste with some water.

Measurements	Ingredients
20 g	Red chillies
1 level tbsp	Coriander seeds
1 heaped tsp	Cumin seeds

Method

1. Snip the red chilli into small pieces.

2. Place all the ingredients in a frying pan and roast them on a very slow flame, pressing down with a well-folded kitchen towel or cloth until the spices change colour and give off a strong aroma.

3. Do not allow to burn or discolour.

4. Purée in a blender with a little water or as much as is desired.

5. In the recipe above only 1 tbsp masala is asked for. Reserve the rest for other use later.

Dhana Jeera No Masalo

Method

- Take half the quantity of cumin to coriander seeds, roast them gently as shown above and purée them to a fine paste in a blender or liquidiser but use very little water.

Aadu Lasan No Masalo

- This is a ginger garlic paste (see page 135).

Storage

- These masalas will keep well in airtight jars with a wide mouth or small plastic containers.

- Make sure that each time you use a masala you wipe the edges of the container with a dry paper towel and close the lid tightly.

- Another way of preserving your masalas well is to add some sunflower oil to them on the top. This prevents oxidation and drying out.

- Always remember that if your masala begins to dry up add some oil and not water to make it into a paste again. Raw water will attract mould.

Haddus Kari

Lamb Curry with Yoghurt and Masoor Daal

Chef's Notes

- This is another great classic from my community and one which perhaps may not have been made at a festive celebration for well over 50 years I would imagine. It is rather rich but one can always use sunflower or rapeseed oil instead of ghee to make it lighter on the stomach. Once again I have brought this into the book simply to demonstrate the crossover of cultures. Lamb with yoghurt and saffron plus the lentils is part of our Persian heritage. The spicing along with turmeric and the extra use of onions is most definitely the Indian angle. However, it is a great dish by any measure and one that the diners will remember for a long time to come. This was the very last recipe I made with my father before he passed away. I needed his knowledge to convert my grandmother's measures into grams.

Measurements	Ingredients
500 g	Lamb
5–6 cloves	Garlic
750 g	Onions
7.5 cm piece	Ginger
1 heaped tbsp	Coriander seeds
250 g	Yoghurt (thick)
30 g or as desired	Salt
200 g	Ghee
200 g	Pink lentils (masoor)
12	Cloves
7.5 cm piece	Cinnamon or cassia
10	Cardamom
1 heaped tsp	Turmeric
Few strands	Saffron

Method

1. Clean, wash and set the lamb aside in a colander.

2. Grind together half the garlic, half the onions, all the ginger and the coriander seeds along with the yoghurt and approximately 30 g salt.

3. Once the marinade is smooth and all the ingredients well ground, mix it into the lamb well.

4. Chop half the remaining onions and sauté in half the ghee until golden brown. You can use sunflower or rapeseed oil instead, if you prefer.

5. Add the meat with the marinade and mix well.

6. Sauté until almost dry and very little liquid remains.

7. Wash the lentils and set aside while the lamb is cooking. Add to the lamb when dry.

8. Sauté for a few minutes and add enough water so that the lentils will cook with the lamb, i.e. just enough to cover the lamb.

9. Heat the remaining ghee in a separate pan and add the remaining chopped garlic and onions, the cloves, cinnamon, cardamom and turmeric. Sauté for 2–3 minutes on a medium flame.

10. Remove, cool and grind to a fine paste.

11. Add the saffron when puréeing the above. Use only as much water as may be needed as you do not want to overcook the lamb until all the liquid dries up.

12. Blend this into the cooked lamb and simmer for 2–3 minutes until heated through.

13. This is excellent when eaten with plain pulao or parathas and cachumber (see page 231).

Sheek Kavaab

Chef's Notes

- One of the many great representatives of Indian cuisine, sheek kavaab, or kebab as it is mostly called, is usually a street-side speciality. This Muslim dish can be traced to its Persian roots. Sheek Kavaab also varies in recipe from state to state and region to region. This is one that appeals to most palates and I believe it is one of the simplest and best. Though the meat used should always be lean, a bit of good quality kidney fat will bring out the best flavour and a superb texture.

Measurements	Ingredients
500 g	Lamb shoulder meat
20 g including stalks	Fresh coriander
20 g including stalks	Fresh mint
2.5 cm piece	Fresh ginger (coarsely cut)
6–8 cloves	Garlic
1 tsp	Garam masala powder
1 tsp	Ground cumin
1 tsp	Ground coriander
1–2 large	Fresh green chilli
½ tsp	Ground red chilli
½ tsp	Turmeric powder
1 tsp	Lime juice
To taste	Salt

Method

1. Clean the meat well, removing all sinews and gristle. Do not discard any fat if found. Cut into pieces small enough so as not to jam the mincer.

2. Mince all the ingredients together except the powdered spices, salt and lime juice.

3. Once the mince is done add the powders and lime juice and knead well.

4. To check salt if you do not like tasting raw meat, either deep fry a small ball of the mince or pan fry a small patty-sized piece.

5. Once you are satisfied with the taste, cover the mince and chill in the refrigerator for 4–6 hours (overnight is best).

6. To make the kebabs you either need a tandoor or you can grill them over a barbecue. Ensure that whatever you are cooking over is lit or heated to a high degree before you start forming the mince over the skewers.

7. Thick square skewers are the best if you are not familiar with using rounded ones; thin skewers cannot hold the weight of the mince.

8. Take a 5 cm ball of the mince in one hand and a skewer in the other. Make the mince as smooth as possible by tossing it like a ball in your hand.

9. Now place the mince ball at roughly the middle of the skewer and press around so that the mince is now covering all round that part of the skewer.

10. Apply a little oil or water to the palm that you use for the mince and gently press the meat to make it in the shape of a sausage on the skewer. This does take a bit of practice and you may find that initially the mince falls off the skewer. However, if you form a ring between your forefinger and thumb and use the rest of the fingers to guide the mince you will be fine. The pressure has to be applied gently and the mince pushed upwards so that it thins itself out over the skewer. Ideally the size of the sausage should be 2.5 cm or a bit less in diameter.

11. Once you have achieved this you can suspend the skewer on a small tray so that the skewer rests over the two opposite sides and allows the minced area to remain in the hollow of the tray.

    Complete this with all the skewers.

12. When you are ready suspend the kavabs in a similar way either over the barbecue or insert them in the tandoor as recommended by the manufacturer.

13. Do not overcook as this makes the kavab dry and chewy. The kavab should ideally feel spongy but should show signs of a liquid presence inside.

14. Serve with fresh green chutney and an onion based salad … and enjoy. Alternatively roll in a chappati or a flour tortilla filled with salad and sliced onion and serve.

INTERNATIONAL CUISINE

Shikari Nargisi Kofta

Measurements	Ingredients
200 g	Venison
200 g	Hare
200 g	Wild boar
7.5 cm piece	Ginger
8 cloves	Garlic
2–3 medium	Green chillies
4–5 stalks with leaves and stem	Fresh coriander
10–15 leaves	Mint
1½ tsp	Salt
1 tsp	Garam masala powder
4	Eggs

Chef's Notes

- Nargisi kofta is the classical Indian Scotch egg and dates back centuries. This kofta is a variation of the usual lamb kofta and is made from a combination of game meats. You may combine any meats to make your own kebab depending on what meat you have at your disposal.

Method

1. Mince together everything but the eggs. Preferably do it twice to get a fine mince. Check seasoning and set aside.

2. Hard boil the eggs for 7–8 minutes on the boil and then cool them gently under slow running water.

3. Peel the eggs and cut into halves.

4. Divide the mince into 8 equal portions and work each ball with your hands until soft and supple.

5. Flatten the mince in your palm and place an egg half in the middle.

6. Enclose the mince around the egg and using both hands form a 'Kofta' or ball or egg-shaped rissole. You may shape it like an egg or keep it round.

7. Repeat the process with all the egg halves and make eight koftas in all.

8. These have to be cooked in the gravy below or use another gravy if you like.

9. They can also be fried or baked in a medium oven and then placed in the gravy later. Frying seals the mince quite rapidly. However, if putting in an oven be sure that it is very hot otherwise you will lose too much fluid and the mince will crack.

10. To make the gravy heat the oil in a casserole and sauté the onions on a medium flame.

11. Put the remaining ingredients into a blender and purée to a fine consistency.

12. Stir the onions regularly and brown them to a rich dark brown.

13. When the onions are browned add the masala and stir continuously for 2–3 minutes until the masala as a whole begins to bubble.

14. Lower the flame and cook covered for 15 minutes stirring from time to time and ensuring that the bottom of the pan is scraped clean.

15. If the gravy thickens too rapidly add some stock or water.

16. Check the seasoning and cook until a thin film of oil comes to the surface.

At this stage add the koftas if raw and cook them covered for up to 20 minutes on a slow simmer.

17. If you are adding them already cooked you only have to simmer them for a few minutes until heated.

18. Also both the recipes can be used independently of one another and you can serve the koftas with green chutney, a raita, another rich Indian-style gravy or a coconut-based curry.

Gravy	Ingredients
2 tbsp	Oil
3 medium	Onion (minced)
1 5 cm piece	Ginger (cut small)
8 cloves	Garlic
3–4 large	Red chillies
1 tsp	Cumin seeds
1 tbsp	Coriander seeds
½ tsp	Fennel seeds
5 cm piece	Cinnamon (broke up)
½ teaspoon	Turmeric powder
12–15	Cashew nuts (whole, raw not roasted)
10–12 1 heaped tbsp	Almonds (peeled) or almond powder
200 g	Yoghurt
100–150 g	Tomatoes
To taste	Salt

Ulathu

Dry Fry Beef

Chef's Notes

- This is a Keralan Syrian Christian speciality and recipes do differ from family to family. A friend's sister here in England showed me this style and we have made a few simple adaptations for a better result and for ease of use. While the preparation itself is simple it is important to get the basics right so that you have a tantalising result. This is served best with 'Môr' (page 28) or 'Dahi Bhaat' (page 211).

- To clean a whole coconut in its shell you will find that a cleaver, though not necessarily a sharp one or a large one, is often most apt. First wash the outer shell and wipe it with a kitchen towel. Keep a bowl ready to hold the water inside the shell, which is always quite delicious to drink. Hold the coconut in one hand while you start tapping the coconut down the middle with the

9. Stir from time to time from the bottom up so that you prevent burning or sticking at the bottom.

10. The sauce will gradually thicken and the rabbit meat will cook and soften.

11. When the sauce acquires a consistency that is thick enough to coat the meat completely, melt the butter for the Baghaar in a frying pan and gently sizzle the aniseed.

12. Blend this into the cooked rabbit and mix well.

13. Season now to your taste.

14. Serve either with parathas or a light pulao.

15. This also keeps quite well if chilled and stored in a tight-lidded container. The taste improves the day after cooking.

Badak Kay Tikkay

Duck Tikka

Chef's Notes

- Though duck is not so commonly found on Indian menus, it does exist in Indian cuisine and is often consumed in various forms depending on where the dish originates from in India. Wild duck is hunted during the migration period in northern India and in some parts of southern India. This is a simple yet delicious dish and one that is acceptable to most palates. The recipe may differ from the traditional but it certainly gets the results.

Measurements	Ingredients
800 g approx.	Duck breasts
4 tbsp	Lime or lemon juice
1 heaped tsp	Turmeric
To taste	Salt
100 g	Onions
30–40 g	Fresh ginger
15 g	Whole red chilli (alternatively use red chilli powder)
30–40 g cloves	Garlic
30 g	Ground cumin
30 g	Ground coriander
10–15 g	Garam masala powder
½ teaspoon	Pepper powder (black or white)
50 g	Tomato paste
200 g	Greek style yoghurt
2 tbsp	Vegetable or Sunflower oil

Method

1. Remove some of the skin off the edges of the breasts but leave the skin on in the middle along the entire length.

2. Cut the breast into roughly 2 cm cubes and place them in a bowl.

3. Sprinkle the duck with half the lime juice, half the turmeric powder and some salt. Mix well with a wooden spoon and set aside covered in a cooler.

4. Peel and coarsely cut the onions. Coarsely cut the ginger, break the red chilli (if using) into pieces and put in a blender with the rest of the ingredients then purée to a smooth paste.

5. Blend the marinade into the duck pieces then clean the edges of the bowl, cover and place in the refrigerator. Ideally the meat should stay overnight in the marinade giving it adequate time to penetrate and add flavour.

6. Either get a grill ready on maximum heat or a barbecue or a tandoor depending on what is available.

7. If cooking on a barbecue you may wish to skewer the pieces or place them directly on the steel grate. For a grill place the pieces on a slotted tray and place the tray over another so that the dripping juices can collect in the bottom tray.

    Ensure in both cases that the heat is high. For the barbecue you will have to turn the meat regularly so that It does not get charred on any one side.

8. Duck is best served a little pink inside for great taste and texture. Excessive cooking of duck renders it tasteless and chewy.

9. Serve with a salad and fresh green chutney.

Ostrich Tikka Toofan Mail

Chef's Notes

- This tikka was created by me a few years ago and was primarily used for venison. Ostrich is now on the market and has similar properties to venison which make it such a desirable meat.

- 'Toofan Mail' was India's best known mail train, thundering from Dehradun in the north to Munbai on the south west coast. Boasting a very good dining car, its name became used as a representation for other vehicles that moved fast or a product that sold fast.

- I have put together this tikka for the book, not simply because the product has become famous in our restaurant, but also because several people have said they would like to try it at home.

Method

1. Cut the ostrich meat into 2.5 cm cubes and cut away any sinews, gristle etc. Rub in 1 tsp salt.

2. Gently roast the remaining ingredients with the exception of the yoghurt and the lemon juice in a frying pan, taking care not to discolour any ingredient. The best way is to place them in a warm

fry pan and stir regularly until you find that the heat has penetrated right through and the chillies are gently roasting.

3. Cool and grind in a blender with the yoghurt and the lemon juice. Make sure you get a smooth paste, not lumpy or with spices not fully ground.

4. Marinade the ostrich by mixing in the paste and rubbing it in. Check the salt. Place in another bowl, keep the edges clean and cover. Leave it out for about 2 hours before placing it in the refrigerator.

5. I would suggest that for a dense meat such as this an overnight marinade is essential. Give it at least 8–10 hours in the refrigerator.

6. To cook either grill under a high grill, turning after about 3–4 minutes. Try not to overcook. Once turned over and coloured well on both sides, check one piece for tenderness. It will also cook very well on a barbecue, again do not overcook.

7. Serve with a salad and pulao if you like.

Measurements	Ingredients
500 g	Ostrich (available in certain supermarkets. Either cut from the breast fillet or from the leg)
250 g	Greek yoghurt
1 2.5 cm piece	Cinnamon
3–4	Green cardamon
2–3	Star anise
1 tsp	Fennel seeds
8–10 flakes	Garlic
5 cm piece	Ginger
2 tbsp	Sesame or mustard oil
2–3	Green chillies
3–4 large	Red chillies
1 bunch	Coriander stalks (save the leaves for garnishes, chutneys and additions to several preparations)
1 tbsp	Lemon juice
To taste	Salt

Malai Murg Tikka

Chef's Notes

- This is perhaps the mildest and creamiest of all tikkas. The name 'Malai' itself means creamy. It has several representations but I prefer this recipe, which we have developed and tested over a period of time and which guarantees a great texture, flavour and taste. Its origins are definitely somewhere in the earliest of Persian influences to Mughlai/Indian cuisine.

Method

1. Wash and clean the chicken, drain and set aside.

2. Break the cardamom pods and the mace flower and roast gently in a frying pan on a very low heat.

3. Place all the ingredients except the chicken in a blender and purée to a smooth paste.

4. Stir regularly with a spatula so that all the ingredients get puréed.

5. Marinade the chicken with the paste and leave covered in the refrigerator for 6–8 hours.

6. Chargrill on skewers, broil in a hot oven or skewer and chargrill in the tandoor.

7. It will take between 4 and 6 minutes for the chicken pieces to cook.

8. However, do remember that this chicken colours very rapidly and can even burn so care and observation are key.

9. This can mean that even if the chicken is coloured it may not be cooked, therefore you need to check this physically. One piece of chicken can be cut open to see if the meat is cooked, before removing the rest from the grill, broiler or tandoor.

10. Since the chicken will not take a long time to cook it is advisable to have everything else ready for your meal and then cook the chicken almost at the very end so that it may be fresh out of the fire on to the table.

11. This chicken does tend to dry out very quickly due to the nature of its marinade and it is therefore best not to agitate it too often when cooking and also to avoid reheating as far as possible.

Measurements	Ingredients
400–500 g	Boneless chicken (cubes)
3–4 pods	Green cardamom
1 flower	Mace
30 g	Cashew nuts
30 g	Ground almond
5 cm piece	Ginger
3–4 cloves	Garlic
150 g	Greek yoghurt
3–4 tbsp	Double cream
40 g	Cheddar cheese
1 tsp	Lime juice
1 level tbsp	Salt
2 tbsp	Oil

Murgh Kay Tikkay or Murgh Tikka

Chef's Notes

- Most widely known among all other Indian preparations, this tikka of chicken is a succulent and juicy kebab if well prepared and makes an ideal snack.

Method

1. Cut the chicken into cubes large enough to be skewered roughly, 3 cm × 3 cm.

2. Rub salt and pepper into the chicken and set aside.

3. In a blender add all the other ingredients except the butter and half the yoghurt and blend to a smooth paste.

4. When all the spices are well ground remove to a bowl and whisk in the remaining yoghurt. Check here for spiciness to suit your requirements. Add more chilli only if you so desire.

5. Mix in the chicken and check for seasoning. The chicken is best left overnight in the refrigerator or at least for 4–5 hours.

6. The tikka can either be grilled on the barbecue or under the grill and finished in the oven. Either way it needs to be basted with butter for that juicy appearance. Ensure that the grill is not too high and that the meat is on a wire mesh with a drip tray below.

7. Only if there is no option use a very hot oven. The tikkas will cook well in approximately in 8–10 minutes.

8. There are several variations to the original tikka recipe and you can use your own imagination for more interesting kebabs.

Measurements	Ingredients
800 g	Deboned chicken (both legs and breasts should be used, however in India the legs are preferred)
To taste	Salt and pepper (use white pepper powder)
40 g	Ginger
40 g	Garlic
½ tsp	Cumin seeds
½ tsp	Coriander seeds
½ tsp	Red chilli powder
¼ tsp	Turmeric powder
2 tbsp	Lime juice (lemon juice can be substituted)
½ tsp	Garam masala powder
50 ml	Mustard or groundnut oil
150 g	Yoghurt
As required	Butter for basting

Chicken Tikka Kala Miri Masala

Chef's Notes

- This is a variation of the traditional chicken tikka showing the possibility of hundreds of different flavours and marinades at our disposal. Though the term 'tikka' may be common in its use, the marinating process and the marinade itself may change right across the sub-continent. This one is a hotter variation and is reminiscent of the flavour of crushed black pepper.

Method

1. Wash and clean the chicken and drain well.

2. Rub the salt and the crushed black pepper in the chicken, cover and set aside.

3. Put all the remaining ingredients in a blender and purée to a smooth paste.

4. Blend the marinade well into the chicken.

5. Clean the sides of the bowl and place in the refrigerator for 4–8 hours for the masala to be well absorbed and the flavours well rounded.

6. Remove onto a greased tray making sure that the pieces do not stick together and broil in a very hot oven for 6–7 minutes or until done.

7. You may prefer to turn them over after 3 minutes to get an even colour as well as perhaps to baste a little with some melted butter.

8. Alternatively if possible charbroil them or skewer and chargrill on a barbeque or in a tandoor if available.

9. Serve with a salad and/or a yoghurt dip.

Measurements	Ingredients
400–500 g	Boneless chicken (cubes 3 cm × 3 cm)
1–1½ tsp as desired	Salt
1½ heaped teaspoon	Black pepper (crushed)
2 tbsp	Sunflower oil
1 heaped tbsp	Tomato paste
5 cm piece	Ginger
6–8 cloves	Garlic
1 tsp	Red chilli powder
¼ tsp	Turmeric
1 tsp	Ground coriander
½ tsp	Ground cumin
¼ tsp	Garam masala
1 tbsp	Lime juice

Espetada De Porco

Chef's Notes

- Espetada is essentially a chargrilling marinade for pork fillet or cubes of leg meat. However, the marinade, which has strong properties, is also excellent for roasting large joints and makes a superb main dish. Though much of the culinary terminology is Portuguese this is a fine example of the marriage between Portuguese and Goan cuisine.

- Espetada, the marinade, can also be used to make grilled marinated pork chops, for instance. Diced loin of pork can be marinated and then skewered and chargrilled over a barbeque.

- This marinade is also suitable for chicken but not for lamb or beef.

Measurements	Ingredients
1.5 kgs	Rolled pork shoulder
100 ml	Palm vinegar (cider vinegar is an excellent substitute)
30 ml	Lemon juice
20 g	Whole dried red chilli
2–3 medium	Fresh green chillies
4–6	Black peppercorns
8–10 cloves	Garlic
2.5–3.5 cm piece	Fresh ginger
10 g	Cassia
3–4	Cloves
1 tsp	Cumin seeds
As desired	Salt

Method

1. Purée all the ingredients, except the pork, in a blender/grinder into a fine paste.

2. Marinade the pork well by applying the paste all around. Cover and refrigerate for up to 8 hours or overnight.

3. Preheat the oven to 160–180°C and roast until the desired texture is attained. Either cool and serve or serve sliced warm.

4. Serve accompanied by deep-fried slices of potato approximately 2.5 mm thick.

5. To make gravy with the pan drippings, remove the roasted joint and set aside. Slice one or two medium sized onions and put them in the pan. Add approximately 250–300 ml stock or water and scrape well with a wooden spatula to loosen the residue. Heat the tray slowly while still scraping, until all residues are released.

6. Remove to a small casserole or saucepan and place on the cooker top.

7. Continue to cook on a medium heat until the onions are thoroughly cooked.

8. Season and taste. You can use this as it is with the sliced onions.

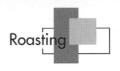

Frango No Espeto Piquanté

Hot Chargrilled/Grilled Chicken

Chef's Notes

- The name above seems more Portuguese than Indian. It is a derivative of the notorious chicken peri-peri from Goa and is a quick and easy recipe for a tantalisingly hot chicken tikka. The masala need take no more than 10 minutes to put together. However, if you marinade overnight in the refrigerator the results will be better. Since the marinade contains vinegar it is advisable to cook on high heat otherwise the chicken will lose too much liquid and turn dry.

Measurements	Ingredients
1 tbsp	Sunflower oil
1 heaped tbsp	Tomato paste
1½ tbsp	Ginger/garlic paste
1 heaped tbsp	Red chilli powder
¼ tsp	Turmeric
1 tsp	Ground coriander
½ teaspoon	Ground cumin
A generous pinch	Garam masala
25 ml	Cider vinegar
2–3 medium	Fresh green chilli
1 tsp or to taste	Salt
400 g	Boneless chicken cubes

Method

1. Put all the ingredients except the chicken in a blender and purée to a smooth paste.

2. Marinade the chicken in a bowl with the paste.

3. Clean the sides of the bowl, cover and place in the refrigerator for 4–8 hours for the masala to be well absorbed.

4. Remove onto a greased tray making sure that the pieces are not sticking together and are well spread out.

5. Roast/broil in a very hot oven for 8–10 minutes or until done.

6. Normally, this type of chicken preparation would not take more than a maximum of 10–12 minutes even if the oven were not quite hot enough.

7. You may prefer to turn the pieces over after 3 minutes, baste with some melted butter and put them back in the oven, to get an even colour.

8. Alternatively, if possible charbroil them or skewer and chargrill on a barbeque or broil in a tandoor if available.

9. Sprinkle some lime juice and freshly chopped coriander on top of the tikkas before serving.

10. Serve with a salad and/or a yoghurt dip.

Galinha Cafreal

Chef's Notes

- A grilled chicken dish of Goan Portuguese origin. It is indeed a variation of the European version and this one is also different to the type often found in Goa. It is something I love and has created waves on all my menus wherever.

Method

1. Grind together the masala ingredients and set it aside. If using a blender ensure you add a little water at a time. This should be a thick yet smooth masala.

2. Blend in salt to taste.

3. Select the cut of your chicken, clean it and apply the masala liberally.

4. If necessary pierce frequently with a fork before applying the masala to allow for better penetration.

5. Cover and leave the chicken in the masala for at least 3–5 hours or overnight in the refrigerator if possible.

6. Take a thick heavy-bottomed frying pan big enough to take all the chicken and pour in the oil.

7. Heat the pan but do not overheat. When still not too hot place the chicken skin side down and gently pan grill until golden brown.

8. Shaking the pan gently from side to side during sautéing will ensure that the skin does not stick.

9. When golden turn over, cover and continue to cook until chicken is more than half cooked. Remove to a baking dish and cook in a moderate oven until done.

Measurements	Ingredients
1	Chicken (cut like a spatch cock, slit lengthwise or cut into pieces with the skin on)
100 ml	Oil
1 large	Onion (cut into thick rings)
1–2 large	Potatoes (peeled and sliced)
1–2	Tomatoes (for salad garnish)
Masala	**Ingredients**
5–6 large	Green chillies
5–6	Black peppercorns
2.5 cm piece	Root ginger
8–10 flakes	Garlic
4–5 large	Dry deep red chillies
4 tbsp	Fresh coriander (chopped)
2 tbsp	Lemon juice
1 tsp	Cumin seeds
2 tsp	Coriander seeds
Sauce (optional)	**Ingredients**
2 medium	Onions (thinly sliced)
2.5 cm piece	Root ginger (shredded)
1 large	Green chilli (shredded)
¼ tsp	Turmeric powder
½ tsp	Cumin powder
½ tsp	Coriander powder
1 small tin *or* 250 ml	Coconut milk

10. To make the sauce put the pan back on the heat and add the onions, root ginger, green chilli, turmeric, cumin and coriander and sauté. Do not wash the pan as the juices will help in the sauce. Deglaze the pan with a little water or stock and continue to cook.

11. When the onions are browned add the coconut milk and cook until the sauce comes to the right consistency. (You may prefer to purée the sauce.)

12. In another pan add a little oil just enough to coat the bottom and sauté the onion rings until brown. Set aside.

13. Likewise sauté the potato slices.

14. When the chicken is ready serve it with the sliced onion rings, the sauté potatoes and the tomato slices. The sauce can either be served separately or poured over.

15. Serving it separate with garlic pulao is an ideal combination.

Roast Chicken Madurai Masala

Chef's Notes

• Madurai is in Tamil Nadu, the state of which Chennai or Madras is the capital. The region of Madurai, unlike other regions here, is noted for its not very hot cuisine and in particular the non-vegetarian element of it. Madurai was the capital of the Pandya Kings and recipes handed down for generations, both ancient and traditional, continue to be popular today. This chicken dish is simple and yet so full of flavour and redolent of the multi-faceted south Indian style of spice blends.

Measurements	Ingredients
750 g	Chicken thighs (with skin)
As desired	Salt
5 cm piece	Ginger
4–6 cloves	Garlic
3 tbsp	Sunflower oil
10–12 leaves	Curry leaves
½ tsp	Cumin
½ tsp	Fennel seeds
2–3	Bay leaves (broken in half)
2	Onions (finely sliced)
2 medium	Tomatoes chopped
1½ tsp	Coriander powder
½ tsp	Red chilli powder
1 tbsp	Fresh coriander (chopped)
10–12 shredded	Mint leaves
¼ tsp	Garam masala
½ tsp	Turmeric powder

- The chicken thighs are actually pan roasted and not oven roasted but once the thighs are well browned on the skin side you can put the pan into the oven until the chicken is well cooked.

Method

1. Clean the chicken, rub in the salt and turmeric and set aside.

2. Purée the ginger and garlic together to a fine paste in a little water.

3. Heat the oil in a heavy frying pan big enough to take all the thighs without them overlapping. A lid for this pan is essential.

3. When the oil is hot but not smoking, add curry leaves, cumin and fennel seeds and keep shaking the pan so they do not burn.

4. Once the fennel is slightly browned add the bay leaves and the onions and sauté until the onions are pale brown.

5. Stir from time to time to prevent uneven browning and sticking at the bottom.

6. Add the ginger garlic paste, sauté for 1–2 minutes longer stirring continuously, then add the tomatoes and continue to cook until almost dry.

7. Add the coriander and chilli powders mixed together in a little water to form a thin paste and sauté for 1–2 minutes longer, or until the oil starts to be released.

8. Now pull the cooked masala to one side of the pan and lay the thighs skin side down, then cover with the masala.

9. You may need to first pull the masala on to one side and then lay all the masala over the thighs on one side before laying the remaining thighs on the opposite side of the pan and then covering them all.

10. Cover the pan, reduce the heat and allow the thighs to brown slowly on the skin side.

11. Check after a couple of minutes and when you are satisfied with the colour, turn them over.

12. At this second turn, the masala is likely to get below the thighs. This is fine, all you have to ensure is that the pan is covered and you may wish to add a little liquid if it begins to burn at the base. This will also create a bit of steam and allow the chicken to cook more evenly.

13. Cook until the chicken is cooked through. For those a bit afraid of the pink, pierce with a knife and check if the fluid released is still pink and not clear.

14. When the fluid is clear the chicken will be thoroughly cooked and if dry, then please do not serve it to me.

15. Check seasoning, add freshly crushed peppercorns if you like as well. Blend the coriander and mint leaves, cover and take pan off the heat.

Murg Bhuna

Chef's Notes

- The word 'Bhuna' often brings forth several thoughts into the minds of people and at once one imagines some meat in deep reddish gravy, hot and greasy with no definitive style or consistency. This is true too as for one thing Bhuna, or Bhoona as it is also called, has various meanings even in the minds of the people who prepare the dish. However, the word itself means 'to roast' or 'to braise'. Roasting in the Indian culinary aspect need not mean to cook something in the oven until it is cooked. It also means the slow cooking of spices, the slow cooking of ground masalas as well as chargrilling in the tandoor or the open spit and so on. Here we have brought to you a classic gravy cooked with chicken but equally suited to red meats. It is by no means a landmark but if well cooked the results are rather addictive.

- Use half oil and half butter if you like for a richer taste. However, browning may occur and you will also have to be extra vigilant when sautéing the onions.

Measurements	Ingredients
100 g	Sunflower oil
400 g	Onion (thinly sliced)
500 g	Boneless chicken breast or leg
20 g	Ginger
20 g	Garlic
1 tbsp	Ground coriander
1 heaped tsp	Ground cumin
1 tsp	Kashmiri red chilli powder
A bit less than ½ tsp	Turmeric
100 g	Yoghurt
20 g	Tomato paste
200 g	Tomato
5 g	Green chilli (chopped)
6 g	Salt
1½ heaped tbsp	Fresh coriander (chopped)

Method

1. Heat oil and add the very finely sliced onions.

2. Sauté gradually until deep golden brown.

3. Add the chicken pieces and do not agitate the pan too much.

4. Sauté chicken until well sealed and browned on all sides. Remove and set aside.

5. Scrape off any browned onion sticking to the chicken and add these back to the pan.

6. Meanwhile purée the ginger and garlic with a little water in a blender to a smooth paste.

7. Lower the heat and add the ginger garlic paste and cook for 1–2 minutes on a medium heat.

8. Mix in a little water to make a paste of the dry ground powders and add to the onion and ginger garlic already cooking.

9. Simmer slowly until the liquid dries out and the masala begins to cook by releasing the fat again.

10. Purée together the yoghurt, tomato paste and the tomato and add this to the pan. Cook until once again you see the fat being released.

11. Add the green chilli and salt and check the seasoning.

12. Return the chicken to the pan and cook until done, approximately 2–3 minutes at boiling point.

13. Add the fresh coriander, mix well and remove.

Seafood

4

ON FISH AND SEAFOOD

The sub-continent of India has a vast coastline reaching from the edge of the Persian Gulf and extending to the coast of Burma (Myanmar) covering two seas and the Indian Ocean at the very southern tip.

The different variations in the coastline, ocean currents, water temperatures and climatic conditions all lend themselves to an abundance of seafood, which leads to a very diverse and interesting cuisine culture. The styles of cooking are so diverse that they differ at every juncture, town, port, location and region and are dominated by religion, area, culture, geographical variations and so on. So much so that it would be impossible to document every type or style prepared across this huge coastline and its surrounding areas.

However, India also has lots of rivers and lakes and a great many varieties of freshwater fish also are available and extremely popular in some regions. For instance, in the region of Bengal river fish is much sought after and certain types of fish such as the hilsa can fetch premium prices. In Madhya Pradesh and Rajasthan where my family comes from river fish was the daily or weekly choice, though as much as one liked river fish the family always went crazy whenever someone could bring in fresh pomfrets or king prawns from Bombay.

It is not uncommon for people from the coastal regions to have a kind of rivalry with those from the hinterland whose preference is to eat freshwater fish, they also compare and criticise the fish itself.

From the rivers, of course, you also get a few shellfish, some varieties of crabs and the crayfish, known the world over as king prawn. This so-called king prawn has extremely large deep blue coloured claws, a bluish tint on its shell and grows to quite a size. It breeds best in brackish water.

The real king prawn, however, is a sea prawn that can be netted either close to shore or in deep waters. The shell of this prawn is white and it has a sleek and slender body. Size, of course, makes the difference in price.

The seas on the other hand offer an immensely large bounty, from large fish to shellfish, from crustaceans to molluscs, vertebrates to invertebrates. And the people of the sub-continent enjoy most types of fish and shellfish immensely, though this is often also limited to coastal tastes and habits.

Having had the privilege of spending almost eight years working in Goa I had the good fortune of seeing, working and also experimenting with some of the very best seafood in the world. The knowledge one acquires about tastes, textures, likes and dislikes cannot be measured or taught so easily – it is learnt through trial and error and experience and the sheer advantage of fresh availability.

RELIGION AND RELIGIOUS OCCASIONS

Most of the Hindus of India are vegetarians. However, Hindus from the coastal regions of the sub-continent are not necessarily so and will eat fish and seafood; some will also eat poultry and lamb. This need not be a common factor but along the coastal fringes it is not uncommon.

During certain times of the year these fish-eating Hindus also turn vegetarian and it is during this period that the remaining fish-eating public enjoys the benefits of cheaper fish in the markets due to a drop in demand.

It is important to understand why certain meats or foods became taboo to eat in certain religions or, as in the case of seafood, in India at certain times of the year.

My own theory, and this may or may not be entirely true or factual, is that these reasons are totally scientific. Humans by their very nature are defiant and as in the case of Adam and Eve we all enjoy a certain amount of defiance and indiscipline. To deter people from eating certain meats, for instance pork, the elders or the intellectual's leaders decided to brand certain foods disallowed or taboo in the religion to prevent people from eating them and also from falling ill due to the health risks involved at the time.

When I say 'at the time' I mean when religions were established centuries ago, when refrigeration would have been unthinkable. Rearing animals such as pigs in a completely hygienic environment would be unheard of and so on and so forth. The easiest solution was to ban these meats, fish, shellfish, etc.

The Hindu ban on eating fish, etc., is in the month of October. Incidentally, October is one of the hottest and certainly the most humid month of the year along the coastal regions, therefore the harvest of the seas could very easily be contaminated or putrefy in the humidity if not well stored. Naturally these days there is no problem as refrigeration is commonplace and there are also huge storage facilities, but religion dictates the god-fearing Hindus.

FISH AND SEAFOOD: EATING HABITS, STYLES, ETC.

Seafood can be used in pickles and chutneys, hot sizzling curries and dry fries, milder gravies and simple grills and chargrilled dishes, which all represent the huge diversity in styles, variety and creativity. Depending on the region, the local culture, the availability and so on the style of cooking has evolved in each region of the sub-continent with some overlap between neighbouring regions.

Most people living around coastal regions across the sub-continent of India are lovers of most forms of seafood. In the hinterlands of course fish is not such a phenomena and people do not get the cravings for eating fish. In some cultures such as the Bengali and Goan, Karwari and East Indian, Manglorean, for example, one fish or seafood item is a must, if not at both main meals then for one at least.

In Goa, for instance, so great is the love of fish that the veritable fish curry is a daily routine. However, the addiction does not end here. Traditionally the leftover curry of the previous night was kept in an earthenware pot overnight, only to be eaten for breakfast with fresh hot bread. I am positive that even without doing more research on the subject there will be other communities in the sub-continent with very similar habits.

WHAT TO LOOK FOR IN FRESH FISH/SHELLFISH

This is the most commonly asked question and perhaps the easiest to answer. Freshness is the answer. However, practicality is yet another issue and one which defies the norm when buying or storing etc.

What is the meaning of freshness? Would it mean caught in your presence? Would it mean caught a few hours earlier? Could it mean caught earlier but stored in a proper manner such that it still looks freshly caught? Actually it could mean any or all of these. It all depends on what the fish looks like, smells like, and feels like. Experience is the key to all of this and one needs to analyse as much as possible whenever buying fish if only to gain that skill.

COOKING TECHNIQUES

Frying, steaming, poaching, grilling, baking, meuniering, sautéing, barbequing, tandoori, you name it and each style suits several types of marine products. However it is the how of cooking, rather than the method or style, that makes the difference between a great, well done or average and bad product.

Fish, shellfish, crustaceans, molluscs and invertebrates, in fact anything that lives underwater, normally requires delicate handling when cooking. It is quite easy to destroy the best fish simply by not trying to understand the product itself. The same applies to seafood and the other products of rivers, lakes and the sea.

I can recall several occasions when I have been just too excited about getting my hands on new never-cooked-before fish and then making simple, stupid errors that destroy the product completely. My big mistake?

Not taking time to understand the product or not trying a little first in the chosen method and then doing what suits the product best.

I would therefore suggest the beginner should ideally stay with known produce and then gradually, as the experience grows, try different products and enjoy earth's bounty to its fullest.

SPICING AND SEASONING

Spicing and seasoning marine products is common to the cooking culture of the sub-continent, though it may be the reverse when compared to Western styles of cooking.

Marinating marine products may not necessarily always enhance flavour or taste, since all the spices can be added during the cooking process. However, marinating plays another extremely vital role and that is preservation.

Once harvested and processed, tropical climes are no place for marine products to be lying around waiting to be cooked, especially when refrigeration can be a luxury or not necessarily available. Furthermore, power cuts and failures on a daily basis would create an open ground for bacteria to breed. This is one big reason why most sub-continental recipes involve a pre-preparation of marinating prior to cooking.

Turmeric, lime juice and salt all play a vital role in the preservation of raw marine products, as well as ginger and garlic purée.

In the Peruvian Serviche, for instance, it is the lemon that virtually preserves the fish, while turmeric and lime juice destroy surface bacteria, which in the sub-continent becomes essential.

Besides flavouring, preserving and/or adding to the taste, some marinades help towards sealing in the juices of the fish so that when cooked the fish remains soft and juicy. Marinated fish also needs much less cooking than normal, and marine food takes very little cooking anyway.

Marinating has certain drawbacks, of course. For one, bad marinating can destroy everything and take away all the inherent flavour of the product itself. It can make fish dry when cooked.

The marinade can burn on the pan while cooking, thereby creating a residue, which will eventually burn and destroy the product.

If the marinade is too strong or not well planned, it can over-tenderise the product, often making it useless for cooking or eating for that matter.

Marinades need to be distinctive, often light in nature and clearly demonstrating some individual flavour. One cannot simply throw every perceivable spice or condiment from the larder into a bowl, blend it and claim it to be a good marinade. It does not work that way.

Everything around cooking and creativity in cooking needs to be treated scientifically and with great thought, but when you are playing with a very delicate product in the first instance, greater care is the key.

A number of marinades are presented throughout this book. All you need to do is to adjust and adapt to suit. Remember to try, taste and compare before you jump to it. Remember above all that of all the various kinds of meats that we cook, it is the marine product that demands greatest respect when cooking. It can be as simple as tossing prawns in a pan and with a quick flash finishing the cooking. But it is more important to understand the correct temperature, how many prawns to add to the pan at any one time, how long to cook for and how much oil to add. Why the word respect? Quite simply, if you fail to observe any of the above when cooking most shellfish, you are asking for failure.

Of course the reward is in the pleasure of dining on succulent, juicy, tender and flavoursome prawns that have been cooked with respect and are the pride and joy of the chef cooking them.

HEALTH

It is known and understood the world over that eating fish and other marine life is good for you, except where allergies dominate. In general, most marine species we see in the markets and supermarkets today are safe and healthy.

All fish and shellfish have a tendency to contaminate rapidly if not well stored, chilled or presented, packaged and transported. These are the simple basic essential tools to ensure that people get safe and healthy food to eat.

However, things do go wrong, carelessness does happen – often in the households – and people fall sick. The proteins and other minerals in these foods are very delicate and in some cases very rich, therefore while it is good for us, it also is good for bacteria to breed on rather rapidly.

Therefore, when preparing any form of fish, shellfish, etc., one must ensure high levels of hygiene. For instance, you should have a separate board for preparing your fish; instantly wash and clean all tools, boards and surfaces, sterilise where necessary and recommended. Do not prepare any fish or shellfish out in the open unless you have no choice. The instantaneous attraction of flies as though out of nowhere will be proof enough and evidence enough that this product is loved by all, including contaminants and disease carriers.

After preparation, if you are not to cook immediately, the product should be marinated, put away or frozen. Ensure that you place the product in a clean, dry container.

If marinating make sure that once placed in a container the sides are thoroughly wiped with a paper towel, the lid fits well and the product goes into the refrigerator immediately.

If the product is to be cooked later, make all your preparations beforehand so that you do not have to leave it outside for too long. This means that

the pan for cooking, the medium of fat to be used, the flour, egg and breadcrumbs, for instance, should all be well prepared in readiness for the fish to be cooked up.

Also, plan the tray or dish to which it is to be removed after cooking. If draining is required or the tray needs some paper at the base for absorbing excess fat and so on, this needs to be planned.

While most fish, shellfish etc. has some essential oils, certain marine species have higher levels that have been proven to be extremely healthy for the human body. Besides, fish protein is easily digestible and will also suit people who have digestive disorders.

Several vitamin and mineral supplements people buy and take these days are derived from the livers and other parts of various oily fleshed fish.

Whereas most marine species we eat have low levels of cholesterol, most shellfish have higher levels and often items such as prawns, lobsters, etc., are not recommended for people suffering from coronary disorders.

All in all fish and shellfish must be enjoyed, but handled with care. That's the simple rule.

Adrak Lehsun Aur Mirch Kay Scallop

Chef's Notes

- A delicious starter of scallops with ginger, garlic and chilli.

Measurements	Ingredients
20–30	Fresh queen scallops (cleaned (preference is to buy unsoaked scallops. If buying frozen thaw in your refrigerator overnight))
1 tbsp	Oil
1 level tbsp	Fresh ginger (finely chopped)
6 cloves	Garlic (finely chopped)
1–2	Green (chilli chopped)
$\frac{1}{2}$ tsp	Cumin powder
$\frac{1}{2}$ tsp	Coriander powder
$\frac{1}{4}$ tsp	Turmeric powder
$1\frac{1}{2}$ tbsp	Fresh coriander (finely chopped)
To taste	Salt

Method

1. Drain the scallops and keep in a colander or sieve until required.

2. Take a heavy-bottomed fry pan and heat the oil to near smoking point. Put in the scallops and spread them out evenly. Do not stir and keep the flame on high all the time.

3. Almost simultaneously put in the ginger, garlic and chilli. Toss and level out again. Unnecessary stirring will make the pan cold and the scallops will give off their juices and become rubbery.

4. Toss again and add the spice powders.

5. Stir until everything is well mixed and check the seasoning.

6. Add the fresh coriander and mix it in gently. Sprinkle some lime juice if you like.

7. The scallops should be ready in 3–4 minutes maximum. I personally prefer them after about 2 minutes but the flame should not be lowered.

8. Remove and serve immediately with the juices that will now escape.

9. Serve with hot toasted bread and salad.

10. The same recipe can be used with oysters, mussels or any other shellfish. You can use a firm-fleshed fish if you like, such as monkfish, shark, tuna or swordfish. This recipe is very versatile. Use it to make a delicious omelette.

Bada Jhinga Chutt Putta

Chef's Notes

- A hot yet delectable masala that is ideal for king prawns, lobsters, crab and the like for grilling directly over a barbecue, in a tandoor or under a grill.

Measurements	Ingredients
12–15	Large king prawns
1 level tsp	Turmeric powder
3 tbsp	Lime juice
8–10 large	Red chillies
8–10 cloves	Garlic
1.5 cm piece	Fresh ginger
1 tsp	Cumin seeds
1 heaped tsp	Coriander seeds
12–15	Peppercorns
2 tbsp	Tamarind pulp
2 tbsp	Sunflower oil
To taste	Salt

Method

1. Slit the prawns over the shell and remove the vein. You may wish to remove the head but the head grills well, tastes very good and helps prevent too much shrinkage.

2. Wash the prawns and drain them well.

3. To make the tamarind pulp, take 50 g dry tamarind and add a cup of boiling water. Allow it to soak for at least 10–15 minutes. Once the tamarind is soft, mix well with a spoon and stir. Strain through a soup strainer and use a spoon to press the pulp through into a bowl held below. Light brown tamarind is more tart than dark brown tamarind. Either is good but the lighter one will give not only a better colour but also a better flavour.

4. Mix the turmeric powder with half the lime juice and rub it into the slit prawns. This will also prevent them from turning black.

5. Remove and discard the stems from the chillies then put the chillies in a blender. Add the remaining ingredients and purée to a fine paste. Taste for seasoning. The marinade should be hot and tangy.

6. Apply the marinade to the prawns and place them in a bowl in the refrigerator. Ideally the dish should marinate for a few hours prior to cooking.

7. When cooking the prawns directly over a chargrill or barbeque grill, the heat should be high but not intense. If the flames are too high the prawns will char and the marinade will not cook well. If the heat is high it is good so that the prawns seal fast and the liquid does not escape — it is the very high or low heat that is detrimental to the texture.

8. Place the prawns on one side first until they are almost cooked and have coloured well. Turn over onto the other side and cook until done. If the heat is perfect the prawns should not take more than 5–6 minutes to cook through the shell.

9. Peel and enjoy.

Balchao De Camarao

Prawn Balchao

Chef's Notes

- A prawn pickle made with peri-peri masala. Again traditionally Goan, this item can be used as a starter or stored and used as a condiment with curry and rice.

Method

1. Get your peri-peri masala as shown on page 13. Clean the prawns if required, wash, sprinkle with a bit of salt and set aside.

2. Take a heavy-bottomed pan and pour in a thin layer of oil. Remember if you are going to keep the balchao as a pickle then it is essential you have some extra oil so that it acts as a preservative. You can use this oil to sauté other shellfish at a later date.

3. Heat the oil and begin to sauté the onions, stirring regularly until they are a deep golden brown. Do not burn them but get them as dark as possible.

4. When brown sprinkle the curry leaves and the piri-piri masala and continue cooking until the oil has re-surfaced. This is indication that the masala is now fully absorbed and cooked.

5. In a frying pan take a little oil and heat it really hot, just beyond smoking point but not flash point. Drain the prawns and shake off any liquid. Put them into the pan, taking care not to allow any splattering to harm you. Level out the prawns but do not stir immediately. If you stir right away the prawns will cool the pan down and release moisture, thereby boiling instead of sautéing.

Two things are to be noted. The heavier the pan the better the heat retention. The flame must not be reduced to allow for heat to be retained.

Measurements	Ingredients
1 large tbsp for every 200 g shelled prawns	Peri-peri masala (see page 13)
200–300g	Prawns
	Salt
As required (do not use any strong oil)	Oil
3 medium for each 200 g prawns	Onions (finely chopped)
10–12	Curry leaves
1 tbsp	Dry shrimp powder (available in most Oriental stores these days)

6. Once you think the prawns are cooked and the liquid has dried blend them into the balchao masala and just simmer for a couple of minutes.

7. Check the seasoning and add the dry shrimp powder. Mix in well while still on the heat and then switch off.

8. When cold, jar as required and place in the refrigerator uncovered. When the temperature of the pickle is the same as that of the refrigerator you can cover it. If the prawns are tiny, which is what is used in Goa, then the pickle will not need to be refrigerated. If the prawns are large then refrigeration will be necessary as they will contain some moisture that will contaminate the pickle.

9. To make an interesting starter, take either prawn balchao or balchao and some other shellfish such as mussels or clams. Chop tomatoes as required to make it saucy.

10. Take a pan, add a little oil from the balchao or use some fresh oil. Heat and sauté the shellfish, again ensuring that the heat is high. Add the tomatoes and then the balchao as you desire.

11. Sprinkle some fresh coriander and check the seasoning.

12. Served on toasted ciabatta and enjoy.

Bolinhas Pescadore

4 portions

Chef's Notes

- 'Bolinhas' means cakes and 'Pescadore' means seafood. These are simple yet delicious seafood cakes made in a Goan/Portuguese syle. (Remember that you can mix and match and use your own imagination to make variations to the recipe.)

Method

1. Steam the fish if you have the facility. Otherwise poach in very little water until cooked.

2. Drain and chill.

3. The prawns can either be poached in the same liquid after the fish has been removed or steamed lightly. Do remember not to overcook the prawns. they should be spongy and not rubbery. Shelled prawns should not take more than 2 minutes to boil on a simmer.

4. Either steam or boil the potato but allow to drain well then peel and let dry a bit.

5. Take the cumin and place it in the smallest pan you have. Take a double sheet of kitchen towel and form it into a little bag or make it like the shape of an onion. This is for dabbing or pressing the cumin in the pan.

Measurements	Ingredients
200–250 g without bones. Provide for more if using fish on the bone.	White fish (any)
200–250 g	Raw prawns (shelled)
400–500 g	Potato
1 heaped tsp	Cumin (crushed and roasted)
1 tsp	Lime juice
2 heaped tbsp	Fresh coriander (chopped)
1–2 medium	Fresh green chilli
3 cloves	Fresh garlic (finely minced)
As desired	Salt
200 g	Semolina (medium)
3–4	Eggs
50–100 g	Plain flour
To shallow fry. You can deep fry if you prefer	Sunflower oil

6. Place the pan on a slow heat and gently begin to shake the cumin in a circular motion. Every now and again press the cumin with the rounded tissue so that every seed touches the bottom of the pan and comes in contact with the heat.

7. Do this until the cumin turns a deep brown and gives off a terrific aroma. Do not allow it to blacken, but once you feel that the seeds seem roasted adequately remove and allow to cool.

8. When cool crush them in a mortar and pestle or a small grinder. The consistency should be coarse but fully broken.

9. Now get the lime juice, coriander and chilli ready.

10. Mince the fish and prawns together. If you do not have a mincer, break the fish down with a fork and mince the prawns with a knife as in mincing parsley.

11. Mash the potato with a masher or in its absence with a fork but make it fine and smooth.

12. Blend the potato, fish, prawns, lime juice and coriander, and mix well, adding the chilli and garlic.

13. Divide into equal-sized balls. The flatten to form cakes, roll in the flour, dip in the egg, and crumb with semolina.

14. Fry and serve with a dip of your choice.

Crab a la Goa

Chef's Notes

• Crab is found abundantly along all coastal regions of India. The Goans with their Portuguese influence have over a period of time begun to adopt many Western styles. Stuffing a crab is not particularly an Indian style, however in Goa it becomes very Indian with a hint of Europe.

Method

1. Place the oil in a large dry heavy-bottomed frying pan. When the oil is reasonably well heated but not smoking add the ginger, garlic and green chillies, sauté for 1–2 minutes and add the onions.

2. When the onions become pale add the peri-peri masala and cook until the onions are soft and translucent.

Measurements	Ingredients
2 tbsp	Sunflower or light olive oil
2.5 cm piece	Root ginger (peeled and chopped)
5 flakes	Garlic (chopped)
2 medium	Green chillies (finely chopped)
2 medium	Onions (finely chopped)
½ tbsp	Peri-peri masala (see page 13)
½ tbsp	Coriander powder
¼ tsp	Turmeric powder
2–3 medium	Tomatoes (chopped)
6 medium	Dressed crabs (plain crab meat can be substituted and for this you may use something else to put the mixture into)

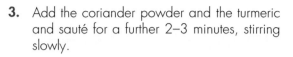

3. Add the coriander powder and the turmeric and sauté for a further 2–3 minutes, stirring slowly.

4. Add the tomatoes and continue to sauté for a few minutes until the moisture has evaporated.

5. Now remove from the heat and season, blend in the crab meat, coriander and green peas. Mix well and check for seasoning. At this stage you may need a few dashes of lemon juice if you desire.

Measurements	Ingredients
1 tbsp	Fresh coriander (chopped)
4 tbsp	Green peas (cooked)
As desired	Lemon juice
As required to cover	Cheese (grated)
To taste	Salt

6. Stuff the cleaned dry shells and cover with cheese then glaze under a grill and serve with a salad.

7. As a variation to this, chopped boiled egg and a few chopped prawns are often added for extra flavour.

Crab, Clam and Beans Porial with Egg

Chef's Notes

• A porial is one of the simplest yet most delicious preparations. I guess it is the simplicity of the ingredients itself that sets it apart. Porials can be made with several products and one must use one's imagination and experiment even further. The best porials are made from greens such as mange tout, sugar snaps, French beans, baby corn, mushrooms and courgettes. A few prawns, squid or other seafood will give it that much extra mileage in impressing your guests.

• The following recipe is one such variation but the basics of preparation must remain constant. If making a vegetarian porial, remember that it is only a side dish and must have more food with it, so also for the seafood porial. Serve with a simple coconut curry and rice.

Measurements	Ingredients
100–150 ml	Sunflower oil
1 level tsp	Cumin seeds
½ tsp	Fennel seeds
10–15	Curry leaves
50 g	White lentils
5–6 cloves	Garlic (crushed)
250 g	Shallots (minced)
½ teaspoon	Turmeric powder
2–3 medium	Green chilli (chopped)
2	Eggs
250 g	Crab meat (white meat preferred)

Method

1. Heat the oil in a wok or a kadhai and add the cumin seeds and fennel seeds.

2. When they splutter add the white lentils then the curry leaves.

3. Sauté slowly, stirring continuously, until the lentils are a pale golden colour. Remember that it colours very quickly and will burn quite quickly if you are not careful, so reduce the temperature after adding it.

Continued

4. Add the garlic, sauté for a minute then add the shallots.

5. Continue sautéing until the shallots turn a pale brown colour.

6. Add the turmeric powder and the green chilli and sauté for 1 minute more.

7. Increase the temperature now and add the clams and French beans.

8. Sauté for a minute or two, still on a high flame to ensure juices are sealed in.

9. Beat the eggs and fold them in, stirring continuously, to achieve a scrambled egg texture.

10. As soon as the eggs are scrambled add the crab meat, clam meat and lime juice a little at a time.

11. Check the seasoning and see if you need to add any more lime juice.

12. Add the coconut and the coriander, blend well and serve.

13. It may be advisable to make the entire mixture except the stage from the eggs onwards, which you can keep for the end. That way you can prepare it all then finish the preparation just prior to service.

Measurements	Ingredients
150–200 g	Small clam meat (Palourde type preferred)
1	Lime (juice only)
120 g	Fresh coconut (grated), (frozen grated coconut available in most Oriental stores these days)
1 tbsp	Fresh coriander (chopped)
150 g	French beans cut into 2.5 cm pieces
As desired	Salt

Daal Jhinga

Lentils with Prawns

Chef's Notes

- This is an unusual dish and there two versions to it. The Maharashtrian version is quite snacky and becomes an afternoon snack but on the other hand it can be an accompaniment to a main meal and would easily form the seafood element of the menu.

- Below I will try to explain the two versions so that you can use them as your menu calls for.

- Indian 'Farsan' and sweet shops will more often than not sell you crispy pan-friend moong beans known either as 'Mogar' or Moong Daal.

- For the Maharashtrian version of this dish this crispy snacky daal is normally used instead of the method I describe below.

Method

1. Soak the mung beans overnight (for 6–8 hours) and add a pinch of bicarbonate of soda or baking soda.

2. The browned onions can be prepared much earlier. Thinly slice the onions evenly, remembering to remove the root stub for best results. Fry in the oil and remove into a colander or strainer over a bowl when pale brown.

3. Loosen with a fork to separate the slices and to reduce the effects of carry over cooking. Remember the onions will brown very rapidly. Remove onto a papered tray and spread out to cool. Strain the oil well and reserve for future use.

4. To make the masala grind together the turmeric, ginger, red chillies and the remaining onion in a grinder or a blender to make a fine purée.

Measurements	Ingredients
250 g	Mung beans
2 medium	Onions (thinly sliced)
100–200 ml	Sunflower oil
$\frac{1}{2}$ tsp	Turmeric
2.5 cm piece	Ginger
8–10 large	Red chillies
1 medium	Onion (for the masala)
1 heaped tbsp	Butter or ghee
12–18	Raw prawns (large)
1–2	Bay leaf (fresh or dried)
$\frac{1}{2}$ tsp	Garam masala

5. Drain the mung beans and wash in the strainer under cold running water until the water runs clear.

6. Heat the ghee or butter until pale gold in colour and fry the mung beans. (It is advisable to melt the butter first and remove any liquid so that you can get a better result from the frying process.)

7. Remove by pouring them into a strainer with a bowl underneath to catch any excess ghee or butter, and reserve.

8. The Maharashtrian will now boil the fried lentils until just soft and drain. You can choose to do that as it gives the dish its authenticity.

9. In the drained ghee or butter sauté the prawns on a brisk flame until just half done and drain again.

10. Add the drained ghee or butter to a medium casserole and if too little add 1 tbsp oil from the fried onions.

11. Fry the bay leaf and then the puréed masala until the oil begins to be released from it. Stir and scrape regularly so that the masala cooks well and does not stick and burn at the bottom of the pan.

12. Once the masala is cooked add the boiled mung beans and after 1–2 minutes when the beans are hot, add the prawns. Season and cook until prawns are done, approximately 2–4 minutes.

13. Add half the fried onions, check the seasoning, add the garam masala, toss, and remove into a dish.

14. Sprinkle with the remaining fried onions and if you like a sprinkling of chopped coriander.

15. You can also drizzle a combination of chopped coriander blended with freshly grated coconut if you can get it.

16. This is best served with hot poories.

Dahi Manchh

Chef's Notes

- This fish curry is one of the most popular of all Bengali fish dishes and believe me there are several. No doubt this will vary from the recipe used in the house by many women who have acquired the fine skills of making this superb dish from their mothers. However, we hope to achieve second place at least; besides this will definitely give the first-time cook the courage and necessary skill to attempt similar dishes as the skills develop.

Measurements	Ingredients
500 g	Rohu or river perch cut into convenient pieces (pomfret or another white fleshed tropical sea fish can also be substituted)
4 tbsp	Mustard oil or ghee
1 2.5 cm piece	Ginger (crushed or finely minced)
5–6 cloves	Garlic (minced fine)
250 g or 3 medium	Onions (finely minced)
4–5 large	Red chillies (minced)
250 g	Thick live yoghurt (beaten)
3	Bay leaves
2	Green cardamom
1–2 tsp	Sugar
½ tsp	Garam masala
To taste	Salt

Method

1. Rub salt into the fish and set aside for 1–2 hours. Retain the liquid that is released and set aside.

2. Rinse and pat dry.

3. Heat the ghee or mustard oil in a frying pan and fry the fish but do not let the pieces brown. This process is simply to seal the fish.

4. Mix the ginger, garlic, onions and chillies into the yoghurt and beat to form a thick liquid.

5. Transfer the ghee to a pan and reheat.

6. Add the yoghurt mixture and gradually bring to the boil.

7. Add the bay leaves and cardamom and then the fish.

8. Add the sugar and sprinkle the garam masala over.

9. Pour in the salt water from the fish marinade and check the seasoning.

10. Simmer for 1–2 minutes and switch off the burner.

11. Remove and serve with plain steamed rice.

Goan Fish Curry

Chef's Notes

- The fish curry is synonymous with Goa. It is a staple part of the daily diet and a vast majority of Goans cannot do without. It is mostly eaten with parboiled or plain steamed rice and when eaten a day old, ciabatta or any crusty bread will do magic .

Method

1. Clean the fish if using whole, wash and drain. Sprinkle with salt and a pinch of turmeric and set aside.

2. Grind the masala ingredients with water in the blender until fine and smooth. Add water a little at a time and ensure that It does not become too runny but looks like a thick paste.

3. Soak the tamarind in the hot water for 1 hour, then pass through the strainer. Retain the pulp.

4. Take a heavy-bottomed casserole pan and add just enough oil to cover the bottom of the pan.

5. Heat the pan and when the oil forms a haze add the onion, ginger and green chilli.

6. Sauté for a while, but do not brown, and then add in the puréed masala. Sauté until the oil begins to escape from the sides again. Stir regularly to prevent sticking. The oil leaving signals the fact that the masala is cooked and absorbed.

7. Blend the water or stock with the coconut powder and allow to simmer. At this stage add the tamarind pulp and the cokums.

8. Boil gently for 5 minutes or so and check the seasoning. Check the consistency and ensure that it is not too thin, more like a pouring sauce. If need be cook for a little while until you have the right consistency.

Measurements	Ingredients
500 g	Firm white fish (use coley, cod or tilapia though pomfret is the best)
Pinch	Turmeric
50 g	Tamarind pulp
100 ml	Water (hot)
As required	Oil
1 medium	Onion (finely sliced)
2.5 cm piece	Root ginger (finely shredded)
2	Green chilli (finely shredded)
500–600 ml	Water or stock
2–3	Cokum or sour plum
Masala	**Ingredients**
8–10	Red chillies (select larger varieties with depth of colour)
1 level tbsp	Coriander seeds
1 tsp	Cumin seeds
6–8 flakes	Garlic
3 cm piece	Root ginger
½ tsp	Turmeric
1 large/ 250 g	Grated coconut or Fine coconut cream powder

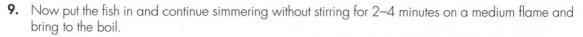

9. Now put the fish in and continue simmering without stirring for 2–4 minutes on a medium flame and bring to the boil.

10. Turn off the heat, cover the pot and allow to rest for at least 5 minutes to allow the fish to cook well in the curry.

11. If the fish is allowed to cook in the heat of the curry it tends to get a perfect texture and will not break up.

Variations

This curry masala can also be used for the following curries:

- Chicken (you will have to sauté the chicken separately, though)
- Prawns, crab, lobster, mussels and even oysters
- Cauliflower and tomato combination with baby potatoes.

The curry is not suitable for red meats.

Imli Ki Machchi/Aamli Maa Machchi

Fish in Tamarind or Tamarind Fish

Chef's Notes

- I honestly do not know the full origins of this dish. We Parsees make something similar and so also would Goans, Maharashtrians, Mangloreans and Keralans because the nature is so similar to all the communities. Keralans perhaps would not add khus-khus (poppy seeds), but that's about it.

- Anyway it is an interesting dish and I have specifically taken it on because the most frequently eaten fish in tamarind sauce would either be Chinese, Thai or Vietnamese and this simply shows certain similarities in the crossover of cultures.

Method

1. Soak the tamarind in hot water for 1 hour then pass through a strainer. Retain the pulp. Alternatively, use ready made light coloured pulp.

2. In a blender grind to a smooth paste the coriander seeds, cumin, poppy seeds, turmeric and garlic with only as much water as required for the blades to catch.

Measurements	Ingredients
2–3 tbsp	Tamarind pulp
1 tbsp	Coriander seeds
½ tbsp	Cumin
1 tbsp	White poppy seeds
½ tsp	Turmeric powder
3–4 cloves	Garlic
1 medium to large	Onion (thinly sliced)
1 tbsp	Sunflower oil
2–3	Green chillies (thinly sliced)
1 small lump, the size of a table tennis ball	Jaggery
250 ml	Water
8–10 5–7.5 cm pieces	Fillet of white fish (wash, sprinkle with a little turmeric and a dash of lime juice, mix well and set aside)

3. Sauté the onion in the oil in a casserole until golden brown.

4. Add the green chillies first and in a few seconds the masala and sauté well to cook the masala. To ensure better cooking of the masala keep adding 1 tbsp water if the masala begins to stick, and loosen the base of the pan of any stuck residue. This also ensures that the spices get well absorbed and cooked and this process can be used in any recipe wherever masala needs to be fried.

5. Once the masala is well browned and oil begins to show at the edges add the tamarind pulp, jaggery and water.

6. Bring to the boil and simmer for a few minutes.

7. Season and taste to see if all the flavours are to your liking, also to check if the masala is thoroughly cooked. This is evident when the chilli in the masala does not hit the throat.

8. Now gently add the fish and simmer for 3–4 minutes.

9. Cover the pan, switch off and let the fish rest for a few minutes to cook thoroughly.

10. Best served with plain steamed rice, flavoured preferably with bay leaf and mace.

Kedgeree

4 portions

Chef's Notes

- A fish and rice dish prepared by the Anglo-Indian community of India. There are several variations but this one is simple to prepare, is excellent when feeling under the weather, very easy to digest and moreover a good filler. It is nutritious and will also give you a lot of scope for being creative and experimentative.

Method

1. Add some salt and approximately 10 g butter to the water. If using parboiled rice add another 500 ml water.

2. Add the bay leaves and bring to the boil.

3. Add the rice and stir continuously for the first 2 minutes or so to separate all the grains.

4. When rice is cooked, drain and retain the liquid. Timing depends on the type of rice you use.

5. Clean the fish and cut into bite-sized cubes.

6. Poach the fish in the rice liquid and/or milk, drain and set aside in a dish. (You can use the rice liquid instead of milk, though milk would authenticate the recipe. I prefer to use half milk and half stock. It gives more taste.)

Measurements	Ingredients
50 g	Butter
1–1.5 litres	Water
2–3	Bay leaves
200 g	Rice
500 g	Fillet of white fish or trout or salmon
100–150 ml	Milk
4	Eggs (organic or free-range)
As desired	Crushed pepper
1 tbsp	Parsley or coriander (chopped)
As desired	Salt

7. Reduce the liquid to a consistency of thin custard.

8. Boil the eggs and shell them. Do not over boil. For best results put the eggs into boiling water and shut off after 8 minutes. Leave the eggs in the water for 3–4 minutes and then drain and chill immediately. Chilling in iced water prevents any further carry over cooking.

9. Sieve the egg yolk and chop the whites and then blend again. The egg whites should be approximately 2.5 mm in size.

10. In a saucepan large enough to hold everything add the rice and gently blend in the fish, half the eggs, the remaining butter, the seasoning, half the parsley or coriander and the milk or combined liquid.

11. Reheat slowly or better still turn out into an ovenproof dish and warm in an oven.

12. This can be either turned out as a portion or if more are sharing it is best served in the dish sprinkled with the remaining egg and either coriander or parsley sprinkled over. I am an avid fan of coriander and prefer it to parsley to give it that little eastern/Indian twist.

Kerala Fish Curry

Vevichathu

Chef's Notes

• This is a different type of curry and one which is best accompanied by the thicker varieties of rice such as parboiled rice or short grain. It is a slightly tart curry and will suit oily fish best. Try sardines or mackerel, but salmon will also do well in this sort of curry.

Method

1. Wash and clean the pieces of fish, drain and keep to one side.

2. Grind the chillies, garlic, turmeric and onions to a fine paste and mix with a cup of water.

3. Put the curry leaves at the bottom of a casserole and put the pieces of fish on top of it with the cokum pieces in between.

4. Add the watered chilli, garlic, turmeric and onion paste.

5. If cokum is not available you can use 2 tbsp tamarind juice.

6. Bring to the boil.

Ingredients	Measurements
500 g (either steaks or filleted)	Fish pieces
4 level tsp	Dry chillies (fried and powdered)
1 tsp	Garlic (chopped and minced)
½ tsp	Turmeric
2 small	Onions (thinly sliced)
10–12	Curry leaves
50 g	Cokum
2–3 tbsp	Coconut oil or sunflower oil
6	Button onions or baby shallots
½ tsp	Mustard seeds
10–12	Fenugreek seeds
300 ml	Water

7. Boil well so that the masala and the onions cook well.

8. When the gravy starts boiling on all sides of the pot, heat a small frying pan and add the coconut oil.

9. Sizzle the button onions or baby shallots until almost browned on all sides, then add the mustard seeds until they crackle and then add the fenugreek seeds and pour into the fish gravy.

10. Allow it to simmer on a slow heat for 30 minutes. When the gravy thickens, add the fish and simmer for 4–5 minutes then remove from the fire to prevent any carry over cooking.

11. As an option you could add some coconut milk to the curry to give it a richer twist.

Keralan Prawn Samosa

Chef's Notes

- The samosa is now so well known that few descriptions are required for it in the UK any more. However, India and its vast cuisines does not have one general recipe for a samosa except for the shape, I suppose. There are different kinds of pastry too, all differing from north to south and east to west. Many communities have their own styles and many cuisines have various styles within themselves. It would be wise to say here that for our many readers and those who may venture out to make samosas for themselves and enjoy them for their simplicity and versatility the best pastry to use is the one readily available in most oriental shops across the UK. This is sold under the name of spring roll pastry. It is available in three sizes and the medium sized will give you best results and minimum wastage.

- The Keralan prawn samosa differs to the Goan prawn samosa by its simplicity of spicing. Whereas the Goan brother is robust and hot the Keralan is mild and simple.

Method

1. Wash, clean and drain the prawns well.

2. If the prawns are too large, cut into half or one-third pieces.

3. Blend them in a bowl in the lime juice, mix and keep cool in the refrigerator. Try not to leave them outside at room temperature unless you are ready with all the other preparations.

4. Boil the peas until just done Drain and set aside.

5. Chop and set aside all your mise-en-place.

6. Keep the condiments such as the turmeric, the asafoetida, the cumin, mustard seeds and white lentils on a small flat plate.

7. Heat the oil in a frying pan (roughly 25 cm diameter) and add the mustard seeds. As soon as the crackling reduces add the curry leaves and the white lentils. Give the pan a little shake then add the asafoetida and the cumin. Shake for a few seconds then add the turmeric and immediately the chillies, ginger and garlic.

8. Sauté until the garlic turns a pale golden then add the onions.

9. As soon as the onions turn soft add the grated coconut and sauté for a few minutes until the coconut gets well roasted and gives off a great toasted smell.

10. Turn up the heat and add the prawns then sauté mixing well for a couple of minutes only. Do not allow the prawns to overcook, as they will get rubbery. Remember that you will fry these samosas in deep oil, which could make the prawns even worse.

11. Sprinkle with salt, taste and mix in the coriander. Taste again and remove immediately to a wide dish to allow for rapid cooling.

12. Refrigerate when cool enough.

13. To make the samosa open the pastry pack and cover the pastry with a clean, damp kitchen cloth.

14. Place a side plate over the pastry stack and cut out a circle, so all the layers have been cut through.

15. Keep the trimmings covered as you can cut and fry them later and serve them as a crisp snack sprinkled with some chaat masala.

16. Now cut the pastry in half to form a semi-circle. Cover one half with the damp cloth and peel the other half in layers of two, cover this also under the damp cloth as you go along.

17. Once you have finished peeling all the pastry (do not forget to keep it covered) take plain flour in a cup and make a very thick paste with it using water.

Measurements	Ingredients
500 g medium or small	Prawns cleaned and deveined
½	Lime (juice only)
200 g	Green peas
1 tsp	Mustard seeds
12–15	Curry leaves
2 tbsp	White lentil
2–3 pinches	Asafoetida
2 tsp	Cumin seeds
½ tsp	Turmeric
2–3 tbsp	Sunflower oil
2–3 medium	Green chilli (minced)
5 cm piece	Ginger
6–8 cloves	Garlic
2 medium	Onions (finely chopped)
200 g	Coconut (grated) (fresh or frozen. If using desiccated, soak in water to rehydrate before use)
1 tbsp	Fresh coriander (chopped)
1 packet or 500 g if using fresh	Samosa pastry
1–2 tbsp	Plain flour
	Water
As desired	Salt
	Oil for deep frying

18. Take one pastry, i.e. two sheets together, form a triangle by bringing one of the edges folded over to one of the round sides in the middle. This will make a pouch.

19. Apply some paste on the open side and then fold over the other end to make a perfect triangle/cone. Make sure that there is no hole or opening at the tip of the triangle or pouch.

20. Put a spoonful of the mixture in the cavity but leave a 12 mm gap at the top.

21. Fold one part in to seal the top and apply some paste to it, then fold over the open edge and press well. Make sure that all of it is well sealed otherwise oil will penetrate when frying.

22. You will get a nice chunky triangular filled pastry. Repeat the process for all until you have finished the filling.

23. If you have any pastry left use it for something else or cut into pieces and fry with the trimmings.

24. When frying make sure that the oil is quite hot otherwise you will get bad results and oil will penetrate the samosa even if your sealing is good. The samosa should float up as soon as it is added to the oil.

25. Serve samosas with fresh green chutney or with tomato ketchup as is commonly done in India.

King Prawns and King Scallops

Ullathiyadh

Chef's Notes

A delicious and very simple preparation, the pre-preparation of which may take longer than the cooking itself. This pre-preparation can be used for various other products including vegetables such as cabbage or chicken, or simply a blend of different types of seafood.

Measurements	Ingredients
10–12	King scallops slit into two horizontally
10–12	King prawns (shell on) (slit over the top, head trimmed and digestive tract cleaned)
½ tsp	Turmeric powder
½ tsp	Chilli powder
To taste	Salt
1 tsp	Lemon juice
2 tbsp	Sunflower oil

Continued

Method

1. Place all the seafood in a bowl and marinate with the turmeric powder, chilli powder, salt and lemon juice. Set aside for up to two hours but no more, otherwise you may lose too much moisture.

2. Once again you must remember that you are cooking delicate seafood and the cooking process needs to be very fast, therefore the pan has to get really hot and be able to sustain the heat.

3. If the seafood is too much for the size of your pan, cook in two batches – it only takes 4–5 minutes at the most. Or cook the seafood separately and then blend the two. This is provided that your mise-en-place or pre-preparation is very good.

4. Place all the ingredients within easy reach so that you do not have to leave the cooking area.

5. Take a wok and heat it really hot. Keeping the heat on high, add the oil and as it begins to smoke add the mustard seeds. Remember they burn quite quickly, therefore as soon as you get a nice nutty aroma you know they are ready.

6. When the crackling stops add the curry leaves.

7. Add the cumin and almost immediately the ginger and garlic. Stir for 1–2 minutes or until the garlic gets a golden colour. Do not allow the garlic to brown.

8. At this stage turn the heat down a bit and add the coconut. Sauté for 1–2 minutes until the aroma gets a bit nutty.

9. Do not allow to brown but just to get a pale golden colour. Now turn the heat on maximum and wait for a few seconds for the pan to get hot again but keep stirring.

10. Toss in the vegetables and sauté for a minute or so. If you like more colour and flavour use both French beans and baby corn.

11. Add the seafood and keeping the heat on high just give it a swirl or two and allow it to sizzle.

Measurements	Ingredients
¼ tsp	Mustard seeds
8–10	Curry leaves, fresh (use dried or frozen if you like but accept a not so good flavour)
½ tsp	Cumin seeds
1 2–3 cm piece	Ginger
5–6 cloves	Fresh garlic (finely chopped)
3 tbsp	Grated coconut (fresh) or
2 tbsp	Dessicated coconut (soak in half a cup water, for 30 minutes before cooking commences)
2 medium	Tomato (pulped and shredded with skin)
8–10	Mangetout cut into half lengthways
1 medium	Carrot cut into 2.5 cm batons or eight to ten small halved lengthways. Blanch them before adding.
6–8 slender	French beans (cut in half) or
6–8	Baby corn (slit lengthways)
¼ of each	Red and green peppers, shredded (optional)
4–5 slender	Spring onions (shredded with greens)
1–2 large	Green chillies seeded and then shredded thinly
1½ tbsp	Fresh coriander (chopped)

12. Do not agitate the pan too much or else the seafood will release all its juices, but toss from time to time allowing all the seafood to touch the bottom of the pan and cook quickly and evenly.

13. Now add some shredded peppers (optional), the spring onions and green chilli and continue to sauté for 1–2 minutes.

14. Your seafood should be almost done by now. Add the fresh coriander and check seasoning. Remove and serve with lemon rice or any other rice of your choice.

15. The illustration on page 125 is just a variation for you to get an idea of how to present the dish.

Kolmi No Patia

Chef's Notes

- This is a much simplified version of the traditional Parsee prawn patia. Patia (or Patio) normally acts as an accompaniment to my favourite dish the Dhaan Daar shown in the illustration on a complete dish. It can also be eaten on its own with fresh hot chappaties.

- Please note that Patia is a classic dish and it will be rare to find this version anywhere in the UK. Most restaurants do not know that a classic recipe exists and go on to make something hot, sweet and sour and bright red in colour, which is not how it should be.

Measurements	Ingredients
500 g	Raw prawns
½	Lemon (juice only)
1 level tsp	Turmeric powder
4 tbsp	Oil
10–12	Curry leaves
1 medium	Aubergine (cut into small dice)
150–200 g	Red pumpkin (cut into small dice)
2 medium	Onions (finely chopped)
1	Green chilli (chopped)
1 heaped tsp	Red chilli powder
1 level tbsp	Coriander powder
1 heaped tsp	Cumin powder
2 level tbsp	Ginger/garlic
2 large	Tomatoes (diced)
2–3 tbsp fresh or 1 tsp concentrated	Tamarind pulp
100 g	Jaggery (or cane molasses or sugar)
2 tbsp	Fresh coriander (chopped)
To taste	Salt

Method

1. Clean the prawns, blend with the lemon juice and turmeric and set aside.

2. In a casserole heat the oil and add the curry leaves.

3. Add the aubergine and remove when well browned.

4. Next add the pumpkin and follow the same procedure.

5. Add the onions and sauté until golden brown.

6. Add the green chilli, the red chilli, coriander, cumin and the ginger/garlic paste.

7. Sauté for 2–3 minutes on a medium to low flame then add the tomatoes.

8. Cook for a further 2–3 minutes and add the tamarind pulp and jaggery.

9. When the tamarind and jaggery are fully dissolved add the aubergine and pumpkin and check for seasoning. The patia needs to be a little hot, sweet and sour.

10. Add the prawns and cook for 2–3 minutes or until they are done to your liking.

11. Finally, blend in the chopped coriander, remove from the cooker and serve.

12. If you are storing the patia as a pickle, use a little extra oil and cook the prawns a little longer so that no fresh prawn moisture remains and the patia begins to look like a thick pickle. You will still have to store it in the refrigerator.

Leeli Machchi Ni Curry

Chef's Notes

- This quite simply translates as green fish curry and is a simple curry that does not need a great deal of preparation.

- We Parsees would use a fish like pomfret in this recipe, which we feel gives the best flavour. Use any fish you like or prefer, only avoid very strong scented fish, as the curry is delicate and would get over powered quite easily.

- You can use fillets or steaks; however steaks are preferred as they do not disintegrate easily in the curry.

Measurements	Ingredients
2 tbsp	Oil
1 medium	Onion (finely sliced)
6 cloves	Garlic (finely crushed)
3.5 cm piece	Ginger (finely crushed)
2	Green chillies (seeded and finely chopped)
½ tsp	Turmeric
1 can or the extract from 1 coconut	Coconut milk
To taste	Salt
4 pods	Green cardamom
4	Cloves

Method

1. Take a casserole and add the oil.

2. Sauté the onions until hazy or translucent. Do not allow to brown, therefore keep the flame on a medium setting.

3. Add the garlic, ginger and green chillies, again taking care not to brown. The above process should not take more than 5 minutes.

4. Add the turmeric and in a few seconds the coconut milk.

5. Do not cover the pan and bring the contents slowly to the boil stirring slowly but effectively. By effectively I mean stirring right from the bottom.

Measurements	Ingredients
5–6	Curry leaves
2.5 cm piece	Cinnamon
2 tbsp	Coriander leaves (chopped)
6–8	Fish (fillets or steaks)

6. Add salt and then the cardamom, cloves, curry leaves and cinnamon.

7. Simmer for 1–2 minutes, add the coriander leaves, cook for a further 1–2 minutes and then add the fish.

8. If you are using fillets then I suggest you allow the pan to be on the heat for only 2 more minutes then cover the pan and turn off the heat. The latent heat in the curry will be adequate to cook the fish through ready for serving within 5–6 minutes.

9. If using thick-cut steaks you can cook for 2–4 minutes and then follow the same procedure.

10. Either way the fish should not be allowed to cook too much.

11. Best served with fried papads and plain rice or a light pulao.

Leeli Kolmi Ni Curry

Chef's Notes

• This simple tasty and creamy light green curry is a great one for whipping up almost at the last minute. It does not ask for a great deal of preparation and once the pre-preparations are done takes no more 10–12 minutes to make. Fresh prawns make the best combination for this style, however fish comes out equally good.

Method

1. Heat the oil in a 15–20 cm diameter saucepan and sauté the onions until soft. Do not let them brown.

2. Add the ginger, garlic and green chillies and sauté for 2–3 minutes. Remember do not keep the heat on high as they will discolour.

3. Add the turmeric, diluted in half a cup of water. Cook for 1–2 minutes then add the coconut milk.

Measurements	Ingredients
2 tbsp	Sunflower oil
1 medium	Onion (finely sliced)
3.5 cm piece	Fresh ginger (crushed)
6 cloves	Garlic (crushed)
2 medium	Green chillies (slit into 4 or 6 each lengthways)
1/2 tsp	Ground turmeric
400 g tin	Coconut milk
4 pods	Green cardamom
4	Cloves
2 cm piece	Cassia/cinnamon
5–6	Fresh curry leaves
1 tbsp	Fresh coriander (chopped)
500 g	Black tiger prawns
As desired	Salt

4. Bring slowly to the boil, stirring gently from the bottom up. As soon as it begins to boil add the cardamom, cloves, cinnamon or cassia and the curry leaves.

5. Add salt to season as desired and simmer for a couple of minutes until the curry begins to thicken.

6. When it is the right consistency add the chopped coriander, stir for a few seconds and add the prawns.

7. Depending on the size of the prawns you can decide how long to cook them. Normally two minutes on boil and then leaving them covered in the curry for a few minutes is adequate. The latent heat in the curry will cook them perfectly.

8. The prawns should always be added just before you are ready to serve as that way they will remain juicy and succulent.

9. Serve with steamed rice, some fresh onion salad and fried papads.

Bhorleley Shayvut

Stuffed Lobster

Chef's Notes

• This simple lobster preparation was created to suit a quick but excellent end product. Though it may take a little more time at home, the results can be very rewarding.

Measurements	Ingredients
4 approx. 300–400 g each	Lobsters (live)
1 tsp	Lemon juice
½ tsp	Turmeric powder
2 tbsp	Butter
8–10 cloves	Garlic (finely chopped)
2 medium	Green chilli (finely chopped and seeded)
2 medium	Onion (finely chopped)
1 heaped tsp	Cumin powder
2 heaped tsp	Coriander powder
2 well heaped tbsp	Coriander (chopped)
4 thin	Spring onions (chopped)
2	Eggs (hard boiled, chopped)
1 medium	Tomato (diced)

Method

1. Place the lobsters in the freezer cabinet until they are dead or almost frozen. This is a more humane way of killing them and I prefer it. Since the cold numbs the brain they tend not to suffer and it prevents you from cutting open live lobsters if you don't like to.

2. Break off the claws and set aside. Crack them so that they cook well and if you are devoid of a 'crackie' then it makes it easier later.

3. With a pointed knife, first pierce the lobster tail just below the base of the head and then with a firm sawing motion slit the lobster into half but do not sever through. By that I mean do not allow the lobster to separate at the bottom. The thin under belly area should not be severed.

4. Next turn the lobster around and slit the head in the same way. If you have a good sawing knife suited for this purpose, use it, if not a regular knife is fine but not as easy to do the job.

5. Remove the meat, coral and other usable bits and discard the rest.

6. Wash the shells well and put them in boiling water along with the claws for 2 minutes.

7. Remove the claws but let the shells remain in the water until they are the desired colour.

8. When the colour is good remove and wash under cold running water, drain, flip them over and open them before they turn firm. This means that you are converting the lobster into a serving dish. To do this, place the thumb of each hand inside the cavity and slowly open the cavity at the tail end. If you exert too much pressure, the bottom collapses.

9. When they are opened fully, tuck the bit just below the head so that the edges of the tail go partially around the head, thereby holding its position.

10. Place some weight over them so that they do not curl.

11. Crack the claws and gently remove the meat. Set it aside.

12. Dice the lobster meat into 12 mm pieces and toss them with the lemon juice and turmeric powder. At this stage add the claw meat.

13. Take either a 23 cm casserole or a large frying pan. A casserole is preferred when cooking at home due to the width of the burners being small.

14. Add the butter and bring it to frothing point. When the butter is hot but not browning add the garlic and chilli and sauté for 2 minutes.

15. Add the onion and continue sautéing until the onions turn soft, but do not increase the flame.

16. Add the cumin and coriander powders and sauté for 1–2 minutes.

17. Turn the heat high then add spring onions and the meat. Do not overwork the meat. After the initial mixing in let it stay in the same position for 1 minute before you turn it around again. Do this only two or three times; the meat to me would be ready in 3–4 minutes after which you are asking for rubber. Season and remove from the heat.

18. If there is too much juice in the pan do not worry. Stuff the meat with the exception of the claws into the shells on individual plates and keep the claws on the side as a garnish.

19. Return the casserole to the heat and slightly dry the juices, then add the chopped coriander and if you like chopped boiled eggs (two) and some diced tomato without juices (one medium).

20. Portion out the mix over all four lobsters and serve immediately with pulao or plain steamed rice.

Machchi Na Pattice Nay Tamota Ni Gravy

Fish Cakes with Tomato Gravy

Chef's Notes

- This is a simple fish cake recipe and one which many Parsee mums can create out of virtually nothing else in the house besides leftovers. No doubt you can plan and execute a memorable dish but don't get bogged down by settling down to copying a recipe bit by bit. However, one needs to know the cultural differences in a recipe to understand the background of the flavouring and the likes and dislikes of a community.

- You can use any white fish you like, however, the taste will change with the fish and its predominance of flavour.

We will deal with the gravy afterwards as it can be an independent recipe. The gravy can be used for various types of croquettes and other snack items.

Method

1. If you have a mincer at home then mincing the fish and the ingredients is simpler. If not then you can chop up the fillets with a cleaver or a large knife. Chop repeatedly as if chopping parsley until you get a fine mince.

2. Blend all the chopped ingredients into the fish mince and mix well, almost kneading it.

3. Add the salt, lemon juice and one egg and mix well.

4. Finally add the bread that has been soaked for a few seonds in water, then squeezed out.

Measurements	Ingredients
250 g	White fish fillet minced
1 large	Green chilli (finely chopped)
2.5 cm	Fresh ginger (finely chopped)
6–8 cloves	Garlic (finely chopped)
2 tbsp	Fresh coriander (chopped)
1 tsp (also check for taste to suit)	Salt
1 tbsp	Lemon juice
3–4	Egg
2 slices	White sliced bread
100 g	Plain flour
As required for shallow frying	Oil

5. The bread is to stabilise the mix and if you find it too soft add one or two more slices until you have a mix that is firm enough to form into balls without sticking to your palms. Too much bread, though, will dilute the flavour of the fish.

6. Taste and add more salt if you need to.

7. If you do not wish to taste raw mince then fry a small piece and taste. Do not make all the cakes before you have approved the taste for yourself.

8. Divide the mix into even sized balls depending on the size you prefer. You may like them large if eating as a main dish or small if serving as a snack.

9. Heat the oil, making sure that it is not overheated.

10. Spread the flour into a flat tray big enough to take all the balls at one time and beat the remaining eggs in a shallow bowl or soup plate.

11. Flatten each ball until about 8 mm thick, smooth the edges, dip each into the egg, wipe off excess egg and shallow fry.

12. Fry a pan full at a time before turning them over to fry on the other side. Raise the heat if the oil begins to foam.

13. They must be a golden brown colour before removing onto to a tray lined with kitchen towel.

14. If the egg is well beaten you will get a nice frilly texture.

15. The cakes will take only a few minutes to cook. Once brown on either side they should be well cooked.

These can also be eaten cold, stuffed in a small cob bread, as a brunch snack or even stuffed when hot.

Method

1. Prepare the ginger garlic paste (see page 135).

2. Heat the oil in a casserole and add the cinnamon sticks. Sauté until deep brown in colour and swollen but not burnt.

3. Add the red chillies and after 15–20 seconds add the onions and sauté until they are opaque but not browned. This should take roughly 3–4 minutes on a medium to high heat.

4. Add the ginger garlic paste and sauté for a further minute or so and add the tomatoes.

5. Add the vinegar, the jaggery or sugar and the tamarind and simmer on a low heat for 15–20 minutes.

6. Stir occasionally but do not allow to discolour. Keep covered when cooking to prevent splattering.

Tamota Ni Gravy	Ingredients
1 heaped tbsp	Ginger/garlic paste
2–3 tbsp	Oil
2 2.5 cm pieces	Cinnamon stick
2 large	Whole red chilli (broken into three or four pieces each)
2 medium to small	Onions (finely chopped)
4–5 medium, *or* 450 g	Tomatoes (chopped) *or* Chopped tomatoes
1 tbsp	Malt vinegar
1 tbsp	Jaggery (grated) *or* substitute with sugar
1½ tsp if freshly removed. If using concentrate use only ½ tsp	Tamarind pulp (optional)

7. Check for salt, remove and cool.

8. Use in the required quantity.

9. This sauce will keep for quite a while in the refrigerator provided it is well covered, you do not insert a wet spoon into it and you keep the edges clean.

10. Tamota ni gravy is excellent with mince croquettes, batter-fried fish, chicken etc.

11. For added flavour you can add fresh green chillies slit over the top and put along with the red chilli as well as three or four cloves.

Masala Ma Taraeli Machchi

Chef's Notes

- This is a classic Parsee fish marinated in a simple masala and shallow fried. This preparation should accompany my all-time favourite 'Dhan Daar nay Vaghar' a simple puréed lentil sizzled with garlic and cumin and served with deep-fried crisp onions and steamed rice.

- Use the fish of your choice. Although pomfret makes the best, plaice, tilapia and coley are also good. Seabass also tops the list.

Measurements	Ingredients
8 small pieces roughly 10 cm long	Fish fillet
¼ tsp	Turmeric powder
1 tbsp	Lime juice
1 tsp	Red chilli powder (medium hot)
1 tsp	Cumin powder
1½ tsp	Coriander powder
1½ tsp (see page 35)	Ginger/garlic paste
To taste	Salt
For shallow pan frying	Oil

Method

1. Rub salt and turmeric into the fillets and set aside for 30 minutes.

2. Make a paste with the remaining ingredients except the oil.

3. Blend in the paste into the fish and set aside in the refrigerator unless you are cooking it straight away. You can leave it overnight if you cover it well. However, the marinade may cure the fish to a degree so less cooking time is required.

4. Taste the paste and check for seasoning. If you like more lime juice or salt go ahead.

5. About 30 minutes prior to serving pan-fry the fish in very little oil. Ensure that you allow each piece to colour well on one side before turning it over. Do not make the pan too hot, as the masala will burn very rapidly. When ready the fish should be crisp on the outside and delicately soft on the inside. It is dead simple and easy.

6. To create a variation from this method, after marinating you can dab the fillets in flour then egg and semolina instead of breadcrumbs. Deep fry as you would a crumbed fillet of fish. Coarse ground rice is also an excellent crumb, and healthy, too.

Ginger/Garlic Paste

Ginger and garlic pastes make the basis of most of India's cooking. I have tried wherever possible to include them chopped, however in most forms a paste is preferred. A Parsee home, for instance, is totally lost if this is not available in the refrigerator at any time. To simplify matters most supermarkets now sell them in individual jars. All you need to do is blend them and use more of one or less depending on how the recipe calls for it. However, these ready-made ones contain an acidic preservative and are not always suitable.

To make your own

Take equal quantities of garlic and ginger, cleaned, and either blend to a paste with a mortar and pestle or in your blender. In the mortar you will not need any liquid but in a blender you will. Add a little water first and a little bland vegetable oil. Do not use olive oil or else it will not be suitable for Indian food. Make a thick paste by stopping regularly and scraping the sides. The addition of oil will prevent the paste from spoiling and it will keep refrigerated for up to two months.

Masala Ma Kolmi Nay Tarela Papeta

Prawns in Masala with Spicy Potatoes

Chef's Notes

- This is another Parsee speciality and the cooking of the potatoes is quite typical though methods may vary. For instance, if my mother were to cook this traditionally she would cook the prawns along with the potatoes thereby lengthening the cooking time for the prawns. Masala na papeta may be made to suit several other items such as fried eggs served on top of them or beaten eggs baked on top and so on.

Measurements	Ingredients
2 tsp	Lime juice
To taste	Salt
500 g	Raw peeled prawns (washed and drained)
500 g	Potatoes (peeled and sliced)
2 tbsp	Sunflower oil
5–8	Curry leaves (fresh shredded, if dry crumble coarsely)
6 cloves	Garlic
2 medium	Green chillies (finely chopped)
100 ml	Water
3 tbsp	Fresh coriander

Method

1. Apply lime juice and some salt to the prawns and set them aside in a bowl.

2. Put all the masala ingredients in a blender and grind to a smooth paste.

3. Mix the potatoes with the masala and let them marinate for 1–2 hours if time permits.

4. Heat the oil in a casserole until hot, but not too hot then sauté the curry leaves, garlic and green chilli for 2–3 minutes.

5. Add the potatoes and the masala.

Continued

6. Keeping the heat on medium sauté well and stir regularly right up from the bottom. A wooden spatula is recommended but use whatever you are comfortable with, though a flat spoon is better.

7. Cover after approximately 5 minutes or so then add the water and simmer until the potatoes are three-quarters done.

8. Check whether the gravy around the potatoes is thick and rich looking. If too wet you need to reduce further until the gravy is really thick.

9. Raise the flame to high and add the prawns.

10. Stir initially only to level the prawns, but do not agitate too much otherwise the prawns will give off too much liquid and turn rubbery.

11. Continue cooking on a high heat for 2–3 minutes, add salt, check for seasoning and sprinkle the chopped coriander and mix it in.

12. The gravy should be thick and quite dry and rich looking.

13. If you have too much liquid remove some and reduce it separately, then add it back.

14. Use this technique whenever cooking any shellfish, which should never be overcooked.

15. Serves best with hot chappaties or crusty bread and some sweet sour and hot chutney.

Masala	Ingredients
6–8	Dry red chillies (cut up and soaked in 2 tbsp malt vinegar)
1 tsp	Cumin seeds
4–5 cloves	Garlic
½ tsp	Turmeric
1 medium	Onion

Mirch Adrak Aur Lehsun Kay Scallop

Method

1. Clean the scallops and slit them horizontally.

2. Apply salt, lemon juice and the turmeric and set aside.

3. Finely shred the vegetables, garlic and ginger and set them aside.

4. Heat a frying pan and add the oil.

5. Turn the heat to high and add the scallops.

6. After a few seconds toss once or twice and throw in the rest of the ingredients with the exception of the coriander. Toss until the moisture quite dries up but keep the heat on

Ingredients	Measurements
2–3 king sized or 6 queen	Scallops
To taste	Salt
1–2 tsp	Lemon juice
¼ tsp	Turmeric
5 cm piece	Ginger (smooth)
3–4 cloves	Garlic
1 medium	Green chilli
1 small to medium	Tomato
¼	Green pepper
¼	Red pepper
1–2 thin	Spring onions
1 tbsp	Fresh coriander (chopped)
2–3 tbsp	Oil

high all along. This way the scallops will not release all their moisture.

7. Check for seasoning, add the fresh coriander, toss and remove.

8. Garnish if required and serve with some salad and toasted ciabatta roll slit in half.

Garnish	Ingredients
	Mixed lettuce
	Melba toast *or* Toasted bread (salamander) *or* Ciabatta

Machli Kay Tikkay

Monkfish Tikka

Chef's Notes

- Most widely known among all other Indian preparations, this tikka, normally of chicken, is a succulent and juicy kebab if well prepared and makes an ideal snack. Ensure that you do not overcook the fish and of course use a very hot oven. If monkfish is not available, select a chunky fish.

Method

1. Cut the fish into 'tikkas', or cubes large enough to be skewered, roughly 3 cm × 3 cm.

2. Rub salt and pepper into the fish and set aside.

3. In a blender add all the other ingredients except the butter and half the yoghurt and blend to a smooth paste.

4. When all the spices are well ground remove to a bowl and whisk in the remaining yoghurt. Check here for spiciness to suit your requirements. Add more chilli only if you so desire.

5. Mix in the fish and check for seasoning. The fish is best set aside overnight in the refrigerator, or for at least 4–5 hours.

6. The tikka can be grilled on the barbecue or under the grill and finished in the oven. Either way it needs to be basted with butter for that juicy appearance.

7. Cook under the grill if you wish to cook right through. Ensure that the grill is not too high and that the meat is on a wire mesh with a drip tray below.

Measurements	Ingredients
800 g	Monkfish tail (deboned)
To taste	Salt and pepper (use white pepper powder)
4 cm piece	Ginger
6–8 cloves	Garlic
½ tsp	Cumin seeds
½ tsp	Coriander seeds
½ tsp	Red chilli powder
¼ tsp	Turmeric powder
2 tbsp	Lime juice (lemon juice can be substituted)
½ tsp	Garam masala powder
50 ml	Mustard or ground nut oil
150 g	Yoghurt
For basting	Butter

8. Only if there is no option use a very hot oven. The tikkas will cook well in approximately in 8–10 minutes.

9. There are several variations to the original tikka recipe and one can use one's own imagination for more interesting kebabs.

Shinanio Chi Salade

Mussel Cocktail

Chef's Notes

• This starter can be eaten as a salad with greens or served as a cocktail.

Method

1. Clean and wash the mussels well. Remove any grit, beards, etc. (Do not use mussels whose shells have opened up.)

2. Sauté the onions, garlic and carrots in the oil in a casserole or saucepan until soft.

3. Add the whole mussels and the green chilli and paprika and sauté for a further 2–3 minutes. All this time the heat has to be high.

4. Now add the wine and salt, cover the pan and cook until all the shells have opened. This should not take more than 2 minutes or so.

5. Put off the flame and allow to cool in the pan.

6. When cool remove the mussels, scraping any of the chopped ingredients back into the pan.

7. Remove the meat from the shells and either discard the shells or use them to present the mussels in. Refrigerate and cover the mussels. By leaving them exposed in the refrigerator you will dry them out.

8. Reheat the residual mix in the saucepan and reduce it until almost dry on a gentle flame.

9. Cool the mix when dry and refrigerate until cold.

Measurements	Ingredients
24 medium or 36 small	Whole mussels
1 tbsp	Olive oil
1 medium onion or 4–5 shallots	Onions *or* shallots (finely chopped)
2–3 cloves	Garlic (finely chopped)
1 small or half	Carrot (finely diced, almost chopped)
1 large	Green chilli (slit and seeded)
½ cup	Dry white wine
2 heaped tbsp	Mayonnaise
2 tsp	Fresh coriander (chopped)
	Lettuce (use as a base if doing a cocktail or assorted lettuce if doing a salad)
½ tsp or less depending on your taste	Paprika powder
To taste	Salt

10. Blend this mixture into the mayonnaise (I prefer to make my own which is always better but you may like to use ready made) a little at a time until you are happy with the flavour. This is because some may find the flavour too strong therefore add in to your individual taste.

11. Mix in the coriander and your dressing is ready.

12. Fold the mussels into the dressing and either spoon each into a half shell or serve on a bed of lettuce on a plate or blend in with lettuce just before serving.

13. Garnish or serve with cut boiled eggs, olives, etc.

Patrani Machchi

Chef's Notes

- Patrani machchi is a classical Parsee fish preparation and is very popular at weddings and other festive occasions. If the banana leaf is not available substitute with aluminium foil or baking parchment. You may also use the chutney for directly grilling the fish under a grill or use a whole fish.

- Pomfret is a flat roundish fish quite like a pompano. You can use filleted plaice or any other white fish if you like but there is no doubt pomfret is the best.

- Banana leaves are available in Thai or Philippino stores and certain Indian stores.

Measurements	Ingredients
3 whole	Pomfrets (cut into 2.5 cm thick slices)
1 200 g	Coconut (grated) *or* Desiccated coconut (Fine ground)
1 large bunch	Coriander (as available in Indian stores, not supermarkets)
4–5	Green chillies
6–8 cloves	Garlic
1 heaped tsp	Cumin seeds
1 tbsp	Sugar
1	Lime (large, juice only)
1 large bunch	Mint (again as available in Indian stores)
½ tsp	Turmeric
To taste	Salt
As required	Banana leaves
As required	Malt vinegar

Method

1. Rub each slice of fish with salt and turmeric and set aside while you proceed with the chutney.

2. Grind all the ingredients except the banana leaves and the vinegar into a paste using only as much water as you think the machine needs to grind. However, if using desiccated coconut you will have to use water when grinding in the blender. Use gradually as required but ensure the chutney is thick.

3. Coat both sides of each slice of the fish with the coconut chutney.

4. Remove the stems from the banana leaves and string the sides and wipe the leaves clean.

5. Cut them into squares big enough to wrap each fish piece.

6. Warm the leaves over an open flame to make them soft and supple. To do this just run them over the burner or hot plate and you will see them change colour and become soft. Do not overdo it, just one pass on either side is often sufficient. This process also destroys any bacteria on the surface.

7. Place the coated fish on the banana leaf and cover the fish with the leaf. Tie with a string to prevent the chutney from coming out. You need to make a neat parcel.

8. Steam the fish till done. To steam you can preheat an oven to 180°C/gas mark 5. Place the wrapped fish on a flat tray, sprinkle some vinegar and a little water over the parcels and put in the oven. Malt vinegar is the preferred choice. The steaming process takes about 20 minutes. If you have a steamer then use that.

9. Just before serving remove the strings. The fish is served with the banana leaf.

10. To avoid all the extra work involved using banana leaves, wrap the fish in foil or greaseproof paper and follow the same principle. However, I cannot guarantee the same flavour.

Pomfret Récheâde

Chef's Notes

- Récheâde is a style typical of Goa and the terminology is Portuguese based. Recheado means 'stuffed' in Portuguese. No doubt the most exotic of all the fish used for Récheâde is pomfret but small sized mackerel, sea bass and grey mullet are as good to use, only the flavour varies. There are variations to Récheâde but this one seems to work extremely well.

Method

1. Place the chillies, garlic, ginger, cassia, cardamom, cloves, coriander seeds, cumin, peppercorns and vinegar in a blender and grind to a smooth paste. Add more vinegar if necessary.

2. Clean the tiny scales from the body of the pomfret and remove the fins. You will find that there are tiny scales below the fin area, too, and these will need to be removed.

3. Now bone the fish. Take a sharp knife and slit them over the top on either side of the central bone structure. Go down gradually until you come to the abdominal cavity, always making sure that you get the flesh off the bone quite cleanly. The best way to achieve this is to keep the blade of the knife tilted towards the bones and not inwards towards the flesh.

4. Once you have gone all the way down to the abdominal cavity you will need to carefully detach the bone at the tail end. To do this simply insert your knife-edge over the bone at either end and with a little pressure cut through it. Make sure that you do not cut through the fish.

5. Gently release the flesh from either side of the cavity. You may wish to remove the bones entirely or leave them inside. It is best to remove the bone, therefore gently lever it out.

6. Clean the entrails and wash out the cavity. If there is a roe, however, keep it.

7. Wash the fish and either dry with a kitchen towel or leave inverted to drain.

8. Blend together the turmeric, lime juice and half the salt and rub this inside the fish.

9. Put 2 tbsp oil in a frying pan and allow to heat up.

10. Toss in the curry leaves and soon after the onions. Sauté the onions until brown then add the masala.

11. Cook the masala until it releases its fat then add the tomatoes.

12. Cook for a few minutes, add the chopped coriander and season.

13. Cool for a few minutes by spreading it out, then fill this into the fish on each side of the cavity. The fish is now ready for pan grilling.

14. Grill each side gently in a large frying pan with a little oil browned on the top side.

15. Some people prefer to tie the fish lightly so that the filling does not come out. However, if you are careful very little will come out anyway.

16. Once cooked, remove and serve with sliced deep-fried potatoes, grilled tomato slices and salad.

Measurements	Ingredients
5–6 large	Whole red chillies (Kashmiri type is best)
5–6 cloves	Garlic
2.5 cm piece	Fresh ginger
2.5 cm piece	Cassia
3	Green cardamom
3–4	Cloves
1 tbsp	Coriander seeds
1 heaped tsp	Cumin seeds
5–6	Peppercorns
250 ml	Palm vinegar or cider vinegar
2 fish, 250 g each	Pomfret
1 tsp	Turmeric powder
1 tbsp	Lime juice
1 level tsp or to taste	Salt
As needed	Sunflower oil
8–10	Curry leaves (fresh)
1 medium	Onions (finely chopped)
2 medium	Tomato (chopped)
1 tbsp	Fresh coriander (chopped)

INTERNATIONAL CUISINE | India

Prawn Fried Rice or Stir-Fried Prawns with Rice

Chef's Notes

- A simple and delicious preparation that most people will enjoy. Kids will just love it and for those who are not familiar with spices this is a gentle introduction, attractive and easy to manage. Also very user friendly.

Method

For this it is always best to use stale rice that has stayed in the refrigerator.

1. Prepare all your ingredients and set them aside ready for the cooking. The pre-preparation is the longest bit in this, cooking will only take few minutes.

2. Heat a wok on the flame and when really hot add the oil. As soon as the oil reaches smoking point and forms a haze toss in all the shredded vegetables including the ginger and garlic.

3. Toss for a minute or so and add the prawns. Keep the flame on high and do not allow the pan to go cold. Also do not stir too much as the heat in the pan will get lost. Toss every now and again to allow all the prawns to touch the bottom of the pan.

4. When the prawns change colour add the salt, pepper and soy sauce. Toss and adjust seasoning.

Measurements	Ingredients
2 tbsp	Sunflower oil or Sesame oil
2 heaped tbsp	Carrot (grated)
1 tbsp each	Green and red peppers (shredded)
2–3	Spring onions (shredded)
2.5 cm	Fresh ginger (finely shredded)
2–3 cloves	Garlic (shredded or finely minced)
200 g	Black tiger prawns (raw peeled)
1 tsp	Dark soy sauce
To taste	Salt and pepper
Made from 200 g raw rice	Pre-boiled rice
1 tbsp	Fresh coriander (optional, chopped fine)

5. As soon as you feel the prawns are almost cooked (2–3 minutes at most) add the rice and toss until the rice is heated through. The prawns will cook fully in the rice as it heats. Alternatively, you may serve the stir-fried prawns with steamed rice or on a bed of noodles.

6. If you like, sprinkle coriander over before service.

Samundari Khazaney Ki Jhalfrazi

Served with Unda Chawal

Chef's Notes

- A combination of seafood tossed with shredded peppers, chillies and onions. The word 'Jhalfrazi' is often spelt 'Jhalfrezi' or 'Jhalfraezi' but what does it actually mean? 'Jhal' means hot as in chilli hot and 'Farzi' means to look like. Therefore this dish actually need not be hot at all. It is the combination of chillies and the other shredded vegetables that give it that extra hot look. 'Unda Chawal' quite simply means egg rice. You may call it an oriental mix but on the streets of India you will be surprised to see several variations of egg-fried rice.

- If monkfish is not available use another firm fish that does not easily disintegrate or add more shellfish.

Method

1. Place all the seafood in a bowl and marinate with the turmeric powder, the chilli powder, some salt and the lemon juice and set aside for no more than 2 hours, otherwise you may lose too much moisture.

2. Once again you must remember that you are cooking delicate seafood and the cooking process needs to be very fast, therefore the pan has to get really hot and be able to sustain the heat. If the seafood is too much for the size of your pan, cook it in two batches as it only takes 4–5 minutes at the most. This is provided that your pre-preparation is very good.

3. Place all the ingredients within easy reach so that you do not have to leave the cooking area.

Measurements	Ingredients
8	King scallops (slit into two horizontally)
8	Tiger prawns (shell on, slit over the top, head trimmed and cleaned)
8 if large green lip or 12 if smaller	Mussels (cleaned)
4–5	Baby squid (cut into rings, tentacles to be left intact)
200 g	Monkfish tail fillet (cut into thin strips along the grain)
½ tsp	Tumeric powder
½ tsp	Chilli powder
1 tsp	Lemon juice
2 tbsp	Sunflower oil
1 tsp	Cumin seeds
2.5 cm	Ginger (finely shredded)
5–6 cloves	Fresh garlic finely chopped
½ medium–large	Green pepper finely shredded
For colour	Red pepper, finely shredded
For colour	Yellow pepper, finely shredded
4–5 slender	Spring onions shredded with greens
1–2 large	Green chillies (seeded and shredded)
2 medium	Tomato (pulped and shredded with skin)
1½ tbsp	Fresh coriander (chopped)
To taste	Salt

4. Take a wok and make it really hot. Keeping the heat on high add the oil and as it begins to smoke add the cumin and almost immediately add the ginger and garlic. Stir for 1–2 minutes or until the garlic gets a golden colour. Do not allow the garlic to brown.

5. Add the seafood and keeping the heat on high just give it a swirl or two then allow it to sizzle. Do not agitate the pan too much or else the seafood will release all its juices, but toss from time to time allowing all the seafood to touch the bottom of the pan.

6. Now add the shredded peppers, spring onions, green chilli, and tomatoes and continue to sauté for 1–2 minutes.

7. The seafood should be almost done by now. Add the fresh coriander and check seasoning.

8. Remove and serve with egg fried rice or any other rice of your choice.

Seafood Ullathiyadh

Seafood with Fresh Grated Coconut and Vegetables

Chef's Notes

- If monkfish is not available use another firm fish that does not easily disintegrate or add more shellfish.

Method

1. Place all the seafood in a bowl and marinate with the turmeric powder, chilli powder, some salt and lemon juice and set aside for no more than 2 hours otherwise you may lose too much moisture.

2. Remember that you are cooking delicate seafood and the cooking process needs to be very fast, therefore the pan has to get really hot and be able to sustain the heat. If the seafood is too much for the size of your pan cook it in two batches as it only takes 4–5 minutes at the most. Or cook the seafood separately and then blend the two. This is provided that your pre-preparation is very good.

Measurements	Ingredients
8	King scallops (slit into two horizontally)
8	Tiger prawns (shell on, slit over the top, head trimmed and cleaned)
8 if large green lip or 12 if smaller	Mussels (cleaned)
4–5	Baby squid (cut into rings, tentacles to be left intact)
200 g	Monkfish tail fillet (cut into thin strips along the grain)
½ tsp	Turmeric powder
½ tsp	Chilli powder

3. If you are using dessicated coconut, select the fine thread type and soak it in half a cup water for 30 minutes before cooking commences.

Continued

4. Place all the ingredients within easy reach so that you do not have to leave the cooking area.

5. Take a wok and make it really hot. Keeping the heat on high add the oil and as it begins to smoke add the mustard seeds. When the crackling ends add the curry leaves.

6. Add the cumin and almost immediately add the ginger and garlic. Stir for 1–2 minutes or just until the garlic gets a golden colour. Do not allow the garlic to brown.

7. At this stage turn the heat down a bit and add the coconut. Sauté for 1–2 minutes until the aroma gets a bit nutty. Do not allow to brown but just to get a pale golden colour.

8. Now turn the heat on maximum and wait a few seconds for the pan to get hot again but keep stirring to prevent the coconut burning.

9. Toss in the vegetables and sauté for a minute or so.

10. Add the seafood and keeping the heat on high just give it a swirl or two and allow it to sizzle. Do not agitate the pan too much or else the seafood will release all its juices, but toss from time to time allowing all the seafood to touch the bottom of the pan.

11. Now add some shredded peppers (optional), the spring onions and green chilli and continue to sauté for 1–2 minutes.

12. The seafood should be almost done by now. Add the fresh coriander and check seasoning. Remove and serve with lemon rice or any other rice of your choice.

Measurements	Ingredients
1 tsp	Lemon juice
2 tbsp	Sunflower oil
½ tsp	Mustard seeds
8–10	Curry leaves (fresh. You can use dried or frozen but accept not such a good flavour)
1 tsp	Cumin seeds
2.5 cm	Ginger (finely shredded)
5–6 cloves	Fresh garlic (chopped)
3 tbsp fresh 2 tbsp	Grated coconut or Desiccated coconut
2 medium	Tomato (pulped and shredded)
8–10	Mangetout (cut into half lengthways)
1 medium cut into 2.5 cm batons or 8–10 Baby carrots halved lengthways	Carrot (blanched before adding)
6–8	French or baby corn (slit lengthways for corn and cut in half for beans. If you like more colour and flavour use both.)
4–5 slender	Spring onions (shredded with greens)
1–2 large	Green chillies (seeded and shredded)
1½ tbsp	Fresh coriander (chopped)
To taste	Salt

Shinanio Ani Tisreo A'la Bardez

Chef's Notes

- In Goa during the mango season, the half-cleaned mussel and clam shells are dumped under a ready to pick mango tree. This attracts all the large red bully ants to the bottom of the tree while the pickers scramble up and do their felling unhampered.

Method

1. Clean and wash the mussels and clams and drain.

2. Toss in a bowl with the lime juice, some salt and the turmeric powder.

3. Put 1 tbsp oil in a casserole and heat until hazy.

4. Add the curry leaves, red chilli and cumin.

5. Add the garlic and sauté for 1 minute then add the onions.

6. Sauté until the onions turn soft and pale, then add the coconut.

7. Stir and cook for approximately 5 minutes until you can smell the nuttiness of the coconut.

8. In a separate large frying pan add the remaining oil and heat it to a high temperature on a high flame.

9. When the oil smokes add the mussels and clams but without the juices. The juices should now be put into the coconut and onion mix.

10. Sauté briskly for 3–4 minutes, stirring or tossing occasionally so that all the shellfish come in contact with the heat. Do not overcook.

Measurements	Ingredients
16 large	Mussels (on or off the half shell)
32 large	Clams (on the half shell if possible)
½	Lime (juice only)
½ tsp	Turmeric powder
2 tbsp	Oil
12–15	Curry leaves
2 medium	Dry red chilli (broken into small pieces)
½ tsp	Cumin seeds
6 medium cloves	Garlic (minced)
2 medium	Onions (finely chopped)
½ 250 g	Grated coconut or Frozen grated coconut (defrost before cooking)
2 tbsp	Fresh coriander (chopped)
To taste	Salt

11. Add the sautéed fish to the casserole and return to the heat.

12. Mix well, add the coriander and check salt. Heat only until the mussels are delicately cooked then remove from the heat and serve.

13. This is best eaten with your fingers and is a bit messy if you do not know how to do this.

14. You may like to have some plain rice and plain curry along with the cleaned clams and mussels or just the coconut mix. Either way this is an experience.

Stuffed Squids

Chef's Notes

- This dish is very commonly found in Goa though recipes differ. We have here a recipe that you will be able to make quite easily and enjoy.

- Always select the smaller squid whose tubes are slender and thin walled.

Method

1. Cut off the eyes from the tentacles. Chop the tentacles.

2. In a frying pan take the drained balchao oil and heat it on a high flame. You only need about 1 tbsp or less so it will be easy when you drain your balchao masala.

3. Once hot add the tentacles and prawns and sauté until dry and once again the oil emerges.

4. Drain off the oil and discard. To do this squeeze the mix against the sides of the pan until you have squeezed out all the oil.

5. Blend the sautéed mix into the balchao masala. Add the eggs and the coriander. Check the seasoning and set aside.

6. Portion out the stuffing into 16 equal parts.

7. Spoon the mixture into each squid tube, pinch where the stuffing ends and run a cocktail stick through in a zig-zag fashion. This is done to look like it has been stitched or skewered and sealed.

Measurements	Ingredients
16	Baby squid (cleaned and washed with tentacles retained)
1 tbsp	Balchao oil (kept from drained masala)
150–200 g	Raw prawns (small, chopped)
4 tbsp	Balchao masala drained (see page 112)
3	Eggs (boiled, whites chopped, yolks mashed)
1 tbsp	Fresh coriander
16	Toothpicks (rounded sharp type)
2 tbsp	Oil
To taste	Salt
Your choice as an accompaniment	Salad

8. Snap off approximately 1 cm at each end or allow the toothpick to jut out only 1 cm at each end of the squid opening.

9. Heat the oil in a fry pan to high and sauté the squids for about 2 minutes on each side. If small the squid will cook very fast. Do not overcook as they will get rubbery.

10. Serve with a salad and perhaps some baked jacket potato. Wow!

Tarleachi Kodi

Sardine Curry

Chef's Notes

- Sardines are commonly found all over the coastal regions of India, however few love them as much as the Goans. I still remember working in Goa and being able to buy sometimes 50 or 100 sardines for a rupee. A rupee is $\frac{1}{80}$ of a pound Sterling. This was, of course, dependent on the season and the landings. Naturally export demands and over fishing can never bring such memories back to reality.

- The sardine is an oily fish and needs to be handled well. It fries extremely well but here we have a curry. The curry needs to work alongside the sardine and not clash with it.

- Murrells/Bhangday/Bhangda or small mackerel are also ideal for this curry.

- In Goa one would also commonly add Sichuan peppers to curries made with oily fish such as sardines and mackeral. Sichuan peppers are known as 'Te flan' or 'Tirphul' meaning 'three fruits'. The tangy yet spicy aroma is ideally suited to these fish. The same recipe can be used for mackeral, grey mullet, shark or tuna.

Method

1. In a large frying pan or wok add 2 tbsp oil and heat over a medium flame.

2. Increase the heat to a haze and quickly sizzle the mustard seeds. As soon as they have crackled, reduce heat to medium and add the sliced onion.

3. Sauté until they become a pale brown, stirring regularly to get an even colour.

4. As soon as the onion is ready add the coconut, chillies, peppercorns, chick pea flour and rice and sauté for a few minutes until the coconut changes to a lightish brown colour and develops a nice nutty aroma. Add the chickpea flour and sauté for another minute or two.

5. Remove onto a tray or a flat dish so that it cools rapidly.

6. Purée to a fine paste in a blender or grinder adding only as much water as is necessary to make a thick paste.

7. In a casserole add the remaining oil and heat.

8. Add the remaining onions and curry leaves and sauté until onions are well browned.

9. Add the puréed masala and the turmeric powder and sauté for a few minutes.

10. Add the tamarind pulp and as soon as the combination begins to splutter and boil, add the hot or boiling water and bring to the boil.

11. Reduce the temperature and simmer until the tamarind loses its smell and the masala gets cooked.

12. Add salt and taste.

13. Now add the sardines and ensure that the liquid completely covers them.

14. Cover and simmer for a few minutes depending on the size of the sardines or mackerels. Approximately 5–6 minutes is normally enough.

15. Switch off, cover and set aside for a few minutes before serving.

16. Serve this with its natural accompaniment – steamed or boiled rice.

Measurements	Ingredients
3–4 tbsp	Sunflower oil
½ tbsp	Black mustard seeds
2	Onions (one sliced thinly for masala, the other chopped)
½ coconut	Fresh grated coconut or
6–7 tbsp *or*	Frozen coconut
6–7 tbsp	Desicated coconut
4–5	Dry red large Kashmiri-type chillies or regular chillies (snipped)
6–8	Black peppercorns (crushed coarsely)
2–3 tbsp	Uncooked rice
1 tbsp	Chickpea flour
8–10	Curry leaves (optional)
1 tsp	Turmeric powder
4–5 tbsp	Tamarind pulp
200–250 ml	Hot water
12–16 or more if small	Sardines (cleaned, gutted, scaled and trimmed)
As desired	Salt

Vegetarian

VEGETABLES, VEGETARIAN COOKING, AND THE VEGETARIAN

It is true enough to say that there is no other nation in the world that can produce so many vegetarian dishes and no other cuisine that has such a significant vegetarian influence in its culture.

India is primarily a land of vegetarians. Up until the introduction of meat in the cuisine by the Mughuls, vegetarianism was the norm except in certain areas.

India even today may have between 400 million and 500 million pure vegetarians. What or who is a vegetarian in the eyes of the Indian?

In the modern world vegetarianism has become a fashionable word and is used by many so-called vegetarians, so it is extremely confusing for an Indian to understand other forms of vegetarianism.

For instance, if you are a vegetarian Indian, you would not eat egg, as they are not considered to be vegetarian at all, since chicken is born out of an egg. All milk products are considered vegetarian and there is no classical vegan except on religious days when certain sects may not eat certain things.

Fish is a meat in one form or another and all seafood is non-vegetarian.

The Jains will not eat roots and tubers at all and their diet is void of basics such as onions, potatoes, carrots, ginger, garlic, etc.

On certain religious days the Jains will not eat anything sour or acidic such as tomatoes, lime, vinegar or yoghurt.

Even canines reared in vegetarian homes are vegetarian and live well and healthily.

The vegetarian or orthodox vegetarian in India is very particular about his heritage and where and how he eats. This needs to be respected and restaurants and hotels have over the years developed their own policies on this issue. For instance, a vegetarian from India, unless well travelled, will not dine next to a non-vegetarian if he is eating any form of meat, fish or poultry.

In most professional kitchens there are always separate pots, pans and other utensils for cooking vegetarian food as well as two tandoors, one of which is reserved for bread making and vegetarian products only.

If a buffet is laid out the vegetarian section must be completely separate from that where non-vegetarian food is displayed.

It may seem strange for someone from a Western background to understand the reason but it is not uncommon to see a vegetarian be ill

at the mere sight of meat. The smell, the look and the blood can set some vegetarians off into spasms.

We non-vegetarians will find that strange but think about it for a moment and you will not find it so difficult to accept. It is like seeing blood for the first time and then suddenly getting dizzy.

Vegetarian cooking is so diverse and has so much scope that one can only begin to imagine feeling exhausted at realising the potential. Try to think about cooking the hundreds of thousands of vegetables, grains, pulses, roots, tubers, plants, leaves, fruits and so on and, you will realise that there are hundreds of items within each category. Now that is variety at just the thought. That is also the sub-continent of India in a nutshell.

Most of us cannot even imagine the different varieties that exist and are cooked on a day-to-day basis.

I consider myself perhaps a few paces ahead of some of my readers regarding knowledge and skills in cooking and it would take someone like me 600–700 years to try to understand Indian cuisine. The depth, the intricacies, the regional nuances, the religious significance, the seasons, the what, why and how? The list simply goes on and I am afraid most of us will not have scratched the surface of the cuisines and diversities of our beautiful and complicated land.

We owe so much to those wonderful women, our mothers and wives, aunts and grannies, friends whom we meet and must learn from. One of my greatest fears is that the cooking of our forefathers will be lost to us forever in the modern changing world where more and more young women are forced to go to work due to family responsibilities and for whom cooking is now a chore.

Certain family traditions, recipes and styles are already lost in the mad rush for success in today's life, which is dominated by the strength of your pockets. While I agree that life has to evolve and change and we live in an ever-changing world, traditions are what keep us together and food is what binds us all together.

I am always hopeful, therefore, that I may enthuse a few people to continue to aspire to become great cooks, be they in their own domestic kingdoms or be they those who will go forth and conquer the world with their skills and talents.

Today in the UK vegetables, fruits, herbs and spices come from all corners of the globe. Young aspiring cooks, housewives (if they still exist), and those who cook for the sheer pleasure of cooking must endeavour to be resourceful and creative. Be bold, try out new things, experiment with flavours and then try to match the cooking style you will adopt for a particular product. This is not only essential, it will bring great pleasure in your life and a continuous feeling of achievement.

The vegetarian in India normally depends on the season for produce and preparation in the house. Even though certain vegetables are now grown

twice or three times a year due largely to modern farming techniques, the well-trained lady of the house will adhere to her seasonality.

It is the hotels and restaurants that need the same things throughout the year and create the huge demands, but for the house and home it is often more fun to cook with foods in season. The family looks forward to the season's favourites and in a sense the non-availability out of season creates a yearning for popular foods as soon as the season for a particular product is in.

Again chutneys, pickles and other preserves such as murabbas (marmalades) are put together for the family to enjoy over a period of time.

I still remember my mother making her mango chutney on our kerosene stove for hours on end until she had the perfect texture and taste. As this book goes to print I still have a jar of her last hand-made chutney, which is now five years old and still as good as new. The mangoes she used were from the tree I had planted as a young boy of perhaps 13 or 14 with my dad. At times I yearn for that time or for our home in Mumbai that I have umpteen memories of, but there is nothing to say that we cannot have as much fun and be just as creative here in the UK or anywhere else in the diaspora. However, we cannot get the same quality of mangoes and the same pricing.

Most rural homes, like anywhere else in the world, grow their own few vegetables and get their seasonal supplies and, if they are lucky to have a larger patch or garden, then even more so. In Madhya Pradesh where I spent a few years of my childhood, my maternal grandfather's house had a huge and very well-tended garden. In there were several fruit trees and the gardener always planted a lot of vegetables in season.

This always meant eating a lot of greens and vegetables in season, much to a young boy's disgust, but you had to eat what was on the table and even though you loved to see the vegetables grow, the thought of eating them was never welcome. Today things are different, of course. If we could have a full-time Gujerati Maharaj (cook) or a Keralan cook I would gladly turn vegetarian. Such is the variety, taste, flavour and enjoyment one can derive from high-class creative vegetarian cooking.

That is just one reason why we have selected to have such a large chapter dedicated to vegetarian cooking. The scope is huge, creativity boundless and the flavours unimaginable until tried and tested. Not to forget the main and most important part of it all … the health factor.

VEGETABLES AND HEALTH

Good vegetarian cooking can be extremely healthy and nutritious and if you balance your meal well it will provide all the nutrients you need.

That leads us on to the benefits of a balanced vegetarian diet. Vegetarians know full well that to live healthily you have to eat healthily, and since Vedic times they have learnt how to get the most out of what they eat to have a well-balanced and nutritious diet.

Today you can resort to learning about the nutritional composition of a carrot or beet or any vegetable by referring to a book but in the olden days they learnt by experience and this was handed down from mother to daughter.

Vegetables, grains and pulses can be just as harmful as eating anything else if the food or meal is not balanced, is greasy or poorly cooked. One has to learn by trial and error how each vegetable behaves and how each particular food you eat reacts to your body or vice versa.

In ending all I have to say is simply this, which was said by the great geographer and historian, Dudley Stamp: 'If you have imagination, the whole world lies at your feet.'

Aloo Ki Subzee

Chef's Notes

- This particular recipe is part of a wider national recipe. Potato is a favourite with Indians and the method of cooking can vary from town to town, place to place and definitely region to region.

- This is a simple easy-to-follow method.

Method

1. Peel, wash and cut the potatoes into cubes.
2. Put approx 1mm of oil in a pan big enough to take the potatoes plus all the other ingredients.

Measurements	Ingredients
750 g	Potatoes (any will do, however select older ones for this)
400 g	Onions (finely sliced)
½ tsp	Turmeric
½ tsp	Chilli powder
1 tsp	Coriander powder
½ tsp	Cumin powder
250 g	Tomatoes (chopped)
3 tbsp	Fresh coriander (chopped)
To taste	Salt
Tempering or sizzling spices	**Ingredients**
100–150 g (enough to cover the bottom of your pan by approximately one millimetre)	Oil
½ tsp	Mustard seeds
1 tsp	Cumin seeds
8–10	Curry leaves (if available)
¼ tsp	Asafoetida (if available)
2	Green chillies (slit and cut into two or three)

3. Heat and when you see a haze form on the top add the tempering spices. The mustard seeds will crackle and so will the curry leaves.

4. Do not increase the temperature but allow the crackling to cease before adding the sliced onions.

5. Sauté the onions for a while and then add the potatoes. Continue to sauté until the potatoes are evenly coated.

6. Add the remaining spices then salt enough water to half cover the potatoes. Cover the pan with a tight lid and simmer on a slow flame.

7. Stir from time to time to rotate the potatoes in order to avoid uneven cooking.

8. When three-quarters cooked add the tomatoes and simmer uncovered until cooked and the gravy thickens. Check the seasoning and remove.

9. Just before serving mix in fresh chopped coriander and enjoy.

Aloo Paneer Khorma

Potato and Indian Whey Cheese with Coconut

Method

1. Wash and dice the potatoes then boil in just enough water to cover them, until just done. Drain and reserve the fluid.

2. Peel, halve, core and slice one onion thinly. Cut the other into cubes.

3. Grind together the ginger, chillies, coriander leaves, fennel seeds and half the onion in a blender.

4. Roast and powder the cardamom, cloves and cinnamon.

5. Grate the coconut if using fresh and extract the milk. If using desiccated coconut, soak in a cup of warm water for 30 minutes then purée in a blender, or add the liquid from the boiled potato and purée.

6. Heat the oil, fry the paneer slowly on all sides and remove.

7. In the same oil sauté the potatoes until light brown and remove.

8. Sauté the sliced onion once the potato has been removed.

9. When soft add the powdered spices and the ground spices.

Measurements	Ingredients
450 g	Potatoes
2 medium sized	Onions
2.5 cm	Ginger
2 medium	Green chillies
3 tablespoons when chopped	Coriander leaves (chopped)
1 tsp	Fennel seeds
10 g collectively	Cardamom, cloves and cinnamon
200 g	Fresh coconut (grated)
4 tbsp	Sunflower oil
125 g	Indian whey cheese (paneer)
½	Lime
As desired	Salt

10. Sauté for a few minutes, stirring well until you see the oil being released at the edges, which indicates that the masala is cooked.

11. Add the fried paneer to the potatoes.

12. Add the coconut milk and bring to the boil on a medium heat.

13. Add lime juice and salt to suit your taste and serve.

14. Serve with a vegetable pulao or a simple cumin pulao.

Avial

Mixed Vegetables with Yoghurt and Coconut

Chef's Notes

- A light vegetable curry typical of Kerala.

- Drumsticks are long beans, thick and stringy. They impart a superb flavour and only the little pulp inside is edible. The rest is too hard to eat.

Method

1. Put all the vegetables in a casserole, add the turmeric, salt and red chillies and enough water to just cover the vegetables. Cook until half done.

2. Grind (liquidise in a blender) together the green chillies, coconut and cumin seeds.

3. When the cumin is well ground add the yoghurt and after a few whirls blend into the half-cooked vegetables.

4. Stir continuously for 2 minutes or so then bring back to the boil slowly.

5. Heat the coconut oil in a frying pan and when hazy add the mustard seeds and curry leaves.

6. When the mustard seeds stop cracking add this to the casserole then stir, check seasoning and remove.

7. Served best with plain steamed rice or hoppers (steamed pancakes made from fermented rice and coconut butter).

Measurements	Ingredients
1 medium	Potato (cut into cubes)
1 small	Aubergine (cut into cubes)
6–8	Okra cut into 2.5 cm pieces
1 small	Unripe banana (cut into cubes. These are available in Indian stores, and can be purchased singly)
1	Drumstick stringed and cut into 5 cm pieces
1 medium	Onion (sliced)
1 small or 15–22.5 cm piece	Snake gourd (peeled, seeded and cut into pieces)
½ tsp	Turmeric powder
3–4	Red chillies
2–3 large	Green chillies
300 g	Grated coconut (fresh or frozen) or
250 g	Dessicated coconut
½ tsp	Cumin seeds
200 g	Thick yoghurt
2 tbsp	Coconut oil (sunflower oil can also be used)
½ tsp	Black mustard seeds
15	Curry leaves
To taste	Salt

Baby Corn and Broccoli Usli

Chef's Notes

- The 'Usli' is once again an example of the greatness of south Indian vegetarian cooking. If somebody were to cook for me recipes from the Gujerati and the south Indian styles of vegetarian food daily, I would very happily give up being the carnivore I am. The term 'Usli' also exists in Goan vegetarian cooking, though it is not similar. A Goan usli can also be a salad. There is no hard and fast rule about the vegetables you can use and the recommendation is that you should use the rest of the recipe and change the vegetables. Squashes, marrows, carrot, gourds and cauliflower are just some examples. If you like eating onions then try this with small onions. It is fab.

Method

1. Soak the split yellow peas (channa daal) for at least an hour to soften it.

2. Drain the split yellow peas and grind coarsely. Your grinder attachment will do that quite easily. You may wish to discard the water but remember that it has nutrients and makes for excellent soup if you use a bit of imagination. What follows next will help.

3. Either take fresh water with a touch of salt and some lime juice and give the vegetables a quick blanch or boil so that they half cook but remain crisp and crunchy, or strain and use the soaking water. This way you will get a very rich stock after the vegetables are done, full of nutrition and ready for a light soup.

4. Once the split peas are ground spread them out on a tray and steam for 10–12 minutes. If a steamer is not available and you have a microwave and a plastic strainer then place the split peas in the strainer over a bowl with a little boiling water and microwave so that the steam rising will steam it. Full power for 5 minutes should do it.

Measurements	Ingredients
300 g	Split yellow peas
1 tsp	Lime juice
250 g	Baby corn
250 g	Broccoli
Sizzling	**Ingredients**
100 ml	Sunflower oil
1 tsp	Black mustard seeds
5–6 large	Dry red chillies (broken into pieces)
6–8	Curry leaves
1 tsp	Cumin seeds
1 medium	Green chilli (finely minced)
1 small	Onion (finely chopped)

5. Otherwise do it in a pressure cooker for a few minutes with the pressure valve open.

6. Once steamed remove and cool to room temperature. Now powder them between the palms of your hands, rubbing well.

7. If you have a wok or a kadhai now place it on the stove and pour the oil into it. If you don't have one of the above just use a saucepan.

8. Once the oil is hot add the mustard seeds until they stop crackling and give off a nutty aroma. Then add the red chillies, curry leaves, cumin and allow a few seconds before adding the rest of the ingredients.

9. Add the powdered split peas and sauté for 1 minute and then add the vegetables. Check the seasoning and serve.

Bhareli Bhindi

Stuffed Okras (Ladies Fingers)

Chef's Notes

*   This item may vary from place to place but this is a standard recipe and one which I feel works very well indeed.

Measurements	Ingredients
20–30	Okra (long slender ones)
¼ tsp	Turmeric powder
½ ½	Grated coconut *or* Frozen coconut (available from Chinese and Thai or Filipino stores)
2 large	Fresh green chillies (finely chopped)
1–2 tbsp	Fresh coriander (chopped)
½ tsp	Coriander seeds (finely crushed but not powdered)
½ tsp	Cumin seeds (finely crushed but not powdered)
2 tsp	Chaat masala (available in Indian and Bangladeshi stores)
3–4 tbsp	Oil
To taste	Salt

Method

1. Wash and wipe the okra first. If you do not wipe them they will get gooey when worked on.

2. Slit them lengthways and apply salt and turmeric powder inside.

3. Blend all the other ingredients together and season lightly.

4. Stuff the okra until they are well swollen but do not let them tear.

5. Sauté them in a heavy-bottomed pan with as little oil as you can permit each time. The oil must coat the bottom of the pan.

6. Sauté them until golden brown and serve sprinkled with any remaining stuffing or make some for the garnish.

7. Served with thick yoghurt it makes a lovely accompaniment or starter.

Cabbage and Beans Jeera

Method

1. Heat the oil in a flat pan large enough to hold the contents.

2. When the oil is hot add the chilli and cumin seeds.

3. When the cumin browns add the onions and sauté for a few minutes then add the turmeric.

4. Raise the heat to maximum and add the cabbage and the beans.

5. Sauté and toss well but do not allow the pan to cool down too fast. This should not be for more than 3–4 minutes, stirring and turning the contents over and over until the cabbage begins to turn a bit opaque.

6. The beans should not wilt and nor should the cabbage.

7. Add the tomatoes, the seasoning and the fresh coriander, taste and remove.

Measurements	Ingredients
100 ml	Sunflower oil
25 g	Green chilli (Slit and seeded)
30 g	Cumin seeds
500 g	Onion (sliced)
5 g	Turmeric
2 kg	Cabbage (shredded)
1 kg	Fine French beans
250 g	Tomatoes (diced and seeded)
To taste	Lime juice
50 g	Fresh coriander
	Salt

Cabbage and Beans Foogath

Chef's Notes

- A simple quick and easy preparation cooked with grated coconut. The quantities given here are sufficient for a side dish to serve four to six people.

Method

1. Shred the cabbage after removing the central stub and prepare the beans as required. Do not mix the two.

2. Heat the oil in a casserole and when hazy add the mustard seeds.

3. After they stop crackling, reduce the heat to medium, add the curry leaves, cumin and red chilli pieces.

4. Sauté for 1 minute then add the onions.

5. When the onions turn soft add the garlic and sauté for 1–2 minutes then add the turmeric and then the cabbage.

6. Sauté the cabbage for 1–2 minutes then add the coconut.

7. Sauté this for 4–5 minutes. By this time the cabbage will be more than half done.

Measurements	Ingredients
250–300 g	Cabbage
250 g	French beans (cut into 2.5 cm pieces)
2 tbsp	Sunflower oil
¼ tsp	Mustard seeds
10	Curry leaves
½ tsp	Cumin seeds
2	Whole red chilli (cut into 12 mm pieces)
2 medium	Onions (thinly sliced)
6–8 cloves	Garlic (chopped)
¼ tsp	Turmeric powder
⅓ fresh 250 g 150g	Grated coconut *or* Frozen coconut *or* Desiccated coconut (coarse)
A few drops to taste	Lime juice
1 tbsp	Fresh coriander (chopped)
To taste	Salt

8. Mix in the French beans and check the seasoning. Cook only for a further 2 minutes or so.

9. Sprinkle the lime juice over and add the coriander. Cover the pan, take off the heat and leave covered for 4–5 minutes.

10. Serve with hot crusty rolls if not eating as part of a meal.

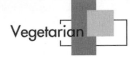

Choley Pindi

Chef's Notes

- A traditional Punjabi chickpea preparation that may vary from place to place and house to house but the method is more or less standard.

- In the Punjab and Pakistan it is essential that this be served on most festive occasions and ceremonies.

Method

1. Heat the oil in a thick-bottomed pan and add the cumin and sauté for 1 minute but do not allow to blacken.

2. Add the onions, then the garlic, ginger and green chillies.

3. Lastly add the tomatoes and the yoghurt.

4. Add the chickpeas. (If using dried, boil them first until soft.)

5. Cook, stirring regularly for a few minutes until the mixture is thoroughly heated.

6. Add the channa or chaat masala if you have it. If not squeeze a few drops of lemon juice and then blend in the coriander.

7. Season and enjoy with hot flour tortillas if you cannot make chappaties or poories.

Measurements	Ingredients
2–3 tbsp (Sunflower or other vegetable oil)	Sunflower oil
2 tsp	Cumin seeds (crushed in a mortar)
1 medium	Onion (finely chopped)
5–6 cloves	Garlic (finely chopped)
2.5 cm	Ginger (peeled and chopped)
2–3	Green chillies (slit lengthwise)
2 medium	Tomato (chopped with the juices)
4 tbsp	Greek style yoghurt
200 g 1 can	White chickpeas or Pre-cooked chickpeas (drained)
1 tsp	Chaat masala powder or Channa masala powder
2 tbsp	Fresh coriander (chopped)
To taste	Salt

Chotta Aloo Rassa

Baby Potatoes in a Tangy Tomato Gravy

Method

1. Peel and parboil the potatoes in only as much water as will cover them.

2. When more than half cooked remove the potatoes and reduce the liquid until it gets to a soup consistency.

3. Heat the oil in a saucepan until it forms a haze then add the mustard seeds and when they crackle add the curry leaves, the cumin and lovage seeds.

4. After a few seconds add the chillies, garlic and ginger.

5. As the garlic begins to colour add the onions and sauté until soft. Add the tomato juice, the potato liquor and the chopped tomato.

6. When slightly thick add the potatoes, check seasoning and simmer until cooked.

7. Sprinkle the coriander and mint over then remove from the heat but keep the pot covered for some time unless it is being consumed immediately.

Measurements	Ingredients
200 g	Baby potatoes
2 tbsp	Sunflower oil
½ tsp	Mustard seeds
6–8	Curry leaves (fresh)
1 level tsp	Cumin seeds
1 level tsp	Carom or lovage seeds
2 medium	Green chillies (seeded and slit)
6 cloves	Garlic (chopped)
20 g	Fresh ginger (chopped)
1 medium	Onions (chopped)
250 ml	Tomato juice
1–2 medium	Tomato (chopped)
2 tsp	Mint (chopped)
1 tbsp	Fresh coriander (chopped)

Dahi Ni Kadhi

Yoghurt Curry

Chef's Notes

- This is a basic simple kadhi and below are mentioned some of the variations of items you can add to it to make a wonderful meal. Kadhis are a plenty but this is as I remember my mother making it. In the industry too we apply different methods and each region of India differs from the other.

Method

1. Beat the yoghurt in a bowl with a whisk and set it aside.

2. Heat the oil in a casserole until it forms a haze then add the mustard seeds.

3. When they stop crackling add the curry leaves and cumin. Stir for a minute without allowing the cumin to burn and add the asafoetida.

4. Pull away from the heat and slowly mix in the chickpea flour, stirring all the time to avoid any lumps.

5. When well mixed return to a slow flame and with the help of a wooden spoon cook the flour until it releases the oil and becomes soft. In the beginning the flour will absorb all the oil and become firm and hard, but with slow cooking it will slowly get cooked and then release the oil.

6. At this stage add the turmeric and green chillies and cook for 1–2 minutes.

Measurements	Ingredients
500 g	Thick yoghurt
2 tbsp	Sunflower oil
½ tsp	Mustard seeds
10–15	Curry leaves
1 tsp	Cumin seeds
¼ tsp	Asafoetida
3 tbsp	Chickpea flour (sieved)
½ tsp	Turmeric powder
2–3	Green chillies (slit lengthways and seeded)
250 ml	Water
To taste	Salt
1 level tbsp	Sugar
1 tbsp	Fresh coriander (chopped)

7. Remove from the heat and allow to cool for a few minutes then add the whisked yoghurt and mix until you see a smooth paste without any lumps.

8. If you add the yoghurt over the fire it is very likely to form several lumps and so spoil the kadhi.

9. Add the water and return to the flame.

10. Increase the flame to medium and bring to the boil.

11. Add the salt and sugar and taste. It should be a bit sour but also a bit sweet and savoury.

12. Boil for a few minutes until thickened to the consistency of a cream soup.

13. Add the coriander and remove.

Variations

- The following are some examples of the myriad items that can be added to a kadhi to give it more complexity. However, a kadhi is perfect without anything. Just enjoy it with plain rice or 'khichdi' (lentil pulao). Or drink it hot with your food.

- Deep-fried thin slices of okra. Fry, drain well and blend in the kadhi before serving. You can also add raw cut okra when boiling the kadhi, but this kadhi will not keep long. Also, for those who fear that the okra may turn gooey, the fried method is best.

- Small onion or plain bhajia.

- Small firm chickpeas fried dumplings or pakodis mixed with chopped cauliflower or broccoli will make an excellent addition. To make these follow the recipe for bhajia but add chopped cauliflower instead. Make a firm batter and fry small balls of the mixture. Remove and boil in the kadhi.

- Fried aubergine pieces can be added.

- Raw banana pieces or thick slices, and pan-fried thick slices of plantain are fantastic.

- Several other items can be added, just use your imagination but do not go overboard. Nothing that you add should get mashed or it will spoil the kadhi.

Dhan Daar Nay Vaghaar

Chef's Notes

- As I mentioned before, this is perhaps my most loved food when eaten with a masala fried fish. It is Parsee in origin, simple to make, nutritious, wholesome and, above all else, delicious.

- My mother makes it better than I do and now my wife makes an excellent product much loved by all of us, though our little son tells me that his 'Bapaiji' (paternal grandmother) still makes the best. You can guess which meal I mentioned when asked by a journalist what I would eat if I were to die the next day.

- This dish also goes well with 'Masala Ma Traeli Machchi' or 'Sukku Bhujelu Gos' or is good on its own. This is actually three recipes in one and each can be used individually. The vaghaar is used for other types of lentils, chickpeas, etc. A sweet hot chutney makes the ideal accompaniment.

Measurements	Ingredients
100 g per person	Basmati rice
2	Bay leaves
2 pods	Green cardamom (cracked at the tip)
200 g	Toover daal (also known as 'Toor' daal, or yellow lentil)
1 level tsp	Turmeric
2 tbsp	Butter
As desired	Salt
1 tsp	Cumin seeds
6–8 cloves	Garlic (coarsely chopped)
1	Green chilli (slit into four)(optional)
5–6 tbsp	Sunflower oil
2 medium	Onions (finely and evenly sliced)
As desired	Salt

Method

1. Take enough water to boil the rice. When boiling add the bay leaves, cardamom and salt.

2. Add the washed rice, stir, boil for 8–10 minutes until rice is cooked but firm, drain and set aside in a covered dish.

The Daar

1. Wash the daal thoroughly and soak in a casserole with water up to 2.5 cm over the level of the lentils. The soaking should be for 2–3 hours or even overnight in cold water. In summer change the water at least once if soaking overnight. Somehow soaking in hot water toughens the lentil and it will take longer to cook.

2. Add the turmeric and bring to the boil.

3. When boiling starts lower the flame and simmer. Remove any scum from the top then add salt and continue cooking until the daal is thoroughly cooked.

4. Add half the butter and then purée the lentils thoroughly into a smooth paste. Keep the consistency to that of a thick pouring sauce.

Vaghaar

1. Take the remaining butter and 1 tbsp oil and heat slowly. Do not let the butter burn or the heat to get too high.

2. Add the whole cumin and 30 seconds later the garlic and continue stirring and cooking gently until the garlic is nice and golden brown in colour.

3. Add the entire mixture to the puréed daal.

4. If you wish to add green chilli, add it after the garlic is a medium gold colour and then cook until garlic is golden brown.

The brown onions

1. The onions will be fried in the remaining oil. Again you have to be careful not to overheat the oil but it will need to be hotter than it was for the garlic.

2. Stir the onions gently but regularly and not continuously until they begin to get light brown. At the stage when they begin to get brown you will notice that oil is oozing out again and the onions are actually frying.

3. This is now a very crucial stage. A slight neglect and the onions will turn black. Stir continuously, breaking up the lumps that the onions are likely to form but keeping all the onions below the oil.

4. You should have a strainer ready placed over a bowl and a fork kept handy. Ensure that the bowl is not plastic.

5. As soon as you see the onions getting a darker shade of brown drain them into the strainer and loosen them with the fork, separating all the strands. If you do not do this, the onions will continue cooking in the strainer and turn black.

6. Later turn them over onto a paper towel to remove any excess oil.

7. Your dish is now ready. Before serving heat the rice either in a microwave or in a steamer. You can even heat it over a double boiler. Heat the Daar very gently over a gentle heat stirring regularly and scraping the bottom as you go along. A wooden spoon or spatula is best.

• Mix chopped coriander into the Daar and sprinkle the fried onions over the top as garnish when serving.

• This can be served with a few fried papads (pappadum).

Enoki or Straw Mushrooms with Ginger, Garlic and Chilli

Chef's Notes

• Straw mushrooms make an ideal dish if well prepared and swiftly done. This is a simple recipe that needs nothing but only dexterity and time.

• Served with crisply fried okra and brown onion it makes a tempting side dish.

Method

1. Take a kadhai or wok and add the oil. Heat until just hot and add the onions. Keep a strainer placed over a stainless steel or a heat resistant glass bowl ready for draining.

2. Stirring almost continuously or very regularly, fry them until light golden brown. As soon as the onions are pale golden evenly pour into the strainer. Do not try to remove a little at a time with a slotted spoon as you will not then get an even colour.

Measurements	Ingredients
250 g	Oil
2 medium	Onions (finely sliced after centre pith is removed)
200 g	Okras
½ tsp	Chaat masala
2 tbsp	Fresh coriander (finely chopped)
1 tsp	Cumin seeds
6–8	Curry leaves (finely shredded)
3.5 cm	Ginger (finely shredded)
4–5	Garlic flakes (finely shredded)
2	Green chilli (seeded and finely shredded)
3 thin	Spring onions (shredded)
100 g	Straw mushrooms (fresh, cut off the roots only)
½ tsp	Lemon juice
1 medium–large	Tomatoes (seeded and shredded)

3. Spread them out in the strainer with a fork to release any trapped heat inside. If this is not done the onions will continue to brown with the latent heat.

4. Meanwhile trim the okra and slice them very thinly almost lengthways. This means that you should get long slices.

5. Return the oil to the kadhai or wok and reheat it to a similar temperature.

6. Fry the okra in the same way and remove when pale golden in colour.

7. Transfer the onions onto a paper-lined plate or bowl and pour the okra into the strainer when ready.

8. When cooled, both will turn crisp. Blend both in a bowl and sprinkle with the chaat masala.

9. Add a dash of freshly chopped coriander before it is served.

10. Clean the wok of any okra residue and return to the fire.

11. Add 2 tbsp of oil and bring to smoking point.

12. Add the cumin and curry leaves then almost straight away add in all the shredded ingredients except the tomato and the mushroom.

13. Toss for 1–2 minutes but do not reduce the flame at all.

14. Add the mushrooms and toss for a further minute.

15. Sprinkle the lemon juice over then add some salt and the tomatoes and check the seasoning.

16. Sprinkle the chopped coriander and remove from the heat.

17. Serve either on top of the crispy okra and onion mixture or mixed with it.

Fansi Jeera Tamatarwala

Chef's Notes

- A simple and yet delicious French beans preparation made with cumin and tomatoes.

Method

1. If buying fresh beans you will have to trim and clean them. If buying frozen you may only need to thaw them in the refrigerator.

2. Take a large fry pan and add the oil.

3. Heat the oil and when reasonably hot add the garlic, onions and cumin.

4. Sauté for 1–2 minutes then add the chilli powder.

5. When the onions turn opaque turn the heat to high and add the beans.

6. Toss not too frequently but so that all the beans get exposed to direct heat at the bottom. The beans need only to cook for 2–3 minutes therefore a high heat is very essential.

7. Sprinkle with salt and the tomatoes, toss for a minute or so, check the seasoning, add the fresh coriander and remove.

8. In less than 10 minutes the beans should be ready. The basic pre-preparation may take a while but if you use the very best quality beans do not let them overcook. If water seeps out it means your flame was too low.

9. The beans are best kept crunchy and just cooked.

Measurements	Ingredients
250 g	Slender French beans (trimmed)
2 tbsp	Oil
3–4 cloves	Garlic (finely chopped)
1 medium	Onion (finely chopped)
1 tsp	Cumin (crushed, i.e. roasted and crushed not powdered)
¼ tsp	Chilli powder
2 medium	Tomatoes (seeded and chopped)
1 tbsp	Fresh coriander (chopped)
To taste	Salt

Gobhi Tamatar Rassa

Cauliflower Florets and Tomato Quarters in a Mild Tomato Gravy

Chef's Notes

• Either blanch the cauliflower florets in just as much water as is required or cook them directly in the sauce. Either way they need to be well washed. If blanching you can retain the liquid and use it in the sauce if it is not too much. If cooking in the sauce you must be aware that sometimes you may end up overcooking part of the batch, particularly if you are cooking in bulk.

Method

1. Heat the oil until almost at smoking point reduce heat and quickly sizzle the mustard seeds. As soon as they stop popping add the cinnamon and bay leaves.

2. When the bay leaves turn almost golden brown add the cumin and sauté for a minute or so until they change colour.

Measurements	Ingredients
2 tbsp	Sunflower oil
½ tsp	Mustard seeds
5 cm	Cinnamon stick
3–4	Bay leaves
1 tsp	Cumin seeds
2 large	Green chilli (slit into half and seeded)
1 tsp	Ginger (chopped)
1 tsp	Garlic (chopped)
300 g	Tomato (chopped and peeled)
250g	Tomatoes (cut into eights)
500 g	Cauliflower florets
½ tbsp	Fresh coriander (chopped)
As desired	Salt

3. Increase the heat slightly again and add the green chillies, ginger and garlic then sauté for a further minute or so until the garlic turns a pale golden brown.

4. Add the chopped tomatoes and the quartered tomato and simmer for 2–3 minutes.

5. Add the florets, cook until done if fully raw, check seasoning, add the coriander and remove.

6. As an option you can also add quarters of potato to the preparation, or red pumpkin dices, or both.

7. If adding raw potato cook till half done before the cauliflower is added.

Gobi Aur Makki Kay Daney

Cauliflower Florets cooked with Sweet Corn Kernels

Chef's Notes

- This can be served as a side dish or with corn tortillas. In Rajasthan the corn tortillas are made soft so that they can be eaten along with the food as chappaties. These are similar to flour tortillas.

- In the north of India where corn grows in abundance a great deal of different breads are made from corn. Instead of tortillas we have corn papads.

- If the Mexicans use sour cream we Indians use yoghurt in our cooking. It is both more nutritious and healthier.

Measurements	Ingredients
1 medium	Onions (chopped)
3 tbsp	Oil
1 tbsp	Ginger/garlic paste (see page 135)
2 medium	Green chilli (chopped)
1 tsp	Cumin seeds (crushed not powdered)
2 tsp	Coriander seeds (crushed not powdered)
200 g	Corn (frozen as available in stores)
1 small	Cauliflower (cut into small florets)
2 medium	Tomato (chopped)
2–3 heaped tbsp	Greek yoghurt
2 tbsp	Fresh coriander (chopped)

Method

1. Sauté the onion lightly in the oil until just about to brown.

2. Add the ginger garlic paste and green chilli and sauté for 2 minutes.

3. Add the coriander and cumin and sauté for 1–2 minutes. These can be lightly roasted in a frying pan and crushed together in a mortar.

4. Add the corn kernels and sauté for 1 minute. If the corn is uncooked you may need to boil it separately first until tender; if using frozen corn which is quite often pre-cooked you will not.

5. When the corn is cooked add the cauliflower florets and sauté for a further 4–5 minutes. Put in half a cup of water and some salt and simmer until the florets are half cooked.

Oyster Mushrooms Sukha Masala

Oyster Mushrooms Tossed with Dry Spices

Measurements	Ingredients
2 tbsp	Oil
¾ tsp	Mustard seeds
10–12	Curry leaves
1 tsp	Cumin seeds
4–5 cloves	Garlic (finely chopped)
3	Green chilli (seeded and sliced)
2 pinches	Asafoetida
½ tsp	Chilli powder
¼ tsp	Turmeric powder
2 medium	Tomato (cut into quarters)
200 g	Oyster mushrooms (I used pink oyster mushrooms for this recipe)
2 tbsp	Lime juice
To taste	Salt
1 tbsp	Fresh coriander (chopped)

Method

1. Heat the oil in a wok or a 22.5 cm saucepan until it forms a haze on top.

2. Add the mustard seeds and allow to crackle for 30 seconds or until they stop.

3. Add the curry leaves along with the cumin, garlic and green chilli, sauté for 1–2 minutes and add the asafoetida.

4. As soon as the garlic changes colour to a pale golden reduce the flame and add the dry powders, stir for 30 seconds and add the tomatoes.

5. Increase the heat again and sauté until the tomato skins begin to peel but they are still firm.

6. Turn the heat onto high and add the mushrooms.

7. Do not overstir but ensure that all the mushrooms are well tossed and coated.

8. Sprinkle a few splashes of fresh lime juice, the salt and fresh coriander and toss.

9. Cook for 2–3 minutes only on high, stirring regularly until you think the mushrooms are cooked.

10. These mushrooms remain firm longer than others therefore you may think they are underdone. They are perfectly cooked in about 2 or 3 minutes. More cooking will destroy them and make them soggy.

11. Check your seasoning and serve.

12. Remember that mushrooms do not take a very long time to prepare, therefore have your preparations ready and cook only when you are ready to serve in 10–15 minutes.

Paneer Bhurjee

Spicy Minced Cottage Whey Cheese

Chef's Notes

• A bhurjee is like a mince or finely chopped and is associated with items such as eggs, paneer, chicken, etc.

• This is a simple yet great recipe for a quick meal made with hard cottage whey cheese or feta (or another cheese that does not melt straight away).

Method

1. Heat the oil in a casserole on a medium flame and add the garlic, ginger and chilli.

2. When the garlic begins to colour add the cumin. Sauté for 1–2 minutes then add the onions.

3. After the onions get soft add the turmeric and chilli powders, increase the flame to high and add the tomatoes.

4. Taking care not to allow sticking at the bottom sauté for a further 2–3 minutes until you see the juices of the tomato drying up.

5. Lower the heat to medium once again and gently fold in the paneer or mashed feta.

6. Saute until well heated and the little water oozing out is almost dry.

7. When heated through add salt and check seasoning. Mix in the fresh coriander, remove and serve sprinkled with the chaat masala.

8. Bhurjee will go well with a peas pulao or bread. Chappati, of course, would be the best partner with some sweetish chutney.

Measurements	Ingredients
2 tbsp	Oil
1 tbsp	Garlic (chopped)
1 level tbsp	Ginger (chopped)
1–2 depending on taste	Green chilli (chopped)
1 heaped tsp	Cumin seeds (crushed)
2 medium to small	Onion (chopped)
1/4 tsp	Turmeric powder
1/2 tsp	Red chilli powder
2 medium	Tomatoes (chopped and seeded)
400 g	Paneer or mozzarella (minced in the case of feta mash with a fork)
1 1/2 tbsp	Coriander (chopped)
1/2 tsp	Chaat masala
To taste	Salt

Paneer Do Piaza/Pyazza/Piazza

4 portions

Chef's Notes

- This is a variation of a very popular preparation in Indian restaurants and is a familiar name. We hoteliers have devised this type of preparation, which is commonly found and accepted all over.

- It is a very simple preparation indeed and can be used for several products, such as okra instead of cottage cheese or diced chicken, prawns, fish, etc.

- Paneer or cottage cheese as we call it, is actually a whey cheese. Boiling milk first, then curdling it with live yoghurt can be easily made at home. It is then to be strained through a fine sieve, placed into a Tammy or muslin cloth, folded neatly and then pressed with a weight on top. This is to be set aside for a few hours until all the moisture has been squeezed out. Later it is to be cut into the desired size and fried.

- Paneer is now available, made in England and sold in several stores.

- Frying paneer and immediately adding it into water as soon as it is lifted out of the hot oil not only makes it spongy but also helps to absorb some flavours from the food.

Measurements	Ingredients
3 tbsp	Oil
1 heaped tsp	Cumin
1 medium	Onion (cut into half, then the halves cut into fours and lastly the dice to be separated)
2.5 cm	Ginger (scraped and shredded)
6–8 cloves	Garlic (finely chopped)
1 tsp	Chilli powder
2 tsp	Coriander powder
A pinch	Turmeric powder
1 large	Green pepper (cut as onion)
1 large	Beef tomato (diced as onion)
250 g	Paneer (cut into cubes, fried and soaked in water and squeezed before adding in)
2 tsp	Fresh Coriander (chopped)
To taste	Salt
5 g	Garam masala powder (optional)

Method

1. Heat the oil, add the cumin then sauté the onion, garlic and ginger.

2. Add the chilli, coriander and turmeric powder and cook for 1–2 minutes.

3. Increase the heat and add the green peppers and tomato and cook for 1–2 minutes.

4. Now add the squeezed paneer cubes and cook for 1–2 minutes until they are heated through.

5. Add the coriander. Finish off with seasoning and top with a few quarters of tomato for garnish.

6. Garam masala can be added at the end (optional).

Potato Bhajee

Chef's Notes

• There are potato bhajees and there are potato bhajees and there are potato bhajees in the subcontinent of India.

• I do not think one can count the innumerable styles and modes of preparation of this most popular, most widely consumed, most common vegetable (root) of them all. With at least 400 million vegetarians you can imagine the quantity of potato consumed across this huge landmass. In our household alone we use some eight different preparations.

• So there is no one standard Indian potato bhajee or one preparation that you can say, is the 'Indian' Aloo Ki Subzee. Mentioned here is just one of the hundreds of preparations that exist.

Method

1. Peel potatoes and cut into quarters or cubes depending on the size.

2. Halve and slice the onions.

3. Wash and slit the green chillies.

4. Heat about half the oil in a wok or casserole.

5. Sauté the onions, green chillies and potatoes.

6. Add the turmeric and continue sautéing for a few minutes.

7. Add the tomatoes and salt and enough water to cook the potatoes.

8. When the potatoes are soft and the gravy is thick, remove.

Measurements	Ingredients
3 tbsp	Sunflower oil
115 g	Onions
2–3 slender	Green chillies
225 g	Potato
¼ tsp	Turmeric
2 medium	Tomatoes
1 heaped tsp	Salt
¼ tsp	Mustard seeds
8–10	Curry leaves

9. Heat the remaining oil in a small frying pan, sizzle the mustard seeds and curry leaves and add to the bhajee.

10. Serve hot with poories or as a vegetable accompaniment.

Saag Aloo

Chopped or Pureed Spinach with Potato

Chef's Notes

- Dried fenugreek gives a very good flavour to this preparation. It is available in packets and is known as 'Kasoori Methi'. It needs to be placed in a tray in a very slow oven until it develops a beautiful aroma. It is then crushed and sieved and used in its powdered form to flavour spinach, etc.

Method

1. Either boil the potatoes or blanch and deep fry until cooked. The latter is definitely tastier but the first is healthier.

2. Blanch the spinach, taking care not to overcook it. Drain and either finely chop or purée. For fine chopping use the method applied for chopping parsley. If puréeing there may be no need to add any water as the spinach will contain a great deal.

3. Heat the oil and butter together in a deep pan or a frying pan large enough to hold all the potato and spinach. A wok would be ideal.

4. When the butter begins to change colour add the cumin and red chilli pieces. After about 30 seconds or so add the ginger and garlic.

5. As the garlic begins to turn a deep golden colour add the spinach and sauté for a few minutes, stirring regularly.

6. Add salt, a touch or more of crushed pepper depending on your taste and the fenugreek if you are using it.

7. Stir in the potatoes and simmer for 1–2 minutes until they are heated through. If adding deep-fried potatoes do so at the very end once they are well drained.

8. Blend in fresh coriander for the final touch.

9. Best eaten with Makki Ki Roti or fresh corn tortillas.

Measurements	Ingredients
For deep frying	Oil (optional)
750 g	Baby potatoes (if not using baby potatoes then use ordinary ones cubed)
10–12 bunches or 1 kg picked leaves	Fresh spinach *or*
1 kg	Frozen spinach (chopped)
20 ml	Sunflower oil
20 g	Butter
10 g	Cumin seeds
2	Red chilli whole (broken into pieces)
20 g	Fresh ginger (chopped)
20 g	Garlic (finely chopped)
To taste	Black pepper (crushed)
For taste	Dried fenugreek (crumbled, optional)
A good tbsp	Fresh coriander (chopped)

Saeb Aur Aloo Ki Subzee

Apple and Potato Bhajee

Chef's Notes

• A unique preparation, this originally stems from Kashmir but without potato. Ours is different. However, together they make an ideal accompaniment with pulao and a rich meat preparation such as Roganjosh or Khadey Masaley Ka Gosht.

Method

1. Heat the oil in a wok until hazy.

2. Add the fenugreek seeds and after 10 seconds or so add the mustard seeds.

3. When the mustard stops crackling add the cumin and coriander seeds. Sauté for a further 1–1½ minutes.

4. Add the green chillies and sauté for 1 minute.

5. Add the spring onions and sauté for 2 minutes then add the potato cubes and apple and toss lightly until well mixed.

6. Add the tomatoes and cook for 2–3 minutes, tossing occasionally.

7. As soon as the apple turns pale check the seasoning and if required add a little sprinkling of sugar and lemon juice.

8. Sprinkle with the coriander, toss and remove.

9. As an option at the last minute throw in some blanched French beans cut into tiny pieces. They will add a crunch to the dish as well as making it look even brighter. For the above quantity 100 g would do just fine.

Measurements	Ingredients
2 tbsp	Oil
Pinch or 8–10 seeds	Fenugreek seeds
¼ tsp	Mustard seeds
½ tsp	Cumin seeds
1 tsp	Coriander seeds (roasted and crushed)
2 medium	Green chillies (slit and chopped)
4–5	Spring onions (sliced thinly with the greens)
2 medium	Potatoes (boiled, peeled and cubed)
3 firm	Cooking apples (not peeled and cut into cubes. Not sour if possible)
1 large	Tomatoes (seeded and diced)
To taste	Sugar
To taste	Lemon juice
1 tbsp	Fresh coriander (chopped)

Padwal Caldeen

Snake Gourd Caldeen

Chef's Notes

- The Caldeen is a great curry and is quite versatile. It goes very well with seafood, poultry and vegetables. It has a creamy texture and a mild and interesting flavour. Curry leaves and a sprinkling of fresh coriander at the end will enhance the flavour.

- To check for tenderness the snake gourd should be felt with the thumbnail and pressed slightly. The softness will determine the tenderness.

Method

1. Wash and cut the snake gourd into 5 cm x 2.5 cm pieces. Parboil with a little salt and water. If snake gourd is not available use courgettes or, better still, another gourd such as sponge gourd or any type of marrow.

2. Grind the coconut, coriander, cumin, turmeric, ginger, green chilli and cinnamon to a fine paste.

3. Do the same if using coconut powder except that you will need at least 250 ml water. Use the water from boiling the gourd.

4. Heat the oil. Add the sliced onion and sauté until the onions are soft.

5. Add the ground ingredients and sauté for a few minutes more.

6. If it thickens too rapidly add a little water to get the consistency of rich single cream.

7. Add snake gourd pieces, more stock if required and more salt if desired. Cook till the gravy is thick and the gourd is tender.

Measurements	Ingredients
150 g	Snake gourd (tender)
½ 300 g	Fresh coconut *or* Coconut powder
1 tsp	Coriander seeds
¼ tsp	Cumin seeds
¼ tsp	Turmeric
2.5 cm	Ginger
1 medium–large	Green chilli
2.5 cm	Cinnamon/cassia
3 tbsp	Oil
1 medium	Onion (sliced)
As desired	Salt

Sub Saeb Subz

Apple Bhajee with Melrose and Johnagold Apples

Chef's Notes

- A unique preparation, this originally stems from Kashmir. Ours is different. However, it makes an ideal accompaniment with pulao and a rich meat preparation such as Roganjosh or Khadey Masaley Ka Gosht.

Method

1. Heat the oil in a wok or kadhai until hazy.

2. Add the fenugreek seeds and after 10 seconds or so add the mustard seeds.

3. When the mustard stops crackling add the cumin and crushed coriander seeds. Sauté for a further 1–1½ minutes.

4. Add the green chillies and sauté for 1 minute.

5. Add the spring onions and sauté for 2 minutes then add the apples and toss lightly until well mixed.

6. Add the tomatoes and cook for 2–3 minutes, tossing occasionally.

7. As soon as the apple turns pale check your seasoning and if required add a little sprinkling of sugar as well as lemon juice.

8. Sprinkle with the coriander, toss and remove.

Measurements	Ingredients
2 tbsp	Oil
Pinch or 8–10 seeds	Fenugreek seeds
¼ tsp	Mustard seeds
½ tsp	Cumin seeds
1 tsp	Coriander seeds (roasted and crushed)
2 medium	Green chillies (slit and chopped)
4–5	Spring onions (sliced thinly with the greens)
3 firm	Cooking apples (not peeled and cut into cubes. Not sour if possible)
1 large	Tomatoes (seeded and diced)
To taste	Lemon juice
To taste	Sugar
1 tbsp	Fresh coriander (chopped)

Subz Bhara Baingan Aur Rassedar Malai

Tamatar Ka Kut

Jeera Akhrod Ka Palav

Stuffed aubergine served with diced apple and creamy tomato gravy and cumin and walnut pulao.

Chef's Notes

- This is a combination of three recipes. Although I would recommend that they be eaten together just for the sheer pleasure of it all, there is nothing to say that you should not use them independently or as individual recipes too. Each one is a complete dish in itself.

Method

1. Heat 1–2 tbsp oil for deep frying. Slit the aubergine into half lengthways and fry flesh in a casserole or fryer until deep brown. Drain well on a paper towel, flesh side down.

2. In a frying pan sauté the green chilli, garlic and ginger until the garlic is golden but not brown. Add the onions and sauté slowly, stirring from time to time.

Measurements	Ingredients
1 medium	Aubergine
1–2 tbsp plus	Oil
1 large	Green chilli (minced)
3–4 cloves	Garlic (minced)
2.5 cm	Ginger (minced)
1 small	Onions (finely chopped)
1 tsp	Coriander seeds
5–6	Peppercorns
½ tsp	Cumin
5–6	Fenugreek seeds
1–2 pods	Cardamom
1 small	Potato (diced)
1 tbsp heaped	Green peas
3–4	Button mushrooms (chopped)
¼ tsp	Turmeric powder
1 tbsp	Fresh coriander (chopped)
To taste	Salt

3. Meanwhile gently roast the coriander seeds, peppercorns, cumin, fenugreek and cardamom pods and crush them to a coarse powder in a mortar and pestle or a small grinder.

4. Once the onions have turned pale brown add the turmeric and potato and cook covered on a slow flame. If necessary add a little water to allow the potato to cook.

5. Meanwhile scoop out the flesh of the aubergine and chop it roughly. Retain the skins for stuffing later.

6. Add the flesh to the pan, check the potato dice then add the green peas once the potato is almost done.

7. Sprinkle the powdered masala and cook covered for 1–2 minutes. Add the coriander, check seasoning and remove from the heat.

8. Stuff the skins only when ready to serve, so that you can use reheated stuffing.

9. You can sprinkle some cheese blended with a little freshly chopped (minced) green chilli and garlic on top and bake the stuffed aubergine shell in the oven under a griller.

Method

1. Heat the oil in a fry pan until almost hazy and add the mustard seeds.

2. When the crackling stops add the curry leaves. Lower the flame immediately and add the chilli and in a few seconds the asafoetida.

3. Almost immediately add the apple dices and the tomato. Cover the pan to allow the juices to escape.

4. Cook for 2–4 minutes, or until you see the tomato cook and thicken. Add the cream, check the seasoning and remove from the heat.

Tomato Gravy	Ingredients
2 tbsp (1 tbsp if using a small saucepan)	Oil
¼ tsp	Mustard seeds
3–4	Curry leaves
½ tsp	Red chilli (crushed)
Pinch	Asafoetida
¼	Apple (diced)
3 medium	Tomato (peeled and diced)
2 tbsp	Cream (single)

Method

1. Heat the oil in a sauce pan roughly 15 cm diameter and sauté the cumin until deep brown. Do not allow the cumin to get dark or burnt.

2. Add the onion and sauté until they are soft and beginning to turn golden.

3. Add the walnuts and sauté for 1–2 minutes then add the rice and sauté for a further minute, stirring regularly.

Pulao	Ingredients
1½ tbsp	Oil
1 level tsp	Cumin seeds
1 small	Onion (finely sliced)
2–3 tbsp	Walnuts (diced)
200–250 g	Basmati rice
As required	Water

8. French beans, beetroot, carrot and beans of every kind are great, they simply need to be well boiled first then just blended in and dried if necessary. Tendli or Tindora, the small marrow, is great and so is all other kind of marrow, red pumpkin, all squashes and various kinds of mushrooms, especially the chestnut and oyster types. Potato is OK but still not so bad.

9. Also note that I like coriander but the Keralans will not add coriander to this dish, as it is not classical. You can if you like the flavour. Just please use your imagination. This is an absolutely fantastic way to cook vegetables and is most enjoyable if you like the flavour of coconut.

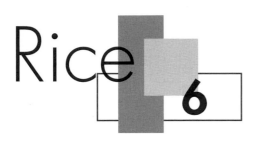

RICE, CHAAWAL, XIT, TAANO, TAANDUL, CHOEKHA

These are just some of the different names for rice.

Rice is consumed across the length and breadth of the sub-continent of India. Though the total population consumes thousands if not millions of tons of it, it is by no means a staple of the daily diet right across the regions. Some eat rice maybe once daily, some as their staple, some only on occasions and celebrations and some maybe once or twice a week. And then there are some who don't eat any.

India is the land where rice originated and there are perhaps a couple of hundred varieties at least if I am not mistaken.

There are hundreds of rice dishes across the Indian sub-continent and it would be impossible to cover even a decent quantity in the book. However, we have taken a few just to give an idea to readers about the diversity and range of dishes one can prepare with rice.

The king of rice is the Basmati, grown predominantly in the northwest and Pakistan. However, the Basmati an Indian selects will not necessarily be the same as what people consume throughout the world when eating the exports of the sub-continent. For one thing good quality rice, any rice, is like good wine. It is best consumed when well-aged. Unfortunately Western labelling laws do not allow the rice to age; in fact quite the contrary – rice is given a use-by date, which for an Indian is quite strange. Moreover, the rice available as Basmati across the globe is overly polished to simplify the cooking process and this process takes out several of the natural nutrients as well as making the grain weak. The older the grain of rice, the better it actually cooks. All Indians believe this.

Much as Basmati is known for its high quality and fragrance and texture, most peoples of the sub-continent will only eat it as a treat. There are several regional favourites. For instance, my parents', and especially my father's, favourite was the Surti Kolum. This is also the Gujerati community's favourite rice. It is a short grain but slender and so full of flavour and taste. My very own favourite, besides the Kolum, is 'Aamba Mohur', which means mango blossom. Believe it or not that rice when cooked has aromas of mango blossom and is absolutely delicious. It is so sought after these days that the good quality grain vanishes from the markets before one can get one's hands on it and is traded privately at a premium.

Whereas Basmati is excellent for making pulaos and biryanis, most of the other rice varieties are not suitable or do not possess the same qualities for that type of cooking. The Kolum may come close because of the nature of its grain but most of the others have a higher starch content, which makes them unsuitable. Long grain, however, is still OK but lacks the depth of flavour and taste.

Rice is a filler and also a poor man's fodder in many parts of the world today. It is nutritious and healthy (unless you have medical complications) and is a superb accompaniment or part of the main food when prepared as a pulao or biryani.

Across the sub-continent the daily rice is cooked in a myriad different ways but mostly plain, with or without salt. Perhaps without the spices that we have shown or with them. With yoghurt or vegetables, nuts or condiments, meat, fish or chicken, the list goes on.

Recipes for rice can go on and on but we have to choose a few only, however we must also have a simple recipe for the most commonly cooked rice of all – boiled rice.

This makes our very first recipe and I feel that it is essential for us to learn this basic preparation first. It teaches us to respect the grain, to understand it and thereafter to take steps to become more creative.

I must tell you this. In 1977, I was on the morning shift at the Shamiana, the coffee shop of the Taj Mahal Hotel in Mumbai. My duties besides à la Carte were also to cook up a host of things including 15 kilos of basmati daily. For this I had to place two large pots of water on the hot plates and divide the quantity. One day, after the water boiled and I had added the rice, one of the fuses blew and the water went off the boil. I did not notice this for some time as I was busy with other things. The rice sank and went from stodgy to pudding. The chef threw up a stink, refusing to accept my explanation that the cooker had stood me up, called the executive chef to give me yet another rollicking and besides being told things like, 'I would never expect you to fail in such a way' he gave me a bill and the money was deducted from my salary. Hard punishment, but food cost was such an over-riding issue that the chef on duty decided to make it up by sacrificing me on the altar. That day I decided never to take rice for granted and you will notice in my recipes certain tips, which have been learnt the very hard way.

Boiled Rice

Baafaela Chawal (Gujerati)

Oobla Hua Chawal (Hindi)

Chef's Notes

- This is the draining method.

Method

1. The rice should preferably be washed gently and set aside for 15–30 minutes.

2. Bring the water to the boil and add the butter or oil and the salt.

3. When the water boils add the rice and stir continuously but slowly for the first 2–3 minutes to separate all the grains.

4. For Basmati sold outside the sub-continent we have noticed that it takes 6–8 minutes for the rice to cook on the boil. It can differ but this is an indicator if you do decide to move away from the cooking area.

5. Keep a colander at the ready.

6. Once you have felt the rice and eaten a few grains to determine that it is cooked drain the rice.

7. Let it cool in the colander for a while by separating the grains with a fork or a roasting fork, before you decide to put it in a bowl or a pan.

8. Now you may decide to retain the liquid and use it for cooking, if so then drain over a pot. In my house it gets converted into nice soups for the family. Either they are soups with diced vegetables, herbs and some meat, or cream soups with the vegetable of your choice diced or puréed. Either way it is a great way to use the liquid or stock.

Measurements	Ingredients
3–4 litres	Water
1–2 tbsp oil *or a* dollop of butter	Oil or butter
500 g (approximately 100 g per person)	Rice
1–2 teaspoons or more if desired	Salt
Optional flavourings	
	Cinnamon
	Green cardamom
	Bay leaves
	Mace
	Cumin seeds

Ausavaela Chawal

Chef's Notes

- Rice cooked by the absorption method

Method

1. In this method you take two parts water to one part rice.

2. You may wish to increase the butter content from the previous recipe.

3. After adding the rice, stir for a while until you see the grains swelling up.

4. At this stage cover the pot, reduce the flame to low and slowly let the rice cook and absorb all the liquid.

5. As soon as the rice is cooked either tip it over into a larger bowl or a tray and loosen the grains. You may also leave it in the pot and serve it straight away. Either way the choice is yours.

6. Also one must remember that due to the high starch content in rice, it has the tendency to spoil quickly and attracts bacteria rather rapidly.

7. Rice must not be toyed with and the health authorities do not recommend reheating rice that has been left out and cooled. Rice attracts bacteria rather quickly once cooked and therefore it demands respect and cautious handling.

Tamatar Ka Bhaat/Tambatar Cha Bhaat

Tomato Rice

- This is another variation of making different types of rice. I have chosen this version to showcase the diversity that is Indian cooking. One might think of Indian cuisine as very closed, narrow, non-creative and ancient and an Indian like me would quite simply say, 'How naïve'. Indian food is as modern as it is ancient. It is perhaps the most creative of all cuisines, if only because of the depth of ingredients used in hundreds of different ways.

- Tomato rice is an interesting addition to a meal and can be accompanied by a great many meats and vegetable dishes.

Measurements	Ingredients
800–1000 g	Tomatoes
1 litre	Hot water
4–6 cloves	Garlic
2.5 cm	Ginger
3 tbsp	Sunflower oil
2 medium	White or pink onion (halved, cored and very finely sliced)
400–500 g	Rice
5–6	Black peppercorns
2–3	Cloves
2 heaped tbsp	Fresh coriander (chopped)
Salt	As desired

Method

1. Take a saucepan or a casserole large enough to hold all the tomatoes at one time as well as the rice when cooked.

2. Wash and halve or quarter the tomatoes and add to the pot.

3. Place on the cooker on a high heat and add approximately half the water and boil for 8–10 minutes.

4. Meanwhile make a paste of the ginger and garlic in a mortar and pestle and add to the tomatoes.

5. Either purée the tomatoes or pass through a strainer. A stick blender will purée it fine, even with the skins.

6. Heat the oil in a small pan, kadhai or wok and gently brown the onions.

7. Meanwhile wash and drain the rice in a strainer.

8. Remove half of the onions to a kitchen towel and reserve, then add the peppercorns and cloves to the pan.

9. Add the rice and sauté with the onions and spices for 2–3 minutes.

10. Add all of this into the puréed tomato with the ginger and garlic paste and return to the heat.

11. Add the remaining hot water and some salt and cover the pot tightly.

12. As soon as boiling commences stir well and see if anything is stuck at the bottom.

13. Scrape the edges with a spatula to clean the sides, then cover the pot tightly and reduce the heat.

14. Let the rice cook on a low heat for 15–20 minutes.

15. Stir occasionally if only to prevent sticking at the bottom.

16. When rice is cooked either remove and serve with the reserved browned onions and coriander sprinkled on the top or blend the onions and chopped coriander into the rice.

17. Tomato rice will also taste good cold served with yoghurt.

Sev Moti Ka Palav

Chef's Notes

- 'Sev' is vermicelli and 'Moti' is the word for pearls. This is an unusual pulao but one which demonstrates the huge diversity that is sub-continental Indian cuisine. It is something of a celebratory rice and is served at happy occasions. Its origins I am not so sure about but it most definitely has Persian roots. With the addition of nuts and raisins and the meatballs along with fine thread vermicelli, it is a bit of a mix of cultures. However, the Muslim cultures and the Parsee culture are fond of something sweet and savoury. It is a clear example that the cuisine of the sub-continent of India derives its nuances from various regions and cultures that have adapted and evolved over the generations into what can be termed as part of the great diversity that is Indian cuisine. The pulao calls for a bit of work and pre-preparation, but I can assure you that the end result is delightful.

- The vermicelli has to be the Indian or Pakistani type only. The Italian one is too thick and unsuitable. You will find these in Indian, Pakistani and Bangladeshi shops.

Method

1. Using the Sheek Kavab (page 84) prepare the mince. Use 500 g lamb mince. This means adding all the ingredients necessary for making the 'Motis'.

2. Put the water in a large pot and bring to the boil.

3. When almost at boiling point add the cinnamon or cassia, cardamom, mace, bay leaves and about 1 tbsp salt or more as desired. Remember no more salt is added later, therefore ensure that you have adequate for your taste.

4. Let the water boil for a few minutes and then add the rice.

5. Stir regularly or continuously for the first 2–3 minutes to ensure that every grain separates and does not stick.

6. Cook until the rice is just slightly undercooked then drain in a colander placed over a pot to collect the water.

7. Break the vermicelli into small tiny pieces before frying it. The procedure below is just a guidance note. I cannot explain it well enough and therefore you will also have to use your imagination a bit. Place the vermicelli in a clean kitchen towel and roll it like a sausage. Now twist the roll until it is taut and the vermicelli is well enclosed inside it. While holding it tightly break the vermicelli by holding the sausage against the edge of the kitchen top and moving it upwards and downwards against the surface. This will break up the vermicelli into tiny pieces.

8. Heat the butter with 1 tbsp oil in a large frying pan and slowly fry the vermicelli to a golden brown on a low to medium heat.

9. Mix the browned vermicelli with the rice with a fork.

10. Form tiny balls the size of small marbles with the prepared lamb mince and place on a greased tray.

Measurements	Ingredients
250–300 g	Lamb mince
4–5 litres	Water
5 cm	Cinnamon/cassia
2–3	Green cardamom (cracked)
1–2 flowers	Mace
1–2	Bay leaves
500 g	Good quality rice
250 g	Vermicelli (see notes)
1 heaped tbsp	Butter
250–300 ml	Sunflower oil
12–15	Whole almonds (sliced lengthways with skin)
15–20	Pistachios (raw, unsalted and sliced)
10–12	Cashew nuts (raw, unsalted and sliced)
1 tbsp	White raisins or sultanas
2–3 large	Carrots (peeled and sliced into roundels 2.5 mm thick)
4–5 medium	Onions (cored and very thinly sliced)
250 g	Sugar

11. Preheat the oven to 200–220°C/gas mark 6–7 and when hot put the kavaabs in the oven for 6–8 minutes, in which time they will be just about half done. Lower the heat of the oven to 150°C/gas mark 3 for later use to make the palav.

12. Heat 3–4 tbsp oil in a small frying pan and fry the nuts and raisins or sultanas. Be very careful as nuts brown very rapidly and the sultanas or raisins burn quickly and go crisp. You must have a strainer over a small glass or steel bowl ready so that you can tip the contents of the frying pan quickly.

13. As soon as the nuts are a pale brown, drain and loosen with a fork to release latent heat, which might otherwise burn the nuts in the carry over cooking process.

14. Blend these into the rice too.

15. Put some of the boiled rice water in a saucepan or casserole and boil.

16. When the water boils, add the carrots and boil for 3–4 minutes and drain, but reserve the water. The carrots need to be par-boiled and not fully cooked.

17. Blend the carrots with the rice.

18. Heat the remaining oil and any left over from the nuts together and fry the onions to a golden brown.

19. Using the water from the boiled carrots, add the sugar to make a thick syrup. You will need roughly 250–300 ml water to make a thick syrup, enough to allow it to boil gently until thickening.

20. Put the rice and all the mixed ingredients into a pot large enough, and with a tight-fitting lid, and slowly blend in the sugar syrup when ready.

21. Wipe the sides of the pot and cover tightly.

22. Either place in the oven tightly covered or use the traditional method on dum with dough. After it has been simmering for 7–8 minutes, transfer to an oven preheated to 190°C/375°F/gas mark 5 and bake for 15–20 minutes.

23. The ovenable method is the safest but if the oven is too hot the rice will not open well and may make the pulao stodgy.

Ghawno Khichdo

Wheat Khichdi

Chef's Notes

• Not very common but it would be a part of a diet in the wheat-growing regions of central and north India. Where my mother's family comes from in Madhya Pradesh, it is common to use either cracked as bulgur or whole wheat as in this recipe. Wheat khichdi, either sweet or savoury, is given to new nursing mothers in particular to help rebuild their strength after delivery.

Measurements	Ingredients
500 g	Wheat
2 litres	Water
250 g	Toover or mung
3 tsp	Salt
½ tsp	Turneric
As required	Ghee or butter

Method

1. Wash the wheat well until the water runs clear.

2. Bring the water to a boil in a deep pan then add the lentils and the drained, soaked wheat and mix.

3. Add the salt and turmeric and continue on a slow boil.

4. The water needs to dry up when the wheat and lentils are thoroughly cooked.

5. If during cooking the water dries but the wheat is still uncooked add a little water at a time until all the water is dry and the wheat is cooked.

6. Remove and blend in some ghee or butter and serve with kadhi, curry or yoghurt

Goan Seafood Pulao

6–7 portions

Chef's Notes

• This is a pulao made after making plain pulao and then adding seafood. The pulao needs to use a light fish stock when cooking for optimum taste. Again this is something that can be finished at the last minute if all the pre-preparation is ready. The vegetables that form the base can be sautéed in advance. The seafood can be marinated in a little turmeric powder and lime juice.

• Cook seafood on a very high flame or heat to avoid it spoiling. Also you must not add all of it at one go if you feel that the flame will let you down. If using monkfish you can add that in first and then the shellfish etc. but try not to agitate the pan too much unless it is a wok where you have to toss naturally.

Method

1. Make a batch of plain pulao (see page 196) using half water and half fish stock.

2. Take a large fry pan or casserole and add the oil. Sauté the garlic until a light golden brown. A wok is ideal provided your cooker could sustain a high heat for a wok.

3. Add the ginger and chilli, the green pepper and lastly the onions.

4. Sauté until the onions turn opaque and limp.

5. Add the curry leaves and coriander and cumin powders. If you like add a pinch of turmeric or a few hairs of saffron.

Measurements	Ingredients
1 batch plain pulao as per pulao recipe using half water and half fish stock	Pulao
2 tbsp	Oil
2.5 cm	Ginger (peeled and cut into fine strips)
6–8 cloves	Garlic (crushed)
1 large	Green chilli (shredded)
½ medium	Green pepper (cut into thin strips)
1½ medium or 1 large	Onion (sliced)
5–6	Curry leaves
½ tsp	Coriander powder
½ tsp	Cumin powder
2 large scallops	Scallop *or*
15–20	Clams
1–2 small squids (also use tentacles)	Squid rings
10–12 medium	Prawns (e.g black tigers)
7.5 cm	Firm white fish (e.g. Monkfish tail fillet, cut into small dice)
2 medium	Tomato (seeded and cut into strips)
2 tbsp	Fresh coriander (finely chopped)
1 tsp	Lemon juice
To taste	Salt

6. Turn the heat on high and sauté the seafood for a maximum of 3 minutes on high so that you do not overcook it.

7. Add the tomatoes. If the pan is small you may need more time, therefore it may be wise to cook in a casserole, unless you have a wok.

8. Add the pulao, fresh coriander, lemon juice and check the salt.

9. Your pulao is now ready to be served.

10. Serve with plain curry from the recipe for Goan Fish (see page 119).

11. You could use olive oil if you like, as many Goans would do.

Aek Halla Ni Khichdi

10 portions

Khichdi Cooked in an Earthenware Pot

Chef's Notes

- I discovered this recipe in my grandmother's cookbook written in Gujerati in her own handwriting. Naturally the traditional methods of cooking can be adapted. This recipe must have been written sometime in the early twentieth century, perhaps 1903 or 1904. I sat for long hours with my dad trying to understand the old measurements and the style and developed this recipe to help people understand our own cuisine culture, much of which we do not use today. You can skip the ghee and use oil instead. This recipe is for 10 persons actually as that was the size of a normal family in those days.

- Chawal no masalo (Rice masala) is made from 1 part cassia, ½ part cloves and ⅓ part cardamom. It can also include peppercorns and black cardamom. Use a combination that you like but make it up to 15 g for this recipe.

Measurements	Ingredients
1 kg	Basmati rice
½ tsp	Turmeric
750 g	Toover daal
250 g	Ghee or butter
15 g	Chawal no masalo (Rice masala)
½	Nutmeg (crushed or powdered)
1 small piece	Mace
10 g	Black cumin
250 g	Lamb (in ½ inch dices)
1	Banana leaf or aluminium foil
1 250 g	Coconut (milked) *or* Rich coconut milk (canned)
Some dough if interested in cooking traditionally	

Method

1. Wash and boil the rice, adding half the turmeric and salt to taste. When the rice is half cooked, drain.

2. Boil the daal separately with the remaining turmeric and salt until it cracks (almost cooked) then drain. Do not use too much water for the daal to avoid excessive draining and losing precious nutrients.

3. In another pan heat half the ghee and fry the rice masala, nutmeg, mace and black cumin. When browned add the lamb and brown well.

4. Cook covered until the lamb is half cooked. Add a little water if you like but only just enough to dry when the lamb is half cooked.

5. Add the coconut milk to the lamb and remove from the fire.

6. Place a cut piece of the banana leaf or foil in the centre of a large flat pan or pyrex type dish (anything oven proof), dividing it into two parts.

7. Place the daal in one half and half the rice in the other half taking care to ensure that they do not mix.

8. Pour the lamb over the rice and cover with the remaining rice.

9. Melt the remaining ghee and pour equally over both halves. Check seasoning.

10. Traditionally this is to be covered and the lid sealed with dough prior to it being very slowly cooked on 'dum' (under pressure). This means that the bottom is placed on a slow fire, preferably embers, and red hot charcoal is placed on the top over a little ash. This allows the food inside to bake very gently.

11. In your kitchen you may prefer to shut the lid tightly, seal the sides with some foil and place in a moderate oven at 170–180°C/gas mark 3–4 for 1–1½ hours.

12. When ready to serve remove the foil or leaf and serve sprinkled with some browned onions, fried nuts and chopped coriander.

13. You may also garnish with some quartered boiled eggs.

Aloo Gobhi Ki Tahiri

Chef's Notes

- This pulao made with potatoes and cauliflower florets is one of my very favourite rice dishes. It has great character and seldom lets you down. I cannot tell you its exact origins though I can tell you I first made it in 1974 and it has stuck in my mind ever since, but as usual I have tweaked a few bits. I cannot explain why I like it so much but it is hugely versatile and will go well with most accompaniments as well as curries or simple plain yoghurt.

Method

1. Peel the potatoes and cut them into cubes.

2. Clean the cauliflower and cut into small florets. Cut the stalk ends into thin slices or half and then slice.

3. Wash the rice and drain (for rice sold outside the Indian sub-continent).

4. Heat the oil in a casserole and while heating add the cloves, cassia or cinnamon and the bay leaves.

5. Fry until the cloves are well swollen and the leaves colour a bit.

6. Add the cumin and after 30 seconds or so add the potatoes and sauté for 1–2 minutes.

7. Next add the rice the cauliflower and sauté well for 2–3 minutes taking care not to let the rice stick at the bottom.

8. Add the turmeric, chilli powder and ginger and stir them in.

9. Now add some salt as you see fit and pour in hot or boiling water up to about 3 cm above the line of the product.

10. Stir gently, cover with a lid and cook on a medium heat

11. Observe from time to time and stir from the bottom up. Always clean the sides with a spatula and cover and continue cooking.

12. If the liquid dries out but the rice has not yet cooked, add a little hot water at a time until the cooking is complete.

13. Remember never add too much water. You can add too much; however, if you follow the simple guidelines you won't come out crying.

14. When cooked and the rice grains have separated, sprinkle with the garam masala powder, mix gently and serve.

15. Best served with spicy mango chutney and the food of your choice.

Measurements	Ingredients
200 g	Potatoes
200 g	Cauliflower florets (do not discard stalk ends)
3–4 tbsp	Sunflower oil
6–8	Cloves
5 cm	Cassia/cinnamon
2–3	Bay leaves
¾ tsp	Cumin
500 g	Basmati rice
1½ tsp	Turmeric powder
1 tsp	Chilli powder
1 tbsp	Ginger (minced)
As desired	Hot/boiling water
½ tsp	Garam masala powder
As desired	Salt

Batata Poha/Pohaybhaat

Flattened Rice with Potato

Chef's Notes

- Poha or flattened rice is very popular across the sub-continent and there are many, many different ways in which it is cooked. Each community has its own style. Sweets, desserts, savouries, snacks and midday quick meals are some of the dishes in which you will often find Poha being made.

- This Maharashtrian recipe of a light midday welcoming snack is appropriate if someone turns up at the doorstep or quite simply as a teatime accompaniment. The Maharashtrians call it 'Batata Poha' and the Gujerati would call it 'Bataka aney Poha Bhaat', whereas in south India in Tamil Nadu it could be called 'Aval Uppuma'. Though the concept is the same the preparations are slightly different.

- The Gujerati version may often have a bit more sugar and lime juice but this can also vary and peanuts need not be added though the Gujeratis do like peanuts. The south Indians would no doubt have their mustard seeds but also urad (while lentil) and/or channa daal (split yellow peas). However, one thing is for certain, this snack is one of my very favourites and I can assure you that it is most enjoyable.

Method

1. Wash the Poha well, squeeze out the excess water and drain in a colander.

2. Heat the oil in a kadhai or a shallow but largish sautéing pan, or even a casserole.

3. When the oil forms a haze add the mustard seeds, reduce the heat to medium and place the lid on top for just a few seconds until the crackling dies down.

4. Add the cumin seeds and as soon as they change colour the asafoetida.

5. Add the garlic, ginger, onion, green chilli, curry leaves and continue sautéing until the onions turn soft.

6. Add the turmeric, chilli powder, salt and the potatoes. Cover tightly, reduce the heat and cook until the potatoes are cooked. Do not add any water just allow the potatoes to cook under their own steam. They will cook well provided you do not keep the heat on high.

7. Once the potatoes are cooked add the optional green peas, though I would certainly recommend them. If you are using fresh peas, cook them with the potato, if using frozen, these don't need cooking and can be added once the potato is cooked.

8. Sprinkle with the Poha, add the lime juice, sugar and the coconut and cook until the Poha turn soft.

9. Serve hot and almost immediately if possible with half the coriander blended and half sprinkled on top.

10. The Maharashtrians also add fried/roasted unsalted peanuts to their Poha. Do this if you like peanuts, as most of we Indians do, and you will notice yet another difference to the overall experience.

Measurements	Ingredients
250 g	Poha (available in most Indian stores)
2–3 tbsp	Sunflower oil
½ tsp	Mustard seeds
¼ tsp	Cumin seeds
A decent pinch	Asafoetida
2–3 cloves	Garlic (minced)
2.5 cm	Ginger (scraped and finely minced)
2 medium	Onion (finely minced)
3–4 (if used to chilli use 5)	Green chillies (finely minced)
10–12	Curry leaves (shredded)
½ tsp	Turmeric powder
As needed	Chilli powder
As needed	Salt
200 g or 1 large	Potatoes (peeled and diced)
150–200 g	Green peas (optional)
1 small	Lime (juice only)
1 tsp	Sugar
½ coconut grated 250 g	Fresh coconut or Frozen coconut
If neither is available, take desiccated coconut, and soak in water, drain and use.	
2 heaped tbsp	Fresh coriander (chopped)

11. Aval uppuma: when making this in the south Indian style, add 1 tsp each of urad daal and channa daal after the mustard seeds have cracked and then continue with the rest of the preparation. Also in the Aval Uppuma there is no need for the sugar, lime juice or the peanuts. However, fried broken cashew nuts are more than welcome.

Gos No Pulao

Chef's Notes

- There has always been a controversy about the difference between a Pulao with meat and a Biryani. I have myself often been greatly confused and sometimes, such as in this recipe, the answer cannot be given. For instance, there are pulaos where the lamb or chicken is blended with the rice, both half cooked and then cooked in a sealed pot together until done. There is a biryani that uses a similar methodology and then the meat is blended in before service. By definition I think that a pulao is the one where the meat and the rice are cooked together. A biryani on the other hand is where the meat and the rice are cooked in layers and then served up from the pot as they would come out straight onto the platter.

- This is a hundred-year-old recipe and it has been altered only to suit modern-day cooking. However, none of the ingredients have been changed or added to. These days we make pulao a bit differently for various reasons, related to the availability of time, to consciousness of fat due to a more sedentary lifestyle and so on.

Measurements	Ingredients
500 g	Lamb
2–2½ litres	Water
400 g	Ghee
1 kg	Basmati rice
20 g	Salt
3 medium	Onion (finely and evenly sliced)
20 g	Garam masala
½	Nutmeg (grated)
5 g	Mace
½ tsp	Caraway seeds
500 g	Yoghurt
A good pinch	Saffron
1	Lime
125 g	Almonds (sliced)
125 g	Sultanas

- The parsees also ate a sweet pulao quite frequently. To try this make a strong sugar syrup of soft ball consistency using 150 g sugar. Add the syrup to the hot pulao only and blend.

Method

1. Clean and wash the lamb.

2. Place in a pot and pour in enough water to cover the lamb. Cook until done (30–40 minutes) and the water is almost dry. When done drain the water and set aside.

3. In another pot place the water and a blob of ghee and bring to the boil.

4. Wash the rice and put it into the boiling water, along with the salt.

5. When the rice is almost cooked, drain in a colander.

6. Take another pot and add 150 g ghee then sauté the onions until brown.

7. Remove some of the onions and set aside for garnish.

8. Add the whole garam masala, nutmeg, mace and caraway seeds. The mace and caraway seeds should be pounded in a mortar and pestle.

9. Blend the yoghurt into the boiled lamb.

10. Heat the saffron and add the lime juice.

11. Sprinkle it over the boiled rice.

12. To the fried masala add the almonds and sultanas and fry for a while until golden.

13. Blend the lamb and yoghurt with all of this and set aside.

14. Alternate the lamb and rice in layers in the pot.

15. Pour over any stock and place in a moderate oven for up to 1 hour.

16. Before serving sprinkle the brown onions on the top.

Laapsi Khichdi A'la Pervin

Wet Khichdi with Onion and Tomato

Chef's Notes

- This is a great khichdi and one that has become a favourite in our family. However, my wife has perfected her very own style by trial and error based on the tastes, likes and dislikes of us all. Laapsi Khichdi does very much exist and you will often notice that, much like our own home, family styles vary with the exception of the onion, garlic and tomato, which are common. 'Laapsi' is another word for 'wet' and a bit of gluten released by the rice, which gives it the texture.

Method

1. Wash, clean well and soak the rice and moong daal together.

2. Chop the onion finely, mince the garlic, wash and chop the tomatoes and set these aside.

3. Add the oil to a 6–8 litre casserole roughly with a tight-fitting lid and heat.

4. Sauté the cumin seeds and when they change colour add the asafoetida and immediately the garlic. Keep stirring.

Measurements	Ingredients
400 g	Rice
200 g	Moong daal
1 medium	Red onions
4 cloves	Garlic
2–3 medium	Tomatoes
2 tbsp	Sunflower oil
1 level tsp	Cumin seeds
$\frac{1}{8}$ tsp	Asafoetida
$\frac{1}{2}$ tsp	Turmeric
$\frac{1}{4}$ tsp	Red chilli powder
$\frac{1}{4}$ tsp	Cumin powder
1200 ml	Water
1 heaped tbsp	Butter
3–4 tsp	Salt
1 heaped tbsp	Fresh coriander (chopped)

5. As soon as the garlic changes colour add the onions and sauté until the onions turn soft.

6. Now add the soaked rice and moong daal, turmeric, tomatoes, chilli powder and cumin powder.

7. Stir for a while and add the water.

8. Add the butter and salt, cover and cook on a medium heat, stirring from time to time but ensuring that you scrape from the bottom up.

9. For best results you must use a good heat-resistant plastic spatula/stirrer or a wooden one.

10. The khichdi will take 30–40 minutes on a medium heat to cook well.

11. For this dish the rice needs to be a little overcooked so do not worry if it gets mushy, that's what Laapsi means. But if the water dries out too quickly add some more but only a very little at a time.

12. As soon as the rice and the moong daal are cooked and the khichdi has the consistency of porridge, add the coriander, stir well and remove from the cooker.

13. Serve as suggested with hot and sweet mango chutney, or shredded mango Choonda (a typical Gujerati-style chutney made by mixing spices and sugar with shredded or grated raw mango and left in the sun to mature), fried papads and some split spring onions if you like.

Choley Palav

Chickpeas Pulao

Chef's Notes

- Chickpeas come in a number of different varieties. The most popular is the large white variety also known as Bengali Channa. High in protein, chickpeas can be cooked in several different ways. This is a simple pulao and makes an excellent accompaniment to many of India's great dishes.

Method

1. If using raw chickpeas, soak them in adequate water in a deep bowl or pan overnight or for a minimum of 6 hours. The longer they are soaked the more they will swell and cook faster. However, prolonged soaking will ferment and thereby spoil the chickpeas. Boil them in the same water, adding more if required with a little salt until fully cooked. Set aside.

2. Heat the oil in a deep pot or pan with a tight-fitting lid.

3. When the oil forms a haze add the cassia, cloves and red chilli. As soon as you see the cloves swell add the cumin and sauté for a minute or so.

4. Add the garlic then 30 seconds later the onions. Sauté until the garlic is almost on the point of browning.

5. Now lower the heat and add the rice and salt and stir for 1–2 minutes, turning well and levelling out each time so that the rice gets an all round heat.

6. Add now the water or stock up to about 2 cm above the height of the rice.

7. Stir for a few seconds and allow to rest covered.

8. Lower the heat to a minimum.

9. Stir again every minute or so until most of the water has been absorbed and you can detect a little water along the sides.

10. Add either the drained canned chickpeas or the drained boiled chickpeas. You may like to use the chickpea in the water or stock when adding to the rice. This will add a lot more flavour but it only discolours the pulao.

Measurements	Ingredients
454 g 250 g	Chickpeas (tinned) or Chickpeas (raw)
3 tbsp	Sunflower oil
5 cm	Cassia
3–4	Cloves
1–2 large	Whole red chilli (broken in half)
00 g	Cumin
5–6 cloves	Garlic (finely chopped)
2 medium	Onions (halved and thinly sliced)
400–500 g	Basmati rice
As desired	Water or stock
For garnish. To make brown onions slice them very thinly then semi-deep-fry them until golden	Browned onions (optional)
To taste	Salt

11. After each stir cover the pot but ensure that all the sides are clean of grains when you are about to cover.

12. Check every 1–2 minutes and give the rice a gentle stir from the bottom up but very gently.

13. Check your seasoning and whether or not the rice is cooked. Approximately 30–40 minutes on a slow fire is often adequate.

14. When serving, top with browned onions and sprinkle some freshly chopped coriander.

Dahi Bhaat

Method

1. Heat the oil in a pan and add the mustard seeds until they stop crackling.

2. Add the urad daal, curry leaves and the cumin and stir gently until the urad daal turns a golden brown. Do not keep the heat too high or allow the daal to brown too much.

3. Keep this (the tadka) aside and cool.

4. Beat the yoghurt in a bowl until smooth.

5. Add the onions, tomato and coriander, blend and taste.

6. Add the rice and then the tadka and check seasoning.

7. Serve chilled as an accompaniment to hot, dry-cooked meats.

8. Eat as a tonic or a coolant for gastric disorders and stomach problems.

Measurements	Ingredients
2 tbsp	Sunflower oil
½ tsp	Black mustard seeds
1 heaped tsp	Urad daal (white lentil)
8–10	Curry leaves
1 tsp	Cumin whole
450 g	Greek yoghurt
1 small	Onion (chopped)
1 medium	Tomato (chopped and seeded)
1 heaped tbsp	Fresh coriander
300 g	Cold boiled rice
To taste	Salt

Egg and Vegetable Fried Rice

Chef's Notes

- There are millions of Chinese in India who now form a part of the Indian people. Chinese food in India was perhaps more popular in restaurants than was Indian food until very recently. The Indian Chinese have developed their own distinct cuisine though, evolving from the provinces of Sichuan, Hunan or Hakka. This is a very simple fried rice preparation, which is ideal made with leftover cold boiled rice.

Method

1. Heat the oil in a wok to smoking point and allow to heat for a little while.

2. Add the beaten eggs and swirl with a ladle or spoon, breaking it up as you go along.

3. Add the spring onions and the peppers and sauté for 1 minute, always keeping the heat high.

4. Add the vegetables and the salt and pepper and sauté for a minute or so.

5. Add the rice and toss gently.

6. If you do not know how to toss with a wok use the frying spoon.

7. Once the rice is heated through it is ready for service.

8. Short and sweet.

Measurements	Ingredients
2 tbsp	Oil
2	Eggs (well beaten)
3	Spring onions (sliced at a slant)
1 small	Green peppers (cut into fine strips or a mix of coloured peppers)
5–6 tbsp	Mixed vegetables (blanched and diced small)
500 g approx	Cold boiled rice (must be cold)
To taste	Salt
To taste	Pepper powder

Sesame Rice

Chef's Notes

- This is a south Indian style of seasoning boiled rice with roasted sesame seeds and spices. However, it goes to show that you can use similar techniques to make other types of rice too. Rice can be made as interesting as one pleases, if one has imagination but keeping within one's means of balance. Over spicing, over seasoning and poor balance can destroy a perfectly good dish.

Method

1. Once boiled and drained, place the rice in a flat tray and spread it out to cool.

2. In a large skillet or frying pan gently roast the sesame seeds and red chilli until the seeds crackle and turn light brown.

3. In a mortar and pestle or a coffee grinder, crush the sesame seeds, red chilli, asafoetida and sea salt to a powder.

Measurements	Ingredients
From 500 g raw rice	Boiled rice (use the recipe for boiled rice (page 196) but without spices if you like)
150 g	Sesame seeds (hulled)
2–3 medium	Dry red chillies (snipped)
Decent pinch	Asafoetida
½ tsp	Sea salt
1 tbsp	Sunflower oil
1 level tsp	Mustard seeds
1 tbsp	Ghee or clarified butter
1 tsp	Urad daal (White lentil)
1 tsp	Channa daal (Split yellow peas)
8–10	Curry leaves (shredded for better flavour)

4. Heat the oil in a smaller frying pan to a haze.

5. Keep a loose lid ready then add the mustard seeds and reduce the heat slightly.

6. As soon as the crackling reduces add the butter or ghee then the two daals and the curry leaves.

7. Sauté and stir gradually until the daals become light and golden brown.

8. As soon as this is ready sprinkle the ground spice mix over the rice and blend well.

9. Serve with yoghurt or warm with a light curry.

10. Some dry vegetable curry goes well with this rice.

11. The sesame powder is also great as a seasoning with salads, sprinkled over yoghurt, an added seasoning for hummus or as a condiment with anything.

Sadi Khichdi

A type of Rice Pulao cooked with Lentils

Chef's Notes

• Khichdis are made in various parts of the sub-continent and always represent the same thing – rice and lentil cooked together. The lentil used may vary and the spice combination will vary but the moment you want to make khichdi you know that it has to be with lentil and rice. The Sadi Khichdi is the basic Gujerati Khichdi and is always made with split moong bean or mung daal, as it is known. Not every culture in the sub-continent will understand the term khichdi, as it is not commonly made everywhere. The Gujerati community is perhaps the best known for its different khichdis and is probably the best at it too.

• Khichdis are made as a quick easy-to-digest and light alternative to meals. They are most enjoyable and our family above all enjoys them immensely. My wife is, however, an expert in making the wet type or Laapsi Khichdi as it is known.

Method

1. Clean and wash the daal separately then drain.

2. Wash the rice and set it aside.

3. Put a pot on the fire with the water and salt and bring it to the boil.

4. As soon as the water boils add the daal, stir a little and allow it to boil.

5. As soon as the daal begins to boil add in all the remaining ingredients, stir and mix well.

Measurements	Ingredients
200 g	Moong/mung daal
400 g	Rice (Select the rice of your choice, either long grain, Basmati or Kolum. Glutinous rice is *not* suitable)
900–1000 ml	Water
1 level tsp	Salt
2 cloves	Garlic (finely minced)
2.5 cm	Fresh ginger (finely minced)
½ tsp	Turmeric powder
1 heaped tbsp	Butter/ghee

6. Cover the pan with a loose lid allowing some steam to escape. This is important because it prevents the water from foaming and overflowing.

7. Stir regularly to prevent sticking at the bottom.

8. This khichdi is a little mushy in nature so cook it until the rice does get a bit mushy. However, you can keep it firm and loose grained.

9. For best enjoyment khichdi is mostly accompanied by kadhi (see page 162), some extra butter or ghee on top, plenty of fried papads and a sweet hot chutney.

Palav, Pulao, Pilav

- These all mean the same thing. The word 'pilaf' is also used in England as well as the USA.

- There are several ways and several styles, there are regional styles and domestic styles. Basically a pulao is rice that is first tempered in a bit of oil with flavourings and then part boiled and part steamed.

- Option two gives you a very simple recipe, one that should not go wrong. Have no fear if you spoil your rice. Make croquettes the next day.

Method

1. Wash the rice if need be and drain. I have realised that in England you do not need to wash the basmati rice available. The rice is so grossly over polished that there is no substance and the grains break up when washed or soaked for too long, unlike in India where we do have to wash well and soak rice well for it to expand and fluff up.

2. Heat the oil or ghee in a 25 cm casserole and fry the spices for 1–2 minutes until they change colour. Remember to crack the cardamom before adding to the oil. This is for two reasons: one, to give a better flavour and two, so that the cardamom does not explode because the air gets trapped inside when frying.

Measurements	Ingredients
500 g	Basmati, or other good long grain rice
3 tbsp 2 tbsp	Oil *or* Ghee
1 tsp	Cumin seeds
2–3	Cloves
2–3	Cardamom
5 cm	Cinnamon stick
1 small	Onion (peeled halved and sliced thinly)
1 litre	Water (boiling)

3. Add the onions and sauté for 1–2 minutes until they go pale but do not colour.

4. Add the rice and sauté for 2–3 minutes, stirring regularly so that all the grains get evenly heated and fried.

5. You must also at this stage keep the water ready in a kettle or another pan. The rice should normally take 1½–2 times the quantity of rice in weight. Therefore for 500 g rice you may need 1 litre water.

6. However, rice does differ in quality and levels of absorption. I therefore recommend that you first add 1 litre, stir well, clean the sides of any loose grains, lower the heat to simmering point, add salt, cover and cook. Once the rice has reached boiling point, always lower the heat to just about simmering level.

7. Stir gently after every minute or so by taking in from each side, and clearing the sides before covering the pan again.

8. If you see that the water is rapidly being absorbed, add a little more water and check at the next turning, after checking the grains.

9. To finish the rice you can also use your oven. Heat to 150–160°C/gas mark 3 and at the half way stage place the casserole in the oven for 25–30 minutes.

10. If you cook the rice on the open flame it has to be finished on a very slow fire, and stirred very gently from time to time so that you do not break the grains. This is done by using the folding method.

11. If you want to try out the rice to see if it follows the required amount of water absorption go for the 1:2 ratio straight away. However, I would still not add all of the water but would give it in two stages just before it is to go into the oven.

12. Also in the oven the rice will need less water and the grains will come out better separated.

13. Once the rice is cooked, stir with a roasting fork loosening all the grains then cover and set aside until you need it.

14. If you feel that the rice is mushy you can return it to the oven for some more time. This happens to the best of us from time to time so do not get too concerned. Try again the next time and back track what you did this time. Avoid what you feel was the problem.

Option Two

- This is sometimes the preferred way to cook a pulao simply because you have less to worry about and the chances of failure are reduced.

1. After frying the spices add the water or stock and season. Once the water begins to boil add the rice and stir in gently.

2. Stir continuously for the first 2–3 minutes to allow the rice to get well mixed and not settle.

3. Then cook as above, covered on a low flame or covered and in the oven.

Masala Bhaat

Masala Rice

Chef's Notes

- It is much more than just Masala Rice and I simply could not do this chapter without including this great Maharashtrian speciality. I grew up eating several versions in several different homes with each friend's mother claiming to have the best of grandma's recipe. How could I not say to them all that each one was the best? After all, I was getting a feast and each recipe was truly spectacular. I am hoping to come a close second with my recipe, using all the hints I picked up as well as being taught by some masters. Naturally no matter how hard chefs like me try we can never match someone else's mother's touch.

- Masala Bhaat is a type of vegetable pulao with a combination of spices and nuts that make it an interesting and flavoursome dish. It is best eaten with a thin daal and of course a good pickle or chutney. The pre-preparation may look immense and the list of ingredients certainly does, but, believe me, it is worth the effort.

Method

1. If the peanuts are not skinned soak them in water for 15–20 minutes then drain and skin them.

2. In a wok or frying pan dry roast the peppercorns, cloves, desiccated coconut, cinnamon, coriander seeds, sesame seeds, and half the cumin seeds.

3. Do this on a slow flame so as not to burn anything and then powder in a coffee grinder or small grinder. You can also preheat the oven to 150–160°C/gas mark 2–3. Place the ingredients on an oven tray and, when hot put them in and switch off the oven after 4–5 minutes. Leave the spices etc. inside for half an hour or so and then cool, powder and set aside.

Measurements	Ingredients
2–3 heaped tbsp	Peanuts/groundnuts (raw) (If you can get skinned ones, even better)
5–6	Peppercorns
3–4	Cloves
2–3 heaped tbsp	Desiccated coconut
12–25 mm	Cinnamon or cassia
1 level tbsp	Coriander seeds
1 heaped tsp	Sesame seeds
1 heaped tsp	Cumin seeds
8–10	Tindlis (This is a small marrow, like a gherkin. If you cannot find this use one courgette)
2 medium	Potatoes
1 medium	Aubergine
4–5 tbsp	Ghee or sunflower oil
½ tsp	Black mustard seeds
A decent pinch	Asafoetida
10–12	Curry leaves
4–5 heaped tbsp	Green peas
3–4 medium	Green chillies
250–300 g	Good basmati rice
½ tsp	Turmeric powder
1 heaped tbsp	Cashew nuts (broken into pieces)
As required	Water
1–2 heaped tbsp	Butter or ghee
A handful	Fresh coriander (chopped)
	Fresh grated coconut (This is for garnish, if you don't have access to it don't worry)
As desired	Salt

4. If you can get the tendlis, or tindoras as they are also known, wash, snip the two tips and then cut lengthways into four. (The tendli has a sticky sap stuck to it normally. It is sold in supermarkets these days and is imported from Kenya into the UK.)

5. Wash the potatoes and aubergine and cut into cubes.

6. In a casserole add the oil or ghee and heat to a slight haze.

7. Add the mustard seeds and, as soon as they crackle, the remaining cumin seeds and the asafoetida.

8. As soon as the crackling (popping) stops add the curry leaves and all the vegetables together.

9. Sauté for 5–6 minutes and then add the rice and the turmeric. Mix well.

10. Sauté for 3–5 minutes and add the powdered spices, the cashew nuts and the peanuts.

11. Spread everything out evenly in the pot and add enough water to cover the rice by just over 2.5 cm. Add salt now and taste the liquid.

12. Once the water comes to the boil reduce the heat to low, cover the pot and cook until the rice is fully cooked and dry.

13. Add the butter and coriander and mix gently but well. If you have any fresh grated coconut sprinkle it on the top before serving.

Dahi Bhaat (two)

Curd or Yoghurt Rice

Chef's Notes

- Though this rice is ever so refreshing and healthy to eat and digest it is often served as a medicinal diet and has always emerged a favourite when someone has an upset stomach, feels poorly, has a high fever, etc. Eaten on its own with a powerful or well-seasoned pickle or chutney it makes for an excellent midday meal, keeping the person light and well nourished.

- Once again this rice has many variations and I am being bold enough to put down my own version to which I am sure several 'Dahi Bhaat' practitioners will find cause for a difference of opinion. This is of south Indian origin, though eating curd and rice is not uncommon right across the regions.

Measurements	Ingredients
400–500 g	Rice (any except very glutinous)
2–3 tbsp	Sunflower oil
1 level tsp	Mustard seeds
½ tsp	Cumin
15–20 leaves	Curry leaves (shredded)
A decent pinch	Asafoetida
2 medium–large	Green chillies (not hot, finely chopped)
1 tsp	Ginger (minced)
1 medium	Tomato (diced small without pulp)
½ tsp	Lime juice
500–600 g	Yoghurt (preferably Greek)
1 tbsp	Fresh coriander (chopped)
1 heaped tbsp	Salt

Method

1. Boil the rice and drain then cool.

2. Heat the oil in a wok or kadhai and keeping a lid or a mesh ready add the mustard seeds.

3. Cover with the mesh and reduce the heat slightly.

4. As soon as the crackling diminishes add the cumin and the curry leaves. As soon as the cumin changes colour add the asafoetida and soon after the chillies and ginger.

5. Sauté for 1–2 minutes then add the tomato and lime juice.

6. After another 2 minutes switch off and remove from the heat.

7. Blend in the yoghurt and chopped coriander and then the rice.

8. Taste and season to your liking.

9. Serve with a hot pickle or chutney.

Bread 7

Breads of varying natures are found across the length and breadth of the sub-continent. When a Westerner thinks of bread they automatically visualise something soft, risen, well baked, either round or square or of a different shape but leavened no doubt in one way or another.

Indian breads have a unique character much unlike our Western counterparts in terms of taste, character and the huge variety. The knowledge and art of bread making in the sub-continent, for instance, is very basic to any cook, in fact it is the first thing a young girl learns from her mother.

Breads are always prepared fresh and hot for every meal or at best carried forward to the next meal. Stale bread is not eaten as a rule and in most households is considered unfit for consumption.

This traditional way of thinking means that the poor housewife in many cultures keeps making and feeding fresh chappaties, poories and the like for her husband and children or guests and then eats last, finishing the remaining bread with her food. No doubt in this modern middle-class society where most women also go to work in the cities, things are changing and one can even buy ready-made chappaties in packets and parathas frozen. This would be unheard of even 15 years ago and might even be considered as a degeneration of our culture and heritage.

The variety of bread is immense, from the humble chappati and roti to the various naans and parathas. Each in turn has several varieties and one can say that in the entire sub-continent there would be no less than 1,000 or so varieties of breads eaten and consumed daily.

Dough for one bread will differ from the dough for another in its composition of fat and liquid, the type of flour used, whether or not 'Khameer', the leavening agent, is used or not, flavourings, the list goes on.

The method or style of making will also alter the characteristics of the bread, be it dry cooked, griddled, made in the tandoor or baked underground or in an oven.

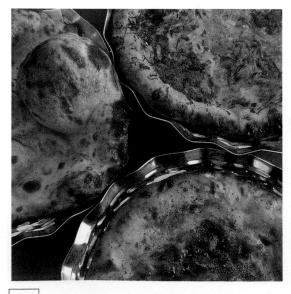

Most Indian breads are not leavened and do not represent the kinds of breads we are used to seeing in the West. Even the naan, which is synonymous with Indian restaurants around the world, is very lightly leavened with baking soda.

Most sub-continental households will eat bread daily; however, the vast majority of it is made from whole-wheat flour.

It is only recently that a woman would have to buy the wheat, clean it and then take it down to the local flourmill to have it milled. It is still a common feature in towns and villages where modern society's laziness or demand for convenience shopping has not yet reached.

Most of the breads cooked daily have to be eaten fresh and on the day, due to the nature of preparation and the low additives in the flour to keep it soft and supple. The breads that have been made using herbs, spices or chopped vegetables or blended with other flours are quite flexible in their nature and will not taste bad or become too hard the following day. These are often eaten with spicy and hot chutneys and pickles.

Normally the shortening such as ghee, butter and oil when added to flours makes them more supple and soft, which makes them longer lasting. However, the quality of the flour and the shortening used are of extreme importance. Chappaties, poories, etc., when made without any shortening such as oil, butter or ghee are served from the griddle or fryer to the table and as such will not keep. This is due to the absence of fat. The same applies to yeast-leavened breads – they are usually very crusty but soft on the inside and as soon as they turn stale or a day old they are no fun to eat.

The phulka or fulka is one type of chappati made and eaten immediately. The chappati in India is much thinner and is normally lifted from the griddle and placed directly over the fire to puff. A little melted ghee or butter may be applied and then it is served.

As a child I spent a few years in my maternal uncle's home where my mother was born. This was a little town in Madhya Pradesh on the border with Rajasthan and phulkas were a daily routine. However, school began at 6.30 am and breakfast before leaving home was yesterday's cold phulka with cream and sugar sprinkled over it and a big mug of hot milk. The phulkas were always crumbly and flaky but once you got used to the taste they were quite enjoyable.

Indian breads are not necessarily wheat-flour dominated. Breads are also made from corn, various kinds of skinned and milled lentils, chickpea flour, millet and rice flour, all depending upon the region and what is grown in the area. Corn chappaties are nothing but tortillas and in India several varieties are made. In the region I spoke of above, corn grows in abundance and papads, or pappadum as they are better known in the UK, are also made from corn meal. Food is cooked with corn meal and so on.

Most breads that do not contain wheat flour are quite difficult to make, especially when rolling (or pinning) out. As there is no gluten in the other flours the dough breaks up and is not supple to handle. Women across the sub-continent have developed tremendous skills in doing this and more often than not a rolling pin is not used and they will pin out a perfect disc with just their palms and not a tear or crack in sight.

Therefore remember practice is the key and, moreover, patience. Do not lose it when making chappaties, parathas etc.: perseverance will bring you immense joy.

Another valuable point to remember is that all types of flour do not necessarily absorb water equally. Even the same brand of flour may have a different intake simply because the grain is different, was harvested differently, and so on. All flours are different and will behave so. Experience will tell you when you have the perfect dough.

Therefore begin by adding a little water at a time until you have the right consistency. Follow a recipe by all means but use the liquid content as a guideline and work your way through the recipe.

Most Indian bread is designed to be eaten with your fingers. Sub-continental Indians, in particular the vegetarian community, break the bread and pick up the food in the bread by using one hand only. The other hand is kept free of food to be able to drink water with clean palms or serve food. The deftness with which this is done is a sight to behold and the neatness and tidiness of it all too.

Breads are a mainstay of the cuisine in general, though in very few regions it can be called the staple food, the same as rice. Since rice also vies for its place in staple diets we can say that both bread and rice play an equally important role in the daily diet of an average household in the sub-continent of India.

The chapters on breads and rice therefore do not necessarily do justice to the huge variety and diversity that the sub-continent has to offer and it is simply not possible to do much more than we have. An entire book may need to be written to simply cover the hundred or more recipes on rice and breads of the sub-continent.

One thing is for certain: bread making is an art which gets better with experience and practice.

Chappaties

Chef's Notes

- There can be no absolute recipe for chappaties. It is merely a matter of experience and how well you understand the dough you are preparing. A guideline recipe is given to ease your initial frustrations.

- Do remember that even the famous chefs and people such as myself with 20 years of experience cannot always roll out smooth, round chappaties as well as our mothers or wives can. This will give you some confidence when you end up plotting the world in different shapes. In hotels and restaurants throughout India where you see chappaties on the menu there is always a specialist employed.

Method

1. Place the flour with the oil mixed in, in a rimmed tray or a large bowl and by adding a little water at a time knead into a firm smooth ball.

2. Knead well for a few minutes until the dough does not stick and feels firm to the touch but not hard.

3. Cover with another bowl or cling film and set aside for 1–2 hours.

4. Divide equally into 2.5cm balls.

5. Heat the griddle and if using ghee melt some in a bowl and place a teaspoon into it, unless you prefer to use a pastry brush.

6. Place each ball on a floured surface and flatten with your palm or fingers.

Measurements	Ingredients
250 g	Wholewheat flour (sifted with 1 level tsp salt)
1 tbsp	Oil (warmed, to be mixed into the flour after sifting while still warm)
As needed	Cold water
As needed for coating one or both sides of the chappati	Ghee or oil
Tawa or flat griddle	

7. With a rolling pin, roll out into a round until 1.5–2mm thick.

8. Dust off any excess flour on the chappati and place it flat on the griddle or tawa.

9. Flip over after 30 seconds or so, apply the ghee on one side and flip over again.

10. If the tawa is too hot the chappati will brown instantly.

11. A good chappati is one that does not show burn marks but cooks through.

12. When done fold over into half and place in a container with a lid.

13. At home we first place a cloth inside the container to avoid steam softening the chappati. You may use a Tammy cloth or paper towel.

14. With experience and after making chappaties a few times the shapes will improve and so also will the roasting process. What you will achieve no doubt is a tasty bread that is suitable for most kinds of foods as an accompaniment. Good Luck.

Makki Ki Roti

Corn Meal Roti

Chef's Notes

- Whereas certain regions of India such as the Punjab and parts of Rajasthan have a particular culture for eating Makki Ki Roti, other regions will prepare them from time to time. This bread is also a typical feature of the harvest festival of Punjab. Indians have been making corn meal rotis for centuries, however it is the advent of the Mexican corn tortilla that has made corn meal bread so popular and it is often difficult to explain to people that Indians too have been making corn meal breads for hundreds of years.

- A simple recipe is given below. However, rolling out the dough balls is the key and care and attention will need to be given. Since corn has no gluten the dough breaks up and cannot hold itself so you will have to make them one at a time. This means each chappati has to be made from scratch. Don't be put off, though, it does not take as long as you may imagine.

Method

1. Sift the flour and mix in the salt or sift together. You will need a medium-holed sieve because a fine one will not be useful here.

2. Remove a small amount of the flour to make one chappati or divide the flour into more or less equal portions on the work surface and take one small mound at a time.

3. Make a stiff dough by adding very little water at a time.

4. Mix and knead.

5. Put the griddle on a low heat.

6. Grease the griddle well with the butter or ghee and place the dough ball in the middle.

Measurements	Ingredients
450–500 g	Maize flour (use medium grain corn meal, much like that used for polenta)
1½–2 tsp	Salt
200 ml plus more if required	Water
2 heaped tbsp	Butter (melted) (use ghee if you prefer)

7. With your flattened palm now flatten the dough ball by pressing down in the middle and outwards until you have a thin pancake-sized chappati. Remember that the griddle gets quite hot so keep your palm well opened. You will also need it well opened to flatten the ball well.

8. Once flattened flip the dough over gently and then cook until you have the desired colour on both sides

9. Apply more butter or ghee if you like.

10. Repeat until you have finished the dough.

11. Best eaten with spinach or mustard greens known as 'Sarson ka Saag' meaning spinach from mustard greens.

Masala Bhakhri

Paratha-like Bread made with the addition of Spices

Chef's Notes

- Bhakhri is made in several different ways. One is the Gujerati way in which spices are not added. The Maharashtrian way would include spices. This is a simple in-between style and is one of those breads that you can even use stale by re-griddling to a crisp texture. Use the recipe for parathas to make the Bhakhri after the dough is kneaded. However, it can be simply pinned out in discs and griddled with a little extra oil when being cooked.

Method

1. Sieve the flour with the turmeric, chilli powder, salt and the asafoetida.

2. Rub in the oil or butter along with the cumin seeds.

3. Add the yoghurt and mix it in well.

4. Knead to form a firm yet smooth dough. If the dough is too hard and does not come together, add a little yoghurt to achieve the right consistency

5. Leave covered for at least 1 hour after kneading.

6. Knead again and roll out into a long sausage.

7. Divide into 10–12 equal portions.

8. Try to roll them out like parathas. Naturally this means a lot of extra fat being used and you may prefer simply to pin them out into discs and griddle them with the addition of oil or ghee to get a crisp texture and even colouring.

Measurements	Ingredients
500 g	Wholewheat flour
½tsp	Turmeric
1 tsp	Chilli powder
1½ tsp	Salt
Pinch	Asafoetida (optional)
3 tbsp 2 heaped tbsp	Oil or Butter
1 tsp	Cumin seeds (powdered coarsely in a mortar)
120 g	Yoghurt (use live yoghurt if you can)
50–100 g	Oil for griddling (use as desired)

9. Bhakhris can be refrigerated if left over and eaten days later by simply reheating them on a hot griddle.

10. They are fantastic eaten with thick yoghurt.

Masala Poori

Poories with Spices

Chef's Notes

- Once again we are in a similar situation with a recipe. A masala as we know by now is a combination of spices and condiments and naturally an item with the word 'masala' attached to it is open to variations. This is a typical recipe for crispy spiced poories, but you can experiment and try it out with different flavoured spicing.

- A poorie, poori or puri is a fried chappati of sorts. Poories come in various shapes and sizes but what they have in common is the frying process, which is constant. Poories can be soft or crisp it all depends on the recipe and the application to food. It can be a snack or it can be part of a main meal. Also poories are a matter of trial and error so do not give up simply because you did not get them right the first time. I can assure you that I am no champion myself and can guarantee that my wife can make them better than me any day. It's all a matter of practice and the first few will not always be good or even shapely for that matter.

Measurements	Ingredients
250 g	Plain white flour
2 heaped tbsp	Fresh coriander (chopped, including stalks)
1½ tsp	Salt
2 medium	Green chillies (finely minced)
1 tsp	Pomegranate seeds (crushed, available in Indian stores in the UK)
½ tsp	Peppercorns (crushed or powdered coarsely in a pepper mill)
½ tsp	Red chilli powder
½ tsp	Cumin (roasted and crushed)
1 tbsp	Butter (melted) or ghee or oil
5–7.5 cm deep in container	Oil for deep frying

Method

1. Sift the flour with the salt in a large steel bowl or in a small dough mixer if you have one.

2. Add all the other dry ingredients and then rub in the shortening (butter, ghee or oil).

3. Add water little by little and begin kneading. Since you need to make a very firm dough, make sure the water is not just poured in on presumption. Knead and add as you go along.

4. Once the dough is formed smooth but firm, take it out and keep it covered in a bowl for 15–20 minutes.

5. Pour the oil in the container in which you are going to fry the poories. At the same time get ready a strainer, some paper kitchen towel spread on a tray in which you will place the poories, your slotted or holed frying spoon, etc. Also remember when frying that you must keep anything flammable or awkward out of the way to prevent accidents as well as keeping the surrounding area tidy and uncluttered.

6. Pin or roll out the dough to approximately 2.5 mm thick or less if you can. Dust the surface lightly with flour if you need to.

7. Heat the oil until hot.

8. Cut out discs of the pinned dough of approximately 5–7.5 cm diameter with a cutter and fry no more than two or three at a time (you can cut them smaller if you like).

9. The idea is to let them puff. For this you need to hold them down in the hot oil for a few seconds and then release them. Flip them over as soon as they bloat, colour lightly and remove quickly as they will cook in seconds.

10. Remember the oil has to be hot. One way to judge is to put in a poorie and see if it rises to the surface immediately. If not the oil is not hot enough and you will get poories that are oil saturated.

11. Drain and serve hot. Enjoy with sweet chutney.

Missie Roti

Chappati with Chickpea Flour and Spinach

Chef's Notes

*   A few variations of this chappati exist, for instance some add plain white flour, some add wholewheat flour and some add cornflour (ground corn). This could be due to local regional staples. Corn is used commonly in some parts of the sub-continent of India because it is the staple crop of the region. The Mexicans may have glorified 'Tortillas', but various forms of this famous bread are commonly prepared in the Punjab, Rajasthan and Madhya Pradesh where corn grows extensively. The recipe below combines all three flours as I like it that way, however you can alternate flours or use any two as available. This one is a popular delight.

Method

1. Sift all three flours together with the salt in a large basin or a small dough mixer if you have one.

2. Add the warm oil to the flours and blend it in well.

3. Now add the spinach and onions and knead.

4. Form a firm dough with as much water as is needed. Remember that all flours vary and some absorb more water and some less.

5. Once the dough is smooth and well kneaded form into a large ball and leave covered for at least 30 minutes. This may soften the dough and this is fine, but if it gets too soft you may need to add some chickpea flour to make it dry again.

227

6. Now make the dough into balls the size of a plum and place on a dusted surface.

7. For the rolling process you now need to practise the turn and fold method. This process is similar to rolling out puff or flaky pastry.

8. Pin one ball out until it is approximately 3.5 mm thick. Apply some oil or melted butter to the surface with a brush and sprinkle with a little flour. It need not be round, oval is just as good.

9. Fold the two edges over, apply some more melted butter and flour and fold over again.

10. Once the pinned roti has become long, stretch it a bit and then hold it between the thumb and forefinger of one hand. Using the thumb and forefinger of the other hand, gradually start to roll it back.

11. You must try to fold layer over layer; in short your roti is wound up like a flat pinwheel. Do this to all the balls you have made.

Measurements	Ingredients
250 g	Chickpea flour
150 g	Wholewheat flour
100 g	Plain wheat flour
1½ tsp	Salt
1½ tbsp	Sunflower oil (warm)
40–50 leaves	Fresh baby spinach (finely chopped)
150 g	Red onion (finely chopped)
200–250ml	Water
2 tbsp	Melted butter
	Sunflower or rapeseed oil as desired when baking on the griddle.
	Tawa or griddle

12. When ready to start cooking, place the griddle on the cooking surface and heat over a medium flame.

13. Roll out your roti balls now. Use flour to dust if you need to, but dust off any excess flour before placing them on the griddle. The roti need be no thinner than 2.5–3.5 mm thick.

14. Once ready put the roti on the griddle and let the side facing the heat colour to a light brown. While this is happening you can begin to roll the next one.

15. Flip the roti over and apply a little melted butter to the surface.

16. Once the other side is browned flip over and apply some butter on this side too. Now flip over once or twice and remove onto a plate or dish with a clean paper kitchen towel at the bottom to absorb any sweating.

17. You may prefer to wipe the surface of the griddle with a paper towel before putting the next roti on.

18. Finish all and either cover the chappaties with a kitchen towel placed on the top, or serve as done. These will keep well and can be reheated later in a warm oven or very quickly in the microwave. They are also very good eaten cold.

Bhatura

Chef's Notes

- The bhatura is a poori made with refined white flour rather than wholewheat flour.

- It is normally larger and heavier. It is eaten as an accompaniment to Channa Masala or Aloo ki Subzi, for example. One or two per person are normally enough, depending on the size of the bhatura as well. My favourite is to fill the bhatura with an onion cachumber and eat that with yoghurt. The recipe given here is very workable indeed and don't fret if you do not always succeed. Bhaturas are temperamental and will give you the intermittent pleasure of getting the perfect one, well puffed and golden brown. However, even the flat ones will taste just as good.

- The only drawback is that you will have to give yourself time for Bhaturas. Make the dough in the morning and make the Bhaturas in the evening.

Method

1. Sift the flour with the salt and the baking powder. If using fine caster sugar add this as well.

2. Beat the egg into the yoghurt in a bowl, add the hot milk, granulated sugar and 2 tbsp of hot water.

3. Gradually add this mixture into the flour and start kneading.

4. If the dough is too hard add a little more water but only 1 tbsp at a time.

5. Knead well to form a smooth, soft and supple dough.

6. Apply butter to your palms and knead to form a large round ball.

7. Place the ball in a bowl, cover with a damp cloth and set aside for 6–8 hours to prove. The dough has to be left at room temperature and not in the refrigerator.

Measurements	Ingredients
400 g	Plain white flour
½–¾ tsp	Salt (castor or granulated)
¾ level tsp	Baking powder
1 heaped tsp	Sugar
1	Egg
100 g	Yoghurt
1–2 tbsp	Hot milk
A few tbsp as needed	Water (hot)
A little to grease your palms	Butter or ghee
	Oil for deep frying

8. To make the final product you must have everything ready, i.e. the oil in a wok or kadhai for frying, a slotted or frying spoon, a colander for removing the Bhaturas placed over a bowl, dusting flour, rolling pin and, of course, the food with which they are to be served.

9. Remove the dough from the bowl and gently smooth it.

10. Divide the dough into equal sized balls. You can decide on the size so that is left to your discretion. Do not overwork the dough. Set the balls aside for 30 minutes or so to overcome the agitation.

11. Heat the oil to almost smoking point.

12. Roll out each ball using only as much flour as needed to stop the rolling pin from sticking.

13. Pin out to about 3.5 mm thick.

14. Fry in hot oil one at a time until golden brown and puffed.

15. Bhaturas may not need to be flipped over but more often than not this has to be done. In restaurants and large kitchens deep oil is always available so it is easy to fry. In the home you may not have that advantage so flipping over may be necessary. However, one idea that works is to push the bhatura with your frying spoon and spin it at the same time. This motion of them spinning in the hot oil will make them puff up quicker and look nicer. If, however, the rolling out is not even, you will have thick edges and a very thin centre and no ballooning.

Mooli Aur Pyaz Ki Roti

White Radish and Onion Roti

Chef's Notes

• In India rotis and parathas are made by adding several vegetables to the flour and forming the dough, thereby adding flavour and giving each a distinct character.

Method

1. Take all the ingredients including the oil and rub them well into the flour.

2. Add a little cold water at a time to form a firm, pliable dough.

3. Knead for 5–6 minutes until the onions and radish have had enough time to give off their juices.

4. If after doing that the dough gets sticky or too soft, add a little flour until you get the desired consistency. Do not be alarmed if the dough takes in more flour than called for. Sometimes the onion can have more moisture depending on its age and the same may go for the radish. The idea, however, is for both to give off their juices to flavour the dough.

5. Rest the dough for at least 30 minutes before dividing it equally into 4 cm round balls.

6. Take the tawa or flat griddle pan and slowly warm it.

Measurements	Ingredients
250 g	Wholewheat flour (sieved)
1 tsp	Salt
1 small	White radish (peeled and finely grated)
1 small–medium	Onion (finely minced)
1 tbsp	Fresh coriander (chopped)
1 small	Green chilli (finely chopped)
1 tbsp	Oil (for the dough, as needed for the tawa when roasting)

7. Take the balls and, after dipping the tips of your fingers in oil, press down firmly on each ball so that it is flattened but covered with oil.

8. Sprinkle a little flour on each ball.

9. Dust the platform or board with flour then take one ball and roll it out as round as you can get to approximately 4 mm width. The chappaties have to be slightly thick otherwise they would crack because of the onions and mooli.

10. Dust off any excess flour from the surface and slap the roti onto the griddle. Do not make the pan too hot as this will result in the roti browning before it is cooked.

11. Flip over once you notice that it is leaving the base of the pan.

12. To make any chappati you must have a flat spoon like a fish slice (this is perfect) so that you can loosen the bread by placing the slice under the chappati and gently moving it round.

13. Sprinkle a little oil on the first side flipped over before you have to flip it over again, to give it a crisp surface and also get it to cook better.

14. When you get an even colour on both sides remove to a plate.

15. You do not have to brown the chappaties thinking that they are only cooked when so. The dough is pinned out flat, therefore 1–2 minutes on each side are often more than enough, even if you do not have a brown colour.

16. What you will definitely get is brown spots all over, which is healthy unless you are a young Gujerati bride demonstrating your skills to the future in-laws, in which case these are forbidden and a certain show of poor cookery skills.

Paratha/Parotha/Prantha

Chef's Notes

- This is a layered chappati with a great deal more fat added to it.

- The idea of making a paratha is that the bread must open out in layers, or rather the layers of rolling must separate. Naturally the layers need to be well made and the fat and flour between each layer must be perfectly done.

- I will try my best to explain how to do it but if you have had any experience in making puff or flaky pastry you will have an understanding of layering. Also remember that when eating and enjoying a paratha one does not also think about calorie intake. With parathas there is no 'good for health' label.

- This recipe is not long; however, due to the multiple instructions I have given to make things easier; it seems rather longish.

Measurements	Ingredients
400 g	Whole wheat flour
½ tsp	Salt
3–4 tbsp	Sunflower or rapeseed oil
200–300 ml	Warm water
100 g	Butter (softened)
	Plain flour (for dusting and sprinkling)
	Oil or ghee (for griddle)

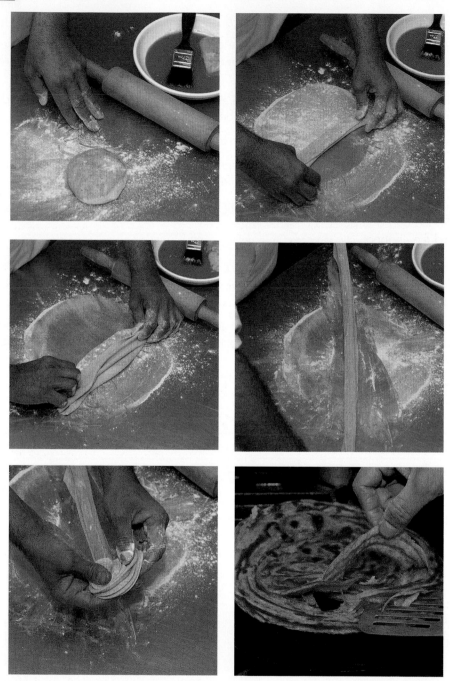

Method

1. Sift the flour and salt together in a large bowl or a thaali or use a small dough mixer if you have one.

2. Gently rub the oil into the flour.

3. Pour in the water a little at a time to make a smooth, supple but firm dough.

4. If using your hands to knead, rub some butter, ghee or oil on your palms and then knead for 10–12 minutes. Set aside for at least 30 minutes.

5. Knead again for 2–3 minutes.

6. Now divide the dough into 8–10 even balls.

7. Roll them in your palms until smooth.

8. To roll out and form a paratha you need to remember that layers are what we want once the bread is griddled.

9. Pin out the ball to approximately 12.5 cm in diameter, making sure that the rolled dough is evenly pinned out, but do not worry about it being perfectly round. That will take some practice.

10. Apply a thin layer of the softened butter all over the rolled sheet and lightly sprinkle some flour over it.

11. Now fold the chappati into a concertina, apply butter again and sprinkle flour.

12. Now twist the narrow end and press down onto the palm to form a twisted yet circular dough ball. Roll out again.

13. Do not knead or handle too much as body heat will disperse the butter inside and the layers will not separate.

14. Griddle on a medium tawa or griddle. If too hot the outside will burn and the inside will not cook well.

15. When griddling you must apply the oil or butter to the surface a little at a time until you get a beautiful golden brown colour and you can see the layers separating.

16. Eat with plain yoghurt.

17. Parathas are made in several different ways. Stuffing them is one of the most common and enjoyable ways of eating them. For stuffing, however, you do not need to go through the process of layering. You can either stuff the dough ball from the base and then roll again into a ball and pin out or you can make two thicker chappaties and sandwich between them a stuffing of mashed spiced potatoes or other finely chopped vegetables with spices, radish grated and blended with fresh coriander, green chilli, salt and lime juice, chopped chicken tikka, lamb, etc. The list is endless – all you need is imagination and to make sure that the bits are almost minced.

Soya Bean Flour Chappati

Chef's Notes

- This is ideal for the person allergic to gluten or the coeliac.

- Soya bean chappati will keep well if wrapped inside a clean cloth or napkin and kept in an airtight container. To do this place the napkin or towel over the mouth of the container and spread it out. Place each chappati one on top of the other until you have finished and then fold the towel over the chappaties and cover with the lid. The cloth stops sweating inside the container from spoiling the chappaties and making them soggy. The steam created and the dampness in the towel will also help to keep any chappati soft. Do this for any and every chappati you make.

Method

1. Sift the flour with the salt into a large basin or dish, or onto a clean work surface.

2. Rub in the ghee, butter or oil.

3. Next rub in the crushed carom or lovage seeds and the cumin. To crush you can gently roast the seeds and then crush to a coarse powder in a mortar. It only takes a few seconds.

4. Add the hot water gradually until you have a clean dough.

5. Do not overknead, as it is not necessary, but just until the flour has absorbed all the water and the dough is not sticky.

Measurements	Ingredients
200 g	Soya bean flour
½ tsp	Salt
1 heaped tsp 2 tsp	Ghee, butter or Oil
¼ tsp	Lovage/carom seeds (crushed in a mortar)
¼ tsp	Cumin seeds (crushed in a mortar)
4–5 tbsp	Hot water

6. Cover and set aside for 30–40 minutes.

7. Divide the dough into 8–10 equal balls.

8. Keep your griddle ready to put the chappati on a medium heat.

9. Pin out on a lightly floured surface and griddle as desired.

10. Remember that if you are making this for coeliacs, use only soya flour for rolling out.

11. This same dough also makes very nice soya poories. Instead of griddling them you could fry them instead.

12. Enjoy and use some other variation in your dough next time, such as chopped coriander, crushed peppercorns, finely chopped green or red chilli, and so on.

Pickles and Chutneys

8

Pickles and chutneys are the mainstay of the cuisine of the Indian sub-continent. Unlike in the UK, where we see them being eaten with papads/pappadums in restaurants, pickles and chutneys are eaten with the main meal.

Mostly the fresh chutneys are eaten with snacks, etc. and used as dips or condiments. Pickles and chutneys are supposed to add flavour and zest to the food you are eating and for this most households take huge pride in their own recipes and secret ingredients.

It is a tradition in every community to make chutneys and pickles from fruits and vegetables in season, for the forthcoming year. Housewives are seen making their selections in the raw mango season, for instance, knowing full well that the mangoes they desire will last for only a few weeks before the season is out or they are sold out. The housewife knows which carrots to buy for pickling or which radish is best.

The art of pickle and chutney making is mind-boggling and the limitations endless. Jars and jars of pickles in the making can be seen on sun-facing balconies and terraces containing different concoctions for the same fruit, and of course, the family speciality too.

The love of preserves is endless and no meal is complete without some condiment on the table.

Young turmeric, ginger, garlic, onions and several roots and tubers do not miss the scrutiny of the ever-watchful housewife who will take a batch home to alter their compositions into delicious, tongue-tingling and flavourful preserves.

The other chutneys are the dry purées. These are hot and mostly have a zing. They are often eaten with dry foods or with snacks.

Then there are the wet purées. These are always of fresh herbs and spices and are eaten either on the day or within a day or two. Freshness for these is the key and a little quantity is made daily as per the needs of the family and the food being prepared.

Some pickles and chutneys are preserved for well near or over a year before the jar is opened with great pride and joy.

Pickles and chutneys can also be made without the power of the sun and are cooked instead. Some of the recipes provided are ideal for cooking and these too should keep very well. Spice balancing is essential and crucial to the very making of the pickle or chutney. Any imbalance can alter the taste and flavour and sometimes spoil the product.

An entire book on the preserving techniques and preserves of the Indian sub-continent could not depict the immense variety and diversity of styles, flavours, etc., and we have been prudent here and brought you just a small handful to try and enjoy.

Bharaela Murcha Nu Achaar/Athanu

Whole Stuffed Chilli Pickle

Measurements	Ingredients
1 tbsp	Fenugreek seeds
2 heaped tbsp	Mustard seeds
1 tsp	Asafoetida
5–6	Cloves
5 cm	Cinnamon/cassia
3–4 tbsp	Sesame seeds
3 tbsp	Salt
2 tbsp	Sugar
1 kg	Chillies (short and thick)
500 ml	Oil

Chef's Notes

- Chilli pickles are enjoyed all over the sub-continent. The chillies differ in size, shape and, above all, in strength. There are numerous types of chilli pickle but this one is easy, quick to prepare and interesting.

Method

1. Lightly roast the spices and the sesame seeds.

2. Powder them finely with the salt and the sugar.

3. Wash and dry the chillies.

4. Slit them down the middle taking care not to cut them open and not letting the knife go through the other side.

5. Fill each chilli with the powder and put them in a large steel or a glass bowl.

6. Heat the oil in a pan until it begins to smoke.

7. Cool slightly and pour over the chillies while still warm.

8. Keep the chillies in the jar with a cloth tied over the bowl for 4–5 days before bottling.

9. The chillies will be best to eat after a week of maturing at least. I would ideally give them 10–12 days before beginning to enjoy them.

Simple Carrot Pickle

Chef's Notes

- In the sub-continent a pickle is normally cured in the sun and then stored to be eaten the following year when the new fruit or vegetable comes back into season and a fresh batch is made for the following year. In the UK, however, sunlight is normally at a premium and systems have to be developed to compensate. The tempering or sizzling of spices and sometimes even cooking the vegetables will ensure that spoilage is minimised and longevity for the pickle is ensured.

Method

1. Peel the carrots and cut into 6 mm batons approximately 3.5–5 cm long.

2. Gently roast the mustard seeds, the fenugreek, the cumin, cinnamon/cassia and cloves.

3. When cold and crisp powder in a coffee grinder or a mortar and pestle.

4. Apply the salt to the carrot batons and set them aside in a bowl for a few hours.

5. Squeeze out all the water and place them in a steel bowl.

6. Heat the oil in a saucepan until it begins to smoke.

7. Switch off and after 1–2 minutes add all the spices.

Measurements	Ingredients
1 kg	Carrots
2 tbsp	Black mustard seeds
1 tsp	Fenugreek seeds
1 tbsp	Cumin seeds
5 cm	Cinnamon/cassia
5–6	Cloves
1½–2 tbsp	Salt
200 g	Sunflower, rapeseed or olive oil
1 level tbsp	Turmeric powder
2 tbsp	Chilli powder
2–3 tbsp	Sugar

8. Keep stirring to prevent them from burning and also to cool the oil rapidly.

9. Mix the sugar into the carrots and then pour in the oil with the spices.

10. Mix well.

11. When cold put in airtight jars and allow to settle for at least a week before eating.

12. The oil will gradually come to the surface and the pickle will gradually take its character.

13. Remember when eating that you do not immerse a wet spoon to remove the pickle. Also as soon as you have taken what you want, wipe the edges with a piece of dry paper towel and then seal again.

14. The pickle should get better with age and you may prefer to leave one of the jars for a few months just to experience the maturing taste developing.

Mixed Vegetable Pickle

Chef's Notes

- Recipes for both pickles and chutneys will vary right across the land and there will most certainly be a few hundred versions readily available if you ask the housewife. However, simplicity is the key and adaptability is an issue for us all.

- Here is a simple recipe but it has an overnight aspect to consider.

- For this pickle use vegetables such as carrots, cauliflower, courgette or tindoras, peppers, even beetroot, turnip and swede.

Measurements	Ingredients
1 kg	Mixed vegetables
3½ tbsp or more	Salt
18–20	Dry red chillies (Kashmiri are best)
5 tsp	Cumin seeds
3 tsp	Mustard seeds
12–14	Garlic cloves
2 level tsp	Fenugreek seeds
2 tsp	Turmeric
200 ml + 100 ml	Cider or malt vinegar
500 g	Oil
20–30	Curry leaves
250 g	Sugar

Method

1. Clean the vegetables, dice those that can be diced and cut the others into small florets.

2. Sprinkle with the salt, mix well in a large bowl and leave them covered for a day. If you have sunlight at the time, leave them in the sun.

3. Meanwhile get the masala ready. Grind the chillies, cumin seeds, mustard seeds, garlic, fenugreek and turmeric in 200 ml vinegar.

4. The following day drain the vegetables in a colander until all the water disappears.

5. Heat the oil and add the curry leaves.

6. Once they finish spluttering add the masala paste and fry for 5–6 minutes.

7. Add the sugar, the remaining vinegar and the drained vegetables.

8. Cook on a slow heat for 20–30 minutes then remove.

9. Bottle hot if possible and seal with a tight lid immediately.

10. Use as desired. If well made there is no reason why this pickle should not last a year.

11. Eat as a condiment with your main meals as pickles are supposed to be eaten.

Bhopla Na Cholta Ni Chutney

Chutney of Red Pumpkin Skin

Chef's Notes

- Often or mostly always this tasty outer covering of the pumpkin is discarded. However it is tasty if cooked well in a bhaji but one can also make, chutney or marmalade from it.

- This is a simple recipe in which the skin is ground to a paste with other ingredients.

Measurements	Ingredients
250 g	Pumpkin skin
3 tbsp	Ghee or oil
4–5 medium	Green chillies
200 g 3–4 heaped tbsp	Grated coconut *or* Desiccated coconut
1½ tbsp	Roasted peanuts
1 tbsp	Sesame seeds
1 tsp or more	Lime juice
1 tsp or more	Salt

Method

1. Chop the pumpkin skin, wash and drain.

2. In a frying pan add the oil or ghee and heat.

3. When hot sauté the skins until fully cooked, stirring regularly to prevent burning.

4. When cooked, mix in all the other ingredients and grind to a smooth paste in the grinder attachment of your blender.

5. Check the seasoning to suit and remove.

6. If necessary use a little vinegar or lime juice when grinding but not too much.

7. Store and use as a condiment with your meals. Preferably refrigerated. Otherwise increase oil by three times.

8. This chutney can also be used to stuff croquettes, etc.

Chayote or Chow-Chow Chutney

Chef's notes

- Chayote or chow-chow is a vegetable grown in abundance in India. It is cooked in several different ways and a chutney with chayote is simply delicious. This is a south Indian version and one that is easy and light. This is a fresh chutney and will keep for only a few days in the refrigerator.

Method

1. Wash and peel the chayote then cut into 1 cm dice.

2. Sauté the chayote pieces in a frying pan with 2 tbsp of oil on a medium heat. Remove and set aside.

3. In the same pan add the remaining oil heat and sizzle the mustard seeds. Remember to hold a lid or mesh over the pan so that the seeds don't pop out and disperse.

4. As soon as they pop reduce the flame slightly and add all the lentils, the red chillies and asafoetida and sauté until the lentils are browned slightly but do not let them burn.

5. Now put all the ingredients in a blender and purée to a paste, or use a mortar and pestle, which may be better considering you should not add any water and you don't want a very smooth paste anyway for this one.

6. If you do not get tamarind, pulp is available instead, use 1 tsp pulp.

7. Check the seasoning and eat with hot steamed rice and yoghurt, or with rice and curry or rice and daal.

Measurements	Ingredients
2 medium	Chayote or chow-chow
3–4 tbsp	Oil
1 tsp	Mustard seeds
2 heaped tbsp	White lentil
1 tsp	Split yellow peas
2–3 medium	Whole red chillies (snipped)
A decent pinch	Asafoetida
20 g	Tamarind (seedless)
1 tbsp	Fresh coriander (chopped)
½ – ¾ tsp	Salt

Fresh Green Chutney

Chef's Notes

- This is one of those chutneys that is made throughout the sub-continent of India and there are several versions (see page 14 for a variation). In short, green chutney means using fresh green ingredients with the exception of some dried spices, which may or may not be added. Green chutney is extremely versatile and will make an ideal accompaniment to several snack items as well as fresh chargrilled tandoor dishes.

- Since bunches of mint and coriander are not standard either by weight or size, I have taken the chopped route to simplify things.

Measurements	Ingredients
4–6 tbsp	Fresh coriander (chopped, wash and use stalks as well)
30–40 leaves	Fresh mint
4–5	Green chilli
4–6 cloves	Garlic
5 cm	Fresh ginger
1 tsp	Sugar
1 tsp	Salt
½ a lime	Lime juice

Method

1. Purée all the ingredients together in a blender until they form a smooth green paste.

2. Add a little water at a time if necessary for the blades of the blender to get a grip on the ingredients.

3. Too much liquid is not necessary.

4. Taste and use.

5. Green chutney can be refrigerated in a jar and will last well over two weeks if kept well and used carefully with a dry spoon and with the edges of the jar kept clean.

Green Coconut Chutney Parsee Style

Method

1. Add to the green chutney ingredients 300–400 g freshly grated coconut and ½–¾ tsp cumin seeds.

2. Purée as above using as little water as possible.

3. If fresh grated coconut is not available take 200 g desiccated coconut, soak in 100–150ml warm water and add when soft and rehydrated. The effect will not be like that of freshly grated coconut but this is one way of coming close to it.

4. Chillies and mint can be added and altered to taste.

5. We Parsees prefer the chutney to be rather minty and a bit on the hot and sour side.

6. It makes a great sandwich when applied with sliced boiled potato and tomato.

7. Parsees also eat this chutney with lentils and rice as an accompaniment.

A South Indian Variation of Green Chutney

Method

1. Make the green chutney (see page 241) and put in a bowl

2. Heat the oil until it forms a haze.

3. Keep a mesh or a loose lid ready then add the mustard seeds.

4. Hold the lid loosely over the pan to prevent the oil from splattering out and the mustard seeds from jumping out.

Measurements	Ingredients
2 tbsp	Oil
½ tsp	Mustard seeds
10–12	Curry leaves
1 heaped tsp	White lentil
A decent pinch	Asafoetida

5. Reduce the heat and add the curry leaves, white lentil and asafoetida.

6. As soon as the white lentil changes colour add this to the chutney and stir the contents in quickly.

7. The quick stirring in infuses all the flavours into the chutney.

8. This method will enhance the life of the chutney and also alter the flavour prepared in the green chutney recipe.

Fudina Ni Chutney

Mint Chutney

Method

1. To make a Gujerati-style mint chutney do the following to the recipe for green chutney (page 241).

2. Firstly double the quantity of mint to coriander.

3. Omit the cumin and the ginger from the recipe.

4. Add a little extra lime juice … and you have fresh mint chutney.

5. This chutney like the others will keep well if refrigerated and looked after.

6. It is good for serving with snacks or as an accompaniment to Indian meals.

Kolmi Nu Achaar

Prawn Pickle

Chef's Notes

- Several coastal communities of India make pickle with different types of seafood including mackerel, sardines, tuna, prawns, fish roe, shark, skate and so on.

- While we cannot give you a huge range of them, this simple prawn pickle can be adapted to suit other seafood too.

Method

1. Clean the prawns but do not wash the prawns in water. Instead, soak them in the malt or cider vinegar for 1–2 hours. Washing them will spoil the pickle but the vinegar will destroy most impurities.

2. Leave them in the vinegar until the rest of the preparations are ready.

3. Roast the spices and chillies gently on a griddle or frying pan then powder them in a mortar and pestle or a grinder.

Measurements	Ingredients
500 g	Raw prawns (cleaned)
250–300 ml	Malt or cider vinegar
12–14	Whole red chillies
1½ tsp	Turmeric powder
2 tbsp	Coriander seeds
6 tbsp	Sunflower oil
2 medium	Onions (finely minced)
1½ tbsp	Salt
2 tsp	Garam masala powder
8 tbsp	Tamarind pulp (thick)

4. Heat the oil and sauté the onions until deep brown.

5. Drain the prawns and put them in a casserole with a tight-fitting lid.

6. Add the spice powder, salt, garam masala and tamarind pulp then and pour over the oil and onions.

7. Cover tightly and cook on a medium heat for 15 minutes or so until the prawns have cooked fully and most of the water has evaporated.

8. Cool and pack in airtight jars.

8. This will keep in the refrigerator for months if care is taken. If left unrefrigerated it will last for about a month.

Lasan Ni Chutney

Simple Garlic Chutney Gujerati Style

Chef's Notes

- Here I will give you two different versions of garlic chutney, one Gujerati style and the other Maharashtrian. Both are hot and zingy.

- Garlic chutneys will keep in a jar for days. They can be used as a condiment to meals, an additive to food if you like or simply eaten with snacks. They are not difficult to make except that the grinding process may need imagination at times.

Measurements	Ingredients
20–24 cloves	Garlic
3–4 tbsp	Red chilli powder (coarse)
4 tsp	Sesame seeds
1½ tsp	Salt

Method

1. Grind all the ingredients to a fine paste.

2. A coffee grinder may do the trick if you stop every few seconds to scrape the sides with a spatula then start again. This is because sesame seeds give off their oil and make the mixture sticky, thereby making it stick to the sides and not fall in the path of the blades. Alternatively, grind in a mortar and pestle or on a chopping block using a rolling pin. The ingredients will also stick to the rolling pin but you can scrape them off and start again.

3. Grind until they form a thick fine paste and all the sesame seeds are fully ground.

4. The chutney will keep for months so it's well worth the hard work.

Lasun Chi Tikhat

Hot Garlic Chutney Maharashtrian Style

Method

1. Roast all the ingredients except the tamarind until the coconut, sesame seeds and peanuts are browned but not burnt.

2. Grind all the ingredients together until you have a smooth paste. You may need to use a coffee grinder or mortar and pestle as the sesame seeds give off their oil and stick to everything.

3. Store and use as desired.

4. This will last for several days if kept well.

Measurements	Ingredients
10–12 cloves	Garlic
200 g	Desiccated coconut
1 level tbsp	Cumin seeds
6–8 large	Dry red chillies
2 heaped tbsp	Sesame seeds
30–36	Peanuts
2 tsp	Salt
Form a ball the size of a large lime	Tamarind (dry)

Mango Chutney Goan Style

Measurements	Ingredients
1500 g	Mangoes (semi ripe but firm)
1 kg	Sugar
250 ml	Cider vinegar
150 g	Ginger
8 cloves	Garlic
6 tsp	Mustard seeds
4 tbsp	Red chilli powder
250 g	Sultanas or raisins
3–4 tbsp	Salt

Method

1. Peel and dice the mango.

2. Put it in a large casserole with the sugar and 190 ml cider vinegar and boil.

3. Purée the ginger and garlic with the remaining vinegar and half of the mustard seeds.

4. Once the mangoes, sugar and vinegar have come to the boil add all the ingredients and continue boiling until the mangoes are soft and fully cooked. The consistency will be thick and jam like.

5. If you have kept any empty jars cleaned, dried and ready, bottle while still hot or boiling and seal the jars.

6. Invert the jars for 1–2 minutes then cool upright.

7. Use as desired.

Sweets 9

Talk about 'the sweet tooth' and the sub-continent of India will feature at the very top of the list. Indians, and when I say Indians, I mean Indians, Pakistanis, Bangladeshis all included, simply enjoy sweets and will create an excuse to eat some or gift some or distribute some at any and every occasion. After food, before food, early morning with tea, you name it, the Indians have got it.

Whereas sweets dominate the culture, there are not many desserts in comparison and most are of a common nature.

When I say common, one has to try to visualise a landmass full of different cultures, cuisines, religions, languages, geographical differences and so on, each having a seriously sweet tooth. One wonders how the dessert has not become a vital part of the daily diet, at least in terms of the creativity.

Perhaps the housewife did not get enough time in between the chores and the cooking to create so many desserts as would be appropriate with such a creative and cuisine-oriented culture. Or perhaps sweets are so abundantly available that, even in the household, the women created more sweetmeats rather than desserts, sweetmeats being more versatile and bearing a longer shelf life in an ambient, domestic environment.

There are recurring combinations in the raw materials and ingredients used. However, variations abound.

Where sweets are concerned, you will find shops at every little distance, selling a huge array of multicoloured sweets that are very seriously made. Seriously, meaning a great deal of time, effort and energy is put into the manufacture, besides the high levels of skills needed to make them to perfection.

Sweet making is an art, as we all know, but in the sub-continent sweet-making techniques are complex and very intricate. Sweet making more often than not runs in the family and the skills are handed down from father to son.

One of India's most famous sweetmeat shops is in Old Delhi and has been in business in the very same location since the 1600s. The forefathers of the present-day owners were sweet makers to the Mughul courts. It is recorded in history that they catered to the courts of the Emperor Aurangzeb, though it is believed that the makers actually pre-dated that era.

Sweet making in the sub-continent is dominated by the use of milk. Though several hundred varieties exist that do not use milk as the prime ingredient, there are many more that do. Sweets are also made from every possible Indian fruit you can imagine and from vegetables such as pumpkin, squash, marrows, lentils and pulses, dried sap or gums of trees, berries and roots such as carrots, etc. You name it, the sub-continent's got it. The different types of fudge made in India are also hugely popular,

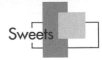

top among them the coconut fudge and the 'Haapshi Halwa' made with milk extracted from soaked wheat, plus buffalo milk. So great is the variety and the diversity that even the most knowledgeable among us will not know the extent to which this creativity extends. I, for one, am no expert at all, though I may be extremely fond of the hundreds of varieties we can sample each time we visit India.

The state of Bengal, for instance, is most famous for its traditional sweets. Here is the only place where you will notice that sweets are not so sweet but perfectly balanced. The Bengalis enjoy the privilege of being the very best sweet makers in the entire land and have introduced to the culture and cuisine some extremely fine specimens. Of course, most of these are milk dominated but the culture in Bengal is one of addiction. I remember distinctly staying at a famous hotel in Calcutta and my room being filled with platters of local sweets brought daily. Too many for one person to enjoy, so several friends and acquaintances made a feast in my room every day.

It is not uncommon to see certain popular sweets such as the veritable 'jalebi' and 'carrot halwa' eaten with tea first thing in the morning, particularly in winter to provide heat to the body. They are also considered tonics for the body during winter and in the north of the sub-continent this is common practice. Loving both of these and craving

them would make me hide from my aunt as a child before eating them in local shops, which she was not particularly happy about. This is in a town called Neemuch, where my mother was born in central India. My aunt, being extremely fussy about local hygiene standards, had banned us from eating from the streets, but the tastes and flavours and a glass of hot milk were too much for a young boy to withstand.

Two of the greatest gifts of Indian sweets from my town (now a city) are the 'gajak' and the 'milk cake'. Gajak is made by boiling raw cane sugar (jaggery) with sesame seeds or peanuts to a toffee consistency and then beating it while still piping hot on a marble tiled wall and platform until the seeds are completely crushed and enough air is incorporated to make it light and fluffy. This is then set and square impressions made. This results in a crisp yet flaky melt-in-the-mouth delicious sweet. However, this is only made between November and early March or until the cold lasts. One needs to know that all of the sub-continent is not hot throughout the year; the cold in the north is extremely severe and dry.

The milk cake is milk gradually condensed with sugar, which, at the appropriate moment, is poured into bread-tin-like moulds and cooled. The latent heat inside the cake begins to caramelise the milk and the sugar and you automatically get a multi-layered sweet, brown and pale brown in the centre and white on the outside ... superb is my verdict, addictive is the negative aspect of it, how they do it is simply masterful.

'Jalebi' is a crisp pinwheel, mostly orangeish in colour, and steeped in rose flavoured sugar syrup. It is made from a fermented batter, which is poured in a cloth bag in which a small hole has been made to act as a piping bag. The pinwheel is directly piped into a skillet of hot oil and it is then fried, picked up and immersed into the coloured and flavoured syrup for a few minutes. When removed it is beautifully crisp but sweet and finger-lickingly good. Very fine lacy and web-like jalebis are also made but these need more specialisation and are more often than not made at festive occasions only.

The sweets from the sub-continent need much control when trying out the myriad varieties at our disposal. They are mostly rich in their make up and naturally sweet. Addiction is not uncommon but one has to be health conscious in this stressful life we lead nowadays. Since most Indian sweets have a reasonable shelf life it is advisable to eat them in small quantities if buying a box full of assorted sweets.

Rose water is used in a number of these sweets. It is available in Indian and Greek or Cypriot stores and is a clear fluid in a longish bottle.

Sabu Daney Chey Aloney

Chef's notes

- A sweet made by both Maharashtrians and Goans alike, made from sago balls, milk and coconut milk.

- The sago balls should be available in most Indian stores as well as Filipino and some Chinese stores.

Method

1. Wash the sago balls lightly and allow to soak in water up to 2.5 cm over the top of the balls for 15 minutes.

2. Drain in a colander. Put in a thick-bottomed saucepan and add the milk and coconut milk.

3. Add the crushed cardamom.

4. Bring it gently to the boil, adding the sugar and salt.

5. Simmer, stirring regularly to prevent sticking at the bottom, until all the milk has been absorbed and the sago balls are swollen and translucent.

Measurements	Ingredients
100 g	Sago balls (Sabudana)
250 ml	Milk
100 ml	Coconut milk (use canned if you like. The rest can be frozen in a jar for future use.)
5	Green cardamom (pressed or crushed)
150 g or more	Sugar
A pinch or two	Salt
1–1½ tbsp 1–1½ tbsp	Ghee or Butter and oil
1 heaped tbsp	Sultanas
1 heaped tbsp	Cashew nuts

6. Meanwhile, heat the ghee or the butter and oil combination in a pan until hot. In the case of the butter, add it after the oil has warmed up. Do not allow to overheat.

7. Add the sultanas and cashew nuts and fry until the cashew nuts are a golden brown.

8. If there is oil in the pan then drain it over a strainer. If the oil is absorbed, empty the contents onto a plate covered with kitchen towel.

9. Check the sugar and taste at this stage.

10. You may add some vanilla essence if you like and better still add a few threads of saffron.

11. Take moulds the size of caramel custard moulds and butter them lightly, ensuring that all sides are coated.

12. Fill them with the mixture up to the level you desire and after a few minutes demould them onto a platter. This should be done prior to the mixture getting cold.

13. Garnish with chopped pistachios and almonds or sprinkle some nutmeg powder on top.

14. This is a very healthy dessert and in several parts of India it is given to nursing mothers. The preparation methods may vary from state to state. I strongly suggest that you use the recipe as a guide and use your own imagination later.

Alle Belle

(Pronounced Allay Bayllay)

Goan Coconut Pancakes

Chef's Notes

- This is a traditional Goan sweet and is thoroughly enjoyable with vanilla ice-cream when served warmed and lightly buttered. It can also be served with cream, however in Goa it is often eaten on its own.

- This filling is sufficient for 6 medium pancakes.

Filling	Ingredients
10–12 tbsp	Grated coconut (If using desiccated, soak in water before using)
1 tbsp	Sultanas
75 g	Palm molasses (or jaggery)
¼ tsp	Cardamom powder
¼ tsp	Nutmeg powder

Method

1. Mix the filling ingredients together gently and use it to stuff the pancakes.

2. Use any good sweet pancake recipe using plain flour. Alternatively the following is a good mix:

Pancakes	Ingredients
1 tbsp	Butter (melted and strained)
200 g	Plain flour
Pinch	Salt
1 tbsp	Caster sugar
150 ml	Coconut milk
As required	Cold water
A few drops	Vanilla essence
Pinch	Lemon rind (grated)

Method

1. Mix the butter into the flour along with the salt and sugar.

2. Add the coconut milk and a little water and mix well to a smooth pouring consistency.

3. Add the vanilla and the lemon zest.

4. Check the consistency and proceed to make your pancakes as you would normally.

5. Stuff and roll the pancake while it is still warm.

6. Brush pancakes with butter and heat prior to serving either on their own or with cream, custard or vanilla ice-cream.

Siru Paruppu Halwa

Chef's Notes

- A sweet made with moong daal, clarified butter and reduced/condensed milk. It is of South Indian origin and classically is rather rich. To suit modern stressful living, however, we have tried to adjust the recipe. If the halwa is well made there is every reason that it should stay very well and will keep at room temperature for up to a week.

- Halwas are good when eaten during winter and act as a source of energy. However, for a traditionally well-prepared halwa I would strongly recommend restraint when feeling peckish. Also in this recipe we are using convenience products, however, one is welcome to reduce and caramelise milk to the same quantity. Milk should generally be reduced by a third at least.

Measurements	Ingredients
500 g	Moong daal (also known as split green moong daal)
1 kg	Sugar
300–400 ml	Water
500 g	Ghee or unsalted butter
100 g	Cashew nuts (split)
50 g	Sultanas
2 450 ml tins	Evaporated milk
1 tin	Condensed milk (sweetened)
15 g	Cardamom powder

Method

1. Wash the moong daal and soak for approximately 1 hour.

2. Meanwhile make syrup from the sugar by adding 300–400ml water and boiling slowly in a saucepan until you have a one-string consistency.

3. Drain the daal and purée it to a smooth paste in a blender.

4. Heat the ghee or butter in a deep saucepan, approximately 3–5 litre capacity. If using butter remove as much of the liquid as possible from it before proceeding any further.

5. Once the fat is heated, fry the cashew nuts and the sultanas then drain and set aside.

6. If any residue remains in the pan clean it out then return the fat to the stove.

7. Add the moong daal and roast it well until it turns a pale golden colour. Remember that you have to stir and scrape it continuously so that it does not stick to the bottom.

8. When it gets a lovely roasted aroma add the evaporated and the condensed milk and keep cooking until the milks dry up. Do not allow the bottom to stick.

9. When almost dry add the syrup and cook until the sugar is all absorbed and the halwa begins to leave the sides of the pan.

10. Mix half the cashew nuts and all the sultanas in the halwa and add the cardamom powder.

11. Remove to a pie dish or a baking dish, flatten the top and garnish with the remaining cashew nuts.

12. Cool and cut the halwa into squares or diamond shapes before serving.

Banana Fritters

Chef's Notes

- An easy way to enjoy a delicious rum-spiked banana dessert. There are ways and ways, but try this for a quick dessert. However, do not use too much rum, otherwise the sauce will get bitter or taste too sharp.

- You can also use plantains but select absolutely ripe ones. This means the skin has to be completely black when buying.

Measurements	Ingredients
2 tbsp	Butter
1 tbsp	Oil (neutral)
4 large	Bananas (peeled and slit into half lengthways)
3 tbsp	Demerara sugar
2–3 tbsp	Black rum
150 ml	Single cream

Method

1. In a large fry pan melt the butter with the oil and bring it gently to a medium heat, taking care not to allow it to caramelise.

2. Add the bananas flat side down and sauté on each side for 1½–2 minutes or until pale golden on each side, unless they become soft and wilted in which case remove.

3. Portion out onto individual plates and keep warm in a previously warmed closed oven.

4. While removing the bananas take the pan from the heat. Return to the heat when emptied and increase the flame to just below high.

5. Add the sugar and then the rum.

6. When the sugar melts tilt the pan forwards a bit and ignite the rum with a lit match or a lighter and allow it to flame for a few seconds or until the flames die.

7. Keep shaking the pan continuously in a circular motion to prevent the sugar from forming lumps.

8. You may find the sugar caramelised into lumps sometimes. If that happens, remove from the heat, cool, add a little cold water, stir to dissolve the sugar and return the pan to the heat.

9. Add the cream and shake the pan in a circular motion continuously for a minute or so until the cream begins to boil.

10. Stir gently with a wooden spatula until the sauce begins to thicken a little. If that consistency suits you, remove and spoon equal amounts onto each portion of banana and serve.

Chawal Ni Kheer

Rice Pudding Parsee Style in its
Simplest Form

Chef's Notes

- Rice puddings have been adopted into the British cuisine naturally from the Indian sub-continent. Rice puddings, or Kheers as they are called, are commonplace, except for subtle changes in flavourings and each community's styles varying slightly. In the south these are known as Payasam.

- The Parsees, true to their Persian heritage, like it rather rich and full of the different flavours brought together by spices such as cardamom and nutmeg or cinnamon.

- Kheers are best eaten during the hot summer months as they are known to have a cooling effect on the stomach after a heavy meal.

- Here is a simple recipe that will help you to add oodles of flavour to the common rice pudding.

Method

1. Crack the cardamoms with the hilt of a chopper or in a mortar and pestle until the pods pop and the seeds get loose inside.

2. Take a casserole or a saucepan and gently heat it on a medium flame.

3. Add the ghee or butter and fry the cardamon and cinnamon.

4. As soon as you feel the spices have swollen a bit add the rice and then the water.

5. As soon as you see the water has been absorbed add the milk and continue to cook. This should take about 15 minutes or so, but make sure you stir well and scrape the sides clean with a spatula regularly. A flat wooden spatula is best as it can keep lifting off what is sticking at the bottom.

Measurements	Ingredients
6–8	White cardamons (or green)
2 heaped tsp	Ghee or butter
5 cm	Cinnamon cassia
200 g	Rice (thick short-grained or pudding rice) (wash well and drain)
600 ml	Water
1 litre	Rich, full fat milk
120–150 g (or more depending on personal tastes)	Sugar
½ tsp	Salt
150–200 g	Sultanas (long, light green)
1 tsp	Rose water
10–12	Almonds (blanched and slivered)
	Vanilla essence (optional)

6. Add the sugar and the salt and continue to cook until all sugar has been dissolved.

7. Feel the rice or eat a little to see if it is thoroughly cooked.

8. Add the sultanas and simmer for 2–3 minutes.

9. Remove and cool to room temperature.

10. Add the rose water and blend well.

11. Remove to a large bowl or individual bowls if serving individually, sprinkle with the slivered almonds and serve cold.

12. As a variation you can add saffron to the pudding and sprinkle some pink rose petals when serving.

Shahi Tukra

Fried Bread in Saffron Milk

Chef's Notes

- A not too difficult dessert made with fried bread and sweetened reduced milk.

Method

1. Heat the butter and oil in a flat pan or frying pan and fry the bread. Do not add too many pieces to the oil as it is likely to absorb too much fat and turn greasy.

2. Remove the fried slices onto a plate with paper towel so that any excess fat may be absorbed.

3. Heat the milk in a medium-sized casserole and bring to the boil.

4. Reduce the heat and simmer for 15–20 minutes or until it begins to change colour.

Measurements	Ingredients
2 tbsp	Butter
4 tbsp	Oil
4	Bread slices (crusts removed and cut in half)
500 ml	Milk
2 tbsp or less	Sugar
1 generous pinch	Saffron
½ tsp	Cardamom powder
1 tsp	Rose water
2–3	Almonds (sliced)
12	Pistachios (sliced)

5. Stir regularly with a flat wooden spoon or spatula and scrape the bottom each time to prevent pan burning.

6. Add the sugar and continue to cook the milk until the colour changes to a light brown and you get a nutty smell. When the milk is ready it will coat the back of the spoon like a thin custard.

7. Ideally you have to reduce the milk virtually by half.

8. Add the saffron and cardamom powder and simmer for a further 2 minutes.

9. Now add the rose water and check the taste. You should not need more sugar but if it is not as sweet as you like it add more and dissolve it in.

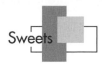

10. Place the bread slices in a flat platter and pour the milk over. Garnish with the sliced nuts and serve either warm or cold.

11. Ideally Shahi Tukras should be eaten the same day. I notice that if bits and pieces of bread break off and mix into the milk the taste is never as enjoyable. When the bread is yet slightly crisp and not fully soaked it is at its best. Therefore pour the milk over when warm just minutes before serving but giving it adequate time to absorb, 5–10 minutes should do it.

Shrikhand

Chef's Notes

- A strained yoghurt dessert served with hot poories or as it is.

- Shrikhand is a hugely popular Indian dessert. It is made across the length and breadth of the sub-continent. What makes them different from one place to the next are the flavouring, the addition of nuts and the sweetness.

Measurements	Ingredients
500 g	Fresh yoghurt (live full-fat curd)
3–4 tbsp	Caster sugar
1 tsp	Cardamom (crushed or coarse ground) powder
A few strands	Saffron (warmed and soaked in 1 tbsp milk)
1 tsp	Rose water
8–10	Blanched peeled almonds (sliced thinly)
8–10	Pistachios (sliced thinly)
1 tbsp	Charoli (a small nut used primarily between the states of Gujarat and Maharashtra)

Method

1. Place the curds in a clean kitchen cloth or muslin and tie the open end loosely.

2. Hang the bag over the kitchen sink or a bowl for 2–3 hours until all the liquid has drained out.

3. Remove into a large bowl and carefully scrape off any bits sticking to the cloth.

4. Beat well with a small whisk, making sure you scrape the edges with a spatula then beat again until smooth.

5. Beat in the sugar until it is completely dissolved.

6. Sprinkle the cardamom powder and mix it in.

7. Now add the saffron milk and rose water and taste.

8. If you need more sugar then remove a little of the Shrikhand and beat in the sugar until dissolved, then return to the bowl and whisk in.

9. Remove to the serving bowl of your choice then sprinkle with the nuts and chill well.

10. Serve as it is or with hot poories for dessert. Remember Shrikhand is not a light dessert and only small quantities are served.

Doodh No Rawo

Chef's Notes

- A Parsee-style semolina pudding that makes a simple, quick and very tasty dessert. Recipes differ from woman to woman, as is the tradition. Rawo is made on festive occasions and is served as a good omen.

- Please note that this is not a woman's recipe but a man's – mine. It looks dreary but let me assure you that semolina will never taste the same again for you.

Measurements	Ingredients
2 tbsp	Sunflower oil
6	Cashew nuts (unroasted, sliced)
6	Almonds (sliced thinly with skin)
6–8	Pistachios (unsalted)
1 tbsp	Sultanas
2 tbsp	Butter
100 g	Semolina (fine to medium, not too coarse)
3–4 tbsp	Sugar
600–750 ml	Milk (cold)
Pinch	Saffron (optional and not always necessary)
¼ tsp	Nutmeg powder
¼ tsp	Cardamom powder
¼ tsp	Vanilla essence
½ tsp	Rose water

Method

1. Take a small frying pan and add the oil.

2. Heat on a medium heat and gently fry the sliced nuts and sultanas.

3. As soon as the nuts have turned a light golden colour pour into a strainer placed over a medium-sized casserole to collect the extra oil and toss the contents lightly so that the latent heat is dispersed.

4. Drain well and remove onto a paper towel for all excess fat to be absorbed.

5. Add the butter to the drained fat.

6. Bring to a medium heat and as soon as the butter is melted and begins to foam add the semolina.

7. With a wooden spoon or flat spatula gently roast the semolina on a heat just above the minimum mark. Stir as continuously as you can. Leaving the semolina unstirred will make it burn in those spots that are in direct contact with the heat. This you do not want.

8. This will take around 7–10 minutes, sometimes more, and the semolina will begin to colour slightly.

9. Add the sugar and continue to roast for 4 more minutes. (You may or may not need more sugar, though I personally do not like it very sweet.)

10. Take it off the heat for just a few seconds then add the milk all at once and stir a bit faster now so that no lumps can form.

11. Continue to cook stirring gently for approximately 6–8 minutes until the semolina is cooked. Certain strains of wheat will absorb more milk, therefore if you notice that the rawo is becoming too thick, add more milk as desired.

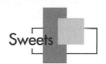

12. The end product is quite thick and it thickens further when cooled. The consistency to note when removing is that of a thick porridge.

13. It is often wise to make it rather thin when removing, as the semolina will always thicken when you are ready to serve.

14. Add all the remaining ingredients to the rawo when cooked except the fried nuts and sultanas. Cook for 1–2 minutes and check the flavouring. If more milk has been added the flavourings may need to be increased to suit your taste.

15. Remove to a serving bowl or dish and sprinkle with the fried garnish. Serve warm, however leftover rawo is great even the following day and is enjoyable cold as well.

16. You can garnish with a few rose petals. Most rose petals are edible and are widely used in India as garnish on sweets.

17. If adding saffron you must first roast the saffron gently in a small bowl or pan on a low heat, shaking the pan about to distribute the heat evenly. When the saffron strands are crisp they are ready.

18. Add the saffron at the same time you add the milk.

Lagan Nu Custard

Chef's Notes

- This a traditional Parsee-style baked custard is a must at festive dinners and at weddings. Its name translates as 'Wedding Custard'. It is rich and flavourful – and great on the calorie count.

Method

1. Heat the milk in a casserole and bring to boiling point.

2. When at boiling point reduce the heat and simmer or boil the milk gently for 1½–2 hours, keeping the sides clean at all time. To ensure this you need a pastry brush and chilled water. Immediately after the milk has risen to boiling point and you put it to a slow boil, clean the sides of the pan with the help of a wet brush. Do this every few minutes. Do not use a dripping brush, as that is likely to dilute the milk.

Measurements	Ingredients
1 litre	Milk (full cream)
100–150 g	Sugar
4	Eggs
1 tbsp	Rose water
½ tsp	Vanilla essence
½ tsp	Cardamom powder
½ tsp	Nutmeg powder
10–12	Almonds (sliced)
1 tbsp	Charoli (a nut typical to the sub-continent, available in Indian stores in the UK)
10–12	Pistachios (unsalted and sliced)

3. Ideally the milk should turn almost a dull nut colour and give off a nutty/toffeeish aroma.

4. Use a flat wooden spatula preferably to keep scraping the bottom so the milk is not allowed to burn. If you notice any formation on the bottom of the pan when you scrape, it is advisable to change pans and check rather than to scrape the bottom and destroy the milk.

5. Reduce the milk to approximately 750 ml.

6. Add the sugar to the milk once it is reduced by almost 30–40 per cent. You may need more sugar if you like your puddings sweet, therefore, check once again after the eggs have been added.

7. To add eggs to the reduced milk, first allow it to cool slightly until just hot but not very hot.

8. Always add the milk to the egg, never the egg to the milk. Pour a little milk into the beaten eggs, mix and whisk rapidly, then gradually mix all the milk in, whisking well.

9. Add more sugar to the mix if desired, and the rose water, vanilla essence, cardamom and nutmeg powders.

10. Butter a baking dish and pour the mixture in.

11. When you are ready to place it in the oven, sprinkle the nuts over evenly.

12. For best results part steam this in the oven by placing the dish inside a larger tray and filling the bottom tray half full with hot water. This will prevent the custard from baking too rapidly, thus acquiring a broken texture when baked.

13. Bake at 180°C/gas mark 6 to start with and after 10 minutes reduce to 150°C /gas mark 4 until done when tested with the tip of a knife. When cooked the knife will come out clean.

14. The colour on top needs to be golden. If you do not get this and the pudding is cooked, apply a little melted butter with a brush on the surface and place under a slow grill until the desired effect is achieved. Be careful to avoid excessive cooling as this will damage the texture.

15. You may have to rotate the dish to get an even colour.

16. Cut into even-sized pieces and serve once totally cooled. You may like to serve it a bit warm if you like but it needs to cool and settle completely before you cut it.

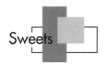

Parsee Pav Makhan Nu Pudding

A Rich Parsee-style Bread and Butter Pudding

Method

1. Heat the milk in a casserole and bring to boiling point.

2. When at boiling point reduce the heat and simmer or boil gently for approximately 1½ hours, keeping the sides clean at all times. To ensure the above you need a pastry brush and chilled water. Immediately after the milk has risen to boiling point and you put it to a slow boil, clean the sides of the pan with the help of a wet brush. Do this every few minutes. Do not use a dripping brush, as that is likely to dilute the milk.

3. Ideally the milk should turn a shade darker and give off a nutty/toffeeish/caramelised aroma.

4. Use a flat wooden spatula preferably and keep scraping the bottom so the milk is not allowed to burn.

5. Beat the eggs and sugar together until light and foamy. You may need more sugar if you like your puddings sweet, therefore, check once again after the milk has been added.

6. To add the reduced milk, first allow it to cool slightly until just hot but not very hot. Always add the milk to the egg, never the egg to the milk. Pour a little milk into the egg mix and whisk rapidly, then gradually mix all the milk in, whisking all the time and for 1 minute extra.

7. Add more sugar to the mix if desired and rose water, vanilla essence, cardamom and nutmeg powders.

8. Take a baking dish and butter it with a brush or a finger. Sprinkle sugar to coat the entire dish wherever buttered. If you see a gap, apply butter and then the sugar until the dish is well coated.

9. Apply butter to both sides of the bread slices (if you like, trim the sides) and arrange one layer at the bottom of the dish, trimming the edges to fit.

10. Over this sprinkle the sultanas and the mixed fruit.

11. Place the remaining bread over this and pour the mix over it.

12. Sprinkle with the almonds and charoli and bake in a moderate oven.

13. Bake at 180°C/gas mark 6 to start with and after 10 minutes reduce to 150°C/gas mark 4 until done when tested with the tip of a knife. When cooked the knife will come out clean.

14. The colour on top needs to be golden and the texture crisp. If you do not get this and the pudding is cooked, place under a slow grill until the desired effect is achieved.

Measurements	Ingredients
1½ litres	Milk (full cream)
5	Eggs
150–200 g	Sugar
1 tbsp	Rose water
½ tsp	Vanilla essence
½ tsp	Cardamom powder
½ tsp	Nutmeg powder
As required	Butter
5–6 (sufficient to form two layers)	Bread slices
1 tbsp	Sultanas
1½ tbsp	Mixed dried fruits
10–12	Almonds (sliced)
1 tbsp	Charoli

Beverages

10

In a hot tropical land like the sub-continent of India both hot and cold drinks are necessary. Like in every other land in the world the sub-continent has its own typical drinks, though these days one finds abundant use of internationally branded pops.

Offering first water or a beverage to a visitor or guest is considered auspicious or bearing a good omen as a blessing for quenching someone's thirst. When visiting friends or relatives in the sub-continent you will first be offered a glass of water and then asked if you would like tea or coffee or any other drink. This is tradition and even a passerby can knock on a door and ask for water, which traditionally should never be refused.

So far as drinking goes inside and outside the home, much of the indigenous population have local favorites and seasons dictate drinks as well, depending on the fruits available.

Cool drinks could be made out of fruits, berries, yoghurt, spice combinations and so on. Hot drinks such as tea and coffee are very traditional and the styles of making the brews vary from region to region, the common factors being milk and sugar.

Coffee, for instance, is also native to India and it is from the south of India that the Arabs first began to trade for spices and coffee. This then reached the Western world and as a result sparked the European nations to seek out the spice-growing world. Tea, however, is thought to have been introduced to India by the British from China, though India has its own varieties and flavours. India remains one of the world's largest exporters of tea and coffee to this day.

Both tea and coffee are consumed extensively throughout the sub-continent. In south India coffee is the preferred beverage but it is virtually non-existent in the households in the north. Tea is preferred brewed instead of being infused normally and is commonly boiled along with the milk and sugar. Sugar is no doubt added in copious quantities due to the common denominator, namely the 'sweet tooth'.

In south Indian restaurants it is advisable to ask for South Indian Filter Coffee and not any other coffee as the experience is simply great. If well made, and it usually is, warm or hot coffee is served in a tiny milk jug and hot milk is served in a large coffee pot. The idea, of course, is that the strong filtered coffee – (which is an espresso brewed with crushed cardamom) – has to be served with lots of milk as we Indians like it to be. The cardamom flavour is an added bonus if you like it. You can, of course, ask them not to add it and also get the exquisite flavour of Indian 'Arabica' beans.

Sugar can be added as desired and these days in most restaurants and tea houses, even the most simple and ordinary ones, there is every chance that both tea and coffee will be brewed for you without sugar. Even drinking instant coffee in India is an experience as it is fully brewed in milk and no water, or very little, is added.

During the hot season street stalls are awash with fresh juices of every nature, milk shakes made with any fruit you like from the exotics like mango, papaya and chickoo to simple all-year fruits like banana and guavas. Cocktails of the same are also available and you can make your own combination either with or without ice-cream. Fresh juices, smoothies and the like have been drunk in the sub-continent even since I can remember and today they are all the rage across Europe. Fresh red carrot juice crushed with fresh ginger is my all-time favourite, followed by fresh sugarcane juice once again crushed with ginger and fresh lime, then 'Mosambi' or sweet lime juice. The sweet lime is a fruit shaped like an orange but with yellow wedges. It is a firmer fruit and is sweet.

The most common and most popular of all is 'Limbu Paani', also known as 'Nimbu Paani' or fresh lime water. This is freshly squeezed lime juice with water or soda water, either sweet or salted, and with black rock salt or crushed roasted cumin or both. Both waters help retain body fluids and give the body a perk when feeling low due to extreme heat and humidity in certain areas.

The other popular drink, though heavier, is 'Lassi', pronounced 'Lussee', which is made from beaten yoghurt with ice and milk, again salted or sweet and with crushed cumin if desired or puréed with fresh fruit of your choice. Lussees are heavier due to the full-fat milk yoghurt used but are very refreshing and can assist in filling the gap for a short light midday meal or snack. Today in the Western world people drink beaten yoghurt drinks with a multitude of flavours, whereas in the sub-continent this drink is centuries old and still as popular. It is simply traditional, not adopted, and the same applies to fresh lime, fresh juices, tea and coffee. Milk shakes became traditional ever since the advent of the blender/liquidiser, which made them possible with 'creativity' being the answer to servicing a need in the market.

Regional variations are always there though most recipes are not commercially viable or sold commercially. For example, the 'Môr' (see page 28) is not sold on the streets but is available in restaurants and cafés. Most, of course, are seasonal and of a domestic nature.

In the chapter we are not discussing other beverages such as beer, wine and spirits but just to touch upon the subject it must be known that within the sub-continent of India a great many alcoholic beverages are made. Naturally in Pakistan and Bangladesh these will not be produced in abundance but in places like India, Sri Lanka and Nepal this is widespread. In India every region perhaps has its own grog or liquor and most of these are extremely potent. Indians as a rule prefer spirits to beer or wine and will mostly drink beer in the afternoons only. Of course, there are exceptions to the rule but by and large the evenings are spirit driven.

India being the world's largest sugar cane producer naturally produces some excellent rum. Other spirits such as whisky, gin, vodka and brandy are also produced as well as some very good wines and sparkling wines.

Ironically, Indians were producing wine hundreds of years before the Western world even grew grapes or knew about viniculture. The perfection in wine making was never developed as an art and wine making was predominantly geared towards medicinal use. Even today some of the best tonics for a sound body and for good digestion are made from fermented grape juice.

Wine in the ancient times was known as 'Soma' or water of the Gods. Wine being intoxicating was not permissible for the general public; the ruling class, ministers and senior officials were the only ones blessed enough to consume it.

Today Indian vine growers have enlisted the expertise of famous wine houses of Europe and Australia and are working closely with them to produce world-class wines. Grapes grow in abundance and the soil, weather and geographical locations are ideal for viniculture. It is only a matter of time before India begins to produce wines in abundance and of a very high quality.

Deshi Pini

Indian Drinks

- A few drinks are given below that are both refreshing and nourishing.

- Most famous of all is the lassi.

Chef's Notes

- A lassi is simply a beaten yoghurt drink. For the best lassi select the best yoghurt, this is essential. A good lassi is not good enough with light yoghurt or fat-free yoghurt. In India buffalo milk is normally used, which yields approximately 10–12 per cent fat. You do not have to go to that extent as then the lassi becomes heavy. Many Indians would go for a good lassi in summer and not eat after that, or go for a light snack.

- To make a lassi you need a good blender or whipper, a few cubes of ice, good yoghurt such as Greek style or full fat and the condiments, flavourings, etc.

Method

1. To make a popular mango lassi take half a glass of yoghurt, $\frac{1}{4}$ glass of mango pulp or one ripe mango peeled and cut into pieces, four ice cubes and maybe some sugar if the yoghurt is too sour.

2. Place everything in the blender and give it a good whip. Pour out into a tall glass and enjoy.

3. Do the same with any fleshy fruit such as strawberries, raspberries, papaya etc.

Masala Lassi

Method

1. Follow the normal procedure for the lassi then add to the blender one small piece fresh ginger, $\frac{1}{4}$ teaspoon cumin seeds, small piece mild green chilli, salt, a little sugar and two or three curry leaves. Give all of this a good whizz in the blender.

2. Finish with a sprinkling of finely chopped mint and coriander. If the two are not finely chopped then they will obstruct drinking. Try puréeing them with the lassi but unlike us Indians you may have to get used to the flavour.

Jeera Lassi

Chef's Notes

- This is a plain lassi but with cumin and salt.

- Both masala lassi and jeera are extremely good for upset stomachs, acidity and general uneasiness.

Method

1. Roast some cumin seeds gently until deep brown in colour, crush coarsely in a mortar and pestle and blend into the yoghurt.

2. Sprinkle some crushed cumin on top.

Chaas

Buttermilk

Method

1. Beat the yoghurt with the water thoroughly until any blobs are dissolved.

2. Add the cumin and salt, mix in well and serve.

3. You may add ice if you like.

Measurements	Ingredients
200 g	Yoghurt
500 ml	Cold water
⅛ tsp	Salt
¼ tsp	Cumin powder (roasted)

Masala Chaas

Chef's Notes

- To make a masala chaas a 'vaghaar' or tadka is added to the chaas above.

Measurements	Ingredients
2 tsp	Oil
¼ tsp	Black mustard seeds
¼ tsp	Cumin

Method

1. Heat the oil in a small frying pan or casserole.

2. Add the mustard seeds and heat until the crackling stops.

3. Add the cumin and sauté until brown.

4. As soon as the cumin browns add this quickly to the chaas.

Limbu Pani

Fresh Lime with Water or Soda

Chef's Notes

- You can see this being sold in almost every major street of every major city in India. Fresh limewaters are very popular again like the lassi but are lighter and more refreshing.

- They replace lost fluids in hot summers and help to control dehydration and nausea brought about by extreme heat.

Method

1. To make a simple fresh limewater, take 2 tbsp of freshly squeezed lime juice in a glass, 2–3 teaspoons sugar and a pinch of salt. Mix well with a little water till the sugar dissolves, then top up with chilled water and drink.

2. Do the same with soda for a fizzy drink.

3. Salt and cumin powder can make another style.

4. In India black rock salt is used specially in summer months.

Tarbooj Ka Pani

Fresh Watermelon Juice

Method

1. Seed the watermelon well taking care not to leave any on the flesh.

2. Whip the flesh in a blender with ice.

3. Remove to a large bowl and add raspberry syrup and stir. Add as much as you need a little at a time until you get the best flavour.

4. Rock salt may be added if you like.

5. The watermelon sometimes tastes a bit bland without the syrup.

Measurements	Ingredients
1 small	Watermelon
To taste	Raspberry syrup or Ribena
To taste	Rock salt
As required	Ice

Masaléwali Chai

Masala Tea

Method

1. Blend the water, milk and spices in a casserole then bring to a boil.

2. Simmer for 2–3 minutes and bring it back to the boil.

3. As soon as it boils add the tea leaves and reduce to a simmer.

4. Cover the pan and switch off.

5. Strain after 1–2 minutes till the leaves settle. Serve.

6. Sugar can be added right at the beginning or served as per individual taste separately. Normally Indians love sweet sugary tea.

Measurements	Ingredients
500 ml	Water
250 ml	Milk (full fat)
2–3 pods	Green cardamom (crushed whole)
2–3	Black peppercorns (coarsely crushed)
2.5 cm	Cassia or cinnamon
3 tsp	Loose tea leaves
	Sugar (optional)

Variations

- For a great taste add a 2.5 cm piece of well-crushed ginger too. More if you have a nasty cold, to open up those nostrils and clear the throat.

- We Parsees love lemon grass and fresh mint in our tea and even here in London you will always find a stash of lemon grass leaves in our freezer. A small piece of lemon grass right at the end before switching off and covering the pot gives a fabulous flavour.

- The same applies to fresh mint. For both do not add too much as you will then lose the flavour of the tea.

Badaam Pusta Nu- Doodh/Badaam Pista Ka Doodh

Milk with Almonds and Pistachios

Chef's Notes

- This is a great treat if you like it rich. The drink is much loved all over the sub-continent.

- You can serve it as a hot or cold welcome drink to people who come to visit.

- It is also served to guests at weddings and happy occasions after a meal or at times even before.

Method

1. In a blender purée the cardamoms, almonds and pistachios in a little of the milk until ground. You may purée it all fine or keep it a bit coarse for a thicker texture. Indians would keep it a bit thicker so as to be able to bite on the nuts when drinking.

2. Pour this with the rest of the milk in a saucepan and heat up slowly, stirring all the time. This is important as the nuts will settle and burn at the bottom.

3. While boiling add some saffron and sugar to taste and continue to cook until the milk comes to the boil.

Measurements	Ingredients
5–6	Green cardamom
6–8	Whole almonds
10–12	Pistachios (unsalted and shelled)
1 litre	Milk (semi-skimmed)
Few strands if desired	Saffron
To taste	Sugar

4. Reduce the temperature and simmer for 5–6 minutes, giving enough time for the nuts to cook and also to impart their flavour and that of the saffron and cardamom.

5. Remove and serve as desired either hot, warm or cold.

Sardai

For 6–8 glasses

Almond and Poppy Seed Drink

Chef's Notes

• This is a speciality in Pakistan and I have had this very rich drink in the house of one of my senior chefs, Babar Salim, who hails from Lahore.

Method

1. Soak whole almonds and poppy seeds in water until both are soft and fully absorbed.

2. Skin the almonds and grind with the poppy seeds and sugar until smooth and silky.

3. Dilute according to taste; the addition of tiny chopped pieces of almonds and pistachios enhances the drink.

Measurements	Ingredients
15–20 g	Almonds (skinned, whole)
½ tbls	White poppy seeds (soaked in 1 litre of water)
To taste	Sugar

4. Add sugar as desired and then drink cold.

5. The milk is derived from the purée of almonds and poppy seeds and not from fresh dairy milk.

6. Some cold milk may be added if desired though this is not often done. Also this will thicken with absorbtion.

Bafloo/Pannaa

Raw Mango or Unripe Mango Drink

Chef's Notes

- Unripe mango is different from raw mango in that the raw mango is plucked while still small and seedy, the unripe mango is a mango ready for ripening but not yet ripe and is often fully grown.

Measurements	Ingredients
2	Mango (raw or partially ripe)
1500 ml	Water
2–3 tbsp to taste	Sugar
½ tsp	Salt
1 tsp	Cumin (roasted and finely ground)

Method

1. Peel and deseed the mango and cut it into pieces. Do not discard the seed.

2. Add the water to a casserole or saucepan and bring to a boil.

3. Add the mango and the seed and boil.

4. When the mango is soft and fully cooked remove the seed with a slotted spoon.

5. Scrape off any flesh sticking to the seed and add to the pot.

6. Purée the mango In the liquid or pass through a strainer.

7. Add the sugar, salt and the cumin and beat until the sugar is dissolved.

8. Chill well in bottles or in a jug.

9. Stir and serve when cold.

10. This is one for the summer and is a great refresher.

Variations

- Rose water can be added to make the drink more flavourful.

- Crushed ice can also be added.

- The drink can also be used as a mixer for long, cool alcoholic drinks.

Adrak Kaa Russ

Adrak Nimbu Ki Thandai

Ginger and Lime Cooler

Method

1. Scrape the ginger and cut it into small pieces

2. Extract the lime juice, squeezing it well

3. Add the water, lime juice, ginger, sugar, mint leaves and crushed ice to a blender and whiz until smooth

4. Either serve as it is in tall glasses or chill and serve as desired.

5. Dilute further if desired.

6. Alternatively do not purée the leaves but snip them and add them to the glass when serving.

Measurements	Ingredients
5–7.5 cm	Ginger
1 large or 2 small	Limes
2 glasses (large tumbler size)	Water
5–6 tbsp	Sugar
6–8	Fresh mint leaves
8–10 cubes	Crushed ice

Glossary

It must be noted that I have preferred to go down the phonetic route rather than the way we Indians normally spell certain products in English. This is so as to let those who do not know the products pronounce them as they should be.

Aaloo, Batata, Bataka, Papeta Potato

Aamchoor Dried raw mango powder

Aam, Kaeri Mango

Aamli, Imli, Aamsaand Tamarind

Aatta Wholemeal flour

Achaar Pickle

Adrakh, Aadoo Ginger

Ajowan, Ajwaain, Ajmo Carom seeds, also known as thymol or lovage

Anaardaana Pomegranate seeds

Ananas Pineapple

Asafoetida Hing

Aubergine Baingan, Egg plant, Ringna, Vaingee

Baadiaan Star anise

Badaam Almond

Badak Duck

Badi saunf, Barri shaep Anise, Fennel

Baesan, Channay kaa atta Chickpea flour

Baghaar, Vaghaar Sizzling of spices, onions, mustard seeds, cumin, etc., fried in hot oil and added to lentils, etc.

Baida, Undaa, Eeda Egg

Baingan, Vengna, Ringna Aubergine, Egg plant

Bataer Quail

Bay leaf Taej Patta, Tej Patta

Bhindi, Bheenda Okra

Boata Cube

Boati Dice

Burtan Vessel

Cachumber Sliced onion salad

Cardamom black Badi elaichi

Cardamom Green or white Elaichi

Cassia bark Jungli daalchini (most commonly used in Indian cuisine as cinnamon)

Cha, Chai Tea

Chaanni, Channi Strainer, sieve

Chaat masala Today an integral part of Indian cuisine. A combination of dried mango powder, black rock salt, pepper, cumin and ginger

Chaawal, Bhaat, Dhaan Rice

Chaawal ka aatta Rice flour

Chappatti, rotli Thin wholewheat bread

Channa, Choalay Chickpea

Channay ki daal Split yellow peas, Chickpea lentil

Chilli green Hari mirch or mirich, tonnio mirsaang, Leela murcha

Chilli red (dried) Laal mirch or mirich. (This would apply to all varieties though each has its own name. India has a few hundred varieties, i.e. laal murcha, taambday mirsaang

Churri, Chaaku Knife

Cinnamon Daalchini. (Name means Chinese bark. Perhaps first introduced to India by the Chinese)

Cloves Lavang, Laving, Loang

Coconut Narial, Naal

Cokum, Kokum 'Garcinia indica', also known as butternut berry, is a sour dark purple fruit when dried. Used to flavour curries.

Cumin Jeera

Curry leaves Curry patta. Kodi chay paan 'mutaya koenigri'

Curry Evolves from the south Indian word 'Kaari' meaning in a lot of sauce

Daal Any lentil; every lentil has its own name, however

Daalchini Cinnamon and cassia bark

Dahi Yogurt

Dhana, Dhania Coriander seeds or powder

Dhania hara, kothmir Fresh coriander

Dhaniya, Dhaana, Kothmiri Chay biyo Coriander seeds

Doodh Milk

Doodhi, Lauki, Ghia, Kaddu White gourd

Dukkar Pig. Also called soover

Dukkar Ka Mass Pork

Eeda, unda, baida Egg

Elaichi Cardamom

Falli, Fansi French beans

Fudina, Pudina, Fudno Mint

Gaanth gobi, Naabil kolsa, Naab Kohl Rabi Knol kholl

Gajjar Carrot

Garam masala Combination of cinnamon, cardamom, cloves, peppercorns, mace, etc.

Ghee Clarified butter

Gosht, Gos, Maas Lamb or mutton or goat's meat (kid)

Gudd, Gore Jaggery/raw cane sugar

Gulaab Jul Rose water

Gurdah Kidney

Haldi, Huldi, Hallad Turmeric

Hara dhaniya, Leeli kothmir Coriander fresh

Heeng, Hing Asafoetida

Hilsa, Bheeng, Paalu Shad

Hiran Ka Gosht Venison

Hundi, Haandi, Degchi Cooking pot

Idli Steamed rice dumpling

Imli, Aamli, Aamsaan Tamarind

Jaavuntri Mace

Jaiphul Nutmeg

Jaithun Olive

Jalaebi Crisply fried fermented batter, sweet

Jeeb, Zabaan Tongue

Jeera, Jeeru, Zeera Cumin

Jhinga, Koalmi, Suncta Prawns, shrimp

Jul, Paani Water

Jungli Wild

Jurdaloo, Khubaani Dried apricots

Kaaju Cashew nut

Kaakdi, Kuckdi, Kheera Cucumber

Kaala mirich, kaara murri Black pepper

Kaanda, Pyaaz Onion

Kabaab chini, Kapur china Allspice/Jamaican pepper

Kabuli Channa Large white chickpea

Kaddu, Koadhu Pumpkin

Kaela, Kaeroo Banana

Kaelay ka patta Banana leaf

Kaesar Saffron

Kairi Mango

Kalaeji Liver

Kalaunji Nigella

Kaloo, Kalwaan Oyster

Kamal kaakri Lotus root

Karaela Bitter gourd

Karai, Kadhai Round-bottomed cooking utensil

Kathore Pulses

Kavaab, Kebab Minced meat balls or skewered mince, chargrilled, deep-fried or grilled

Khaara, Kharu Salty, savoury

Khaekda, Karachla, Kullyo Crab

Khajoor, Khazoor Dates

Khargoash Rabbit, hare

Kheema Mince

Khus-khus Poppy seeds

Kismis Sultanas, raisins

Koakum, Cokum 'Garcinia indica', a small fruit, deep red when dried, added to curries for a zesty flavour. Also known as butternut berry

Kukarmutta, Dhingri Mushrooms

Kulfi Frozen ice cream Indian style

Laal mirich, Laal murcha Dried red chillies

Laep Sole (fish)

Lassi Beaten yogurt drink

Lassun, Lehsun, Loesoon Garlic

Lauki, Doodhi, Ghia Bottle gourd

Lavang, Laving, Loang Cloves

Leeli chai, Hari chai ki patti Lemon grass

Limbu kaa phool Citric acid

Limbu, Nimboo Lime

Loahri, Tawa Griddle

Loancha, achaar, miskoot Pickle

Lobia Black eye bean

Maandki, Maandkyo Squid

Maas, Gosht, Gos Meat (all meats are defined by placing the name of the animal before the word)

Machchli, Machchi, Nishtyay Fish

Maida Refined wheat flour

Makhana Lotus seed

Makkahn, Muska Butter

Makki, Makkai, Bhutta Maize, Corn

Makki ka aatta Ground maize

Masala Individual condiments or spices, or a combination of condiments and spices

Masalay ka patthar Masala grinding stone

Masoor Whole pigeon pea, very similar in appearance to pui but smaller

Masoor daar/daal Pink lentil or split pigeon pea

Mava, Mavo, Khoya Milk evaporated slowly until thick and dry

Methi Fenugreek

Methi bhaaji Fresh fenugreek

Methi quasoori Dried fenugreek leaves

Mirich, Murcha, Mirssang Chillies

Misri, Khaddi Shakkar Rock sugar, Loaf sugar

Mooli, Moora Radish

Mithoo, Namack, Nimackh Salt

Miththu, Meetha, Galyu Sweet

Moong, Mung Whole green lentil (used for making bean sprouts)

Moong daal, Mug ni daar Split mung bean

Murammba, Murabba Sweet preserves

Murgh, Murghi Chicken (pronounced moorghi)

Muska, Makkhan Butter

Mutter, Vatana Green peas

Naariyal, Naal Coconut

Namakh, Nimakh Salt

Narangi, Suntra Orange

Narial ka doodh Coconut milk

Neja, Chilgoza Pine nuts

Nimboo, Limboo Sour lime

Paani, Jul, Udoack Water

Paapri Field beans

Palak Spinach

Paneer Whey cheese

Pao, Double roti Bread

Papad Pappadum

Papeta, Bataka, Aloo Potato

Paratha Layered unleavened bread

Patta, Paan, Patra Leaf, leaves

Phool gobi Cauliflower

Phudina, Phudno, Pudina Mint

Pista, Pusta Pistachio

Poori, Puri, Poorie Thin fried wholewheat bread, crisp or puffed

Pyaaz, kaanda, piyao Onion

Quasuri Methi Dried fenugreek

Raamus Bombay salmon

Rai, Saasuaan, Mustard

Rawa, Rawo, Sooji Semolina

Ravaiyya Baby aubergine

Rotli, Bhakri, Chappati Unleavened griddled bread

Saag Spinach

Saalan, Saakh, Shaak, Salnu Braised vegetables

Saalit Lettuce

Saambaar Lentil and vegetable accompaniment to south Indian snacks

Saboodana Sago, tapioca balls

Saeb, Supperchun Apple

Saev, Semiya, Saeviyaan Vermicelli

Sahnn, Shivut Lobster

Sakkarkun, Ratalu, Kun Sweet potato

Salary, Kurass Celery

Samosa Triangular pastry parcels filled in several styles

Saunf, Variali, Baddi shape Anise, Fennel seeds

Shahi jeera Black cumin

Shikaar Game

Shirka, Surko, Vinagire Vinegar

Sigri, Sigdi Brazier

Singh, Moongphulli Peanuts, groundnuts

Soandh, Soandhia A brackish water crayfish, detentacalised and sold in the UK as king prawn

Subzi, tarkaari, Subjee Vegetables

Sumbhaar Mixed spice powder

Sunchul, Kaala namakh Black rock salt

Sursoan ka tael Mustard oil

Sursoan ki bhaaji Mustard leaves

Tadka, Vaghaar A sizzling of spices in oil

Tael (tail) Oil

Taej patta, Tamaal patta Bay leaf

Tamaturr, Tamota Tomato

Tawa, Lohri Griddle

Teekha, Tikkhu Hot (as in chilli hot)

Tikka Cube

Tisri, Teesreo Mussels

Tittar, Teetar Partridge

Toorai, Tooria, Toori Ridge gourd

Toover, Toor Split pigeon pea lentil

Tul, Til, Tew Sesame, Gingelli

Tulsi Basil

Tupaeli, Haandi, Patila Casserole,

pan, pot without handle

Turkaari, Subzi, Subz Vegetables

Undaa, Eedu, Baida, Taanti Egg

Urad Black lentil

Urad daal Split skinned black lentil, which is white in colour

Vaelan, Baelan Rolling pin

Vaengna, Baingan, Ringna Aubergine

Vaghaar, Baghaar, Tadka A sizzling of spices in oil

Varakh Gold or silver leaf

Variali, Baddi shape, Saunf Fennel seeds

Vatana, Mutter Green peas

Index

ajowan xvi
akoori 33–5
alcohol 264–5
aloo chaat 30
anardana xxxiv–xxxv
apple
  bhajee 183
  and potato bhajee 181
asafoetida xvii
aubergines
  fried 37–9
  stuffed 184–6
Ayurvedic medicine xii,
  xiii

Baffado masala 10
balance, importance of
  xi–xiii, xlvii–xlviii
banana
  cakes 53
  fritters 254
Basmati rice 194–5
bay leaves xvii–xviii
beans see French beans;
  moong beans
beef, dry fry 87–9
beverages
  adding sugar to 263
  alcohol 264–5
  almond and poppy seed
    drink 270
  buttermilk 267
  coffee 263
  fresh juices 264
  ginger and lime cooler
    272
  lassi 264, 266–7
  lime water 264, 268
  mango drink 271
  masala chaas 267–8
  masala tea 269
  milk with almonds and
    pistachios 267–70
  tea-drinking 263
  water 263
  watermelon juice 268
biryani, chicken masala for
  4–5
black cumin xxv
black peppercorns
  xxxiii–xxxiv

braising 61
bread
  corn meal roti 224–5
  dough-making 221–2
  freshness of 220, 221
  fried, with saffron milk
    256–7
  ingredients of 221
  masala bhakhri 225
  poories with spices
    226–7
  poories (white flour)
    229–30
  variety of 220
  white radish and onion
    roti 230–1
  see also chappaties
bread and butter pudding
  261
broccoli
  and corn Usli 157–8
  thimi tarkari masala
    189–90
buffalo meat ix
buttermilk 267
buttermilk soup 28

cabbage
  and French beans foogath
    160
  and French beans jeera
    159
capsicum xx, xxi
cardamom xviii–xix, 263
carrot
  halwa 249
  pickle 238
cashew nut chaat 31
cassia xix–xx
cauliflower
  with potatoes and rice
    204–5
  with sweet corn 169–70
  thimi tarkari masala
    189–90
  in tomato gravy 168–9
cayenne xx
chaat
  masala 3–4
  uses of 30
channa chaat 31

chappaties
  basic recipe for 223–4
  with chickpea flour and
    spinach 227–8
  lamb 51–2
  paratha 231–3
  phulka 221
  soya bean flour 234
chayote chutney 240–1
cheese
  and rice croquette 49
  paneer 178–9
  with potatoes and
    coconut 155–6
  spicy minced 177
chicken
  with cumin and black
    pepper 50–1
  deep-fried in batter 45–6
  grilled 98–9
  hot chargrilled 97–8
  Malayan Poussin Curry
    Parsee style 17
  masala for biryani 4–5
  Murg bhuna 101–2
  roast (Madurai masala)
    99–100
  samosa 43–5
  tandoori malai masala
    (chicken tikka) 11
  tikka (kala miri masala)
    95
  tikka (malai Murg) 92–3
  tikka (Murgh) 94
chicken liver masala 9
chickpeas
  cake 54–5
  channa chaat 31
  chappaties with spinach
    227–8
  choley pindi 161
  hot channa pakora 42–3
  pulao 209–10
chilli powder xx–xxi
chillies
  use of xiii, xx–xxi
  whole stuffed pickled
    237
chôkelo masala 5–6
chutneys

chayote 240–1
  garlic 244, 245
  green 241–2
  green (coconut) 242
  green (masala) 14–15
  green (South Indian
    style) 242–3
  mango (Goan style)
    245–6
  mint 243
  red pumpkin skin 240
  uses of 236
  see also pickles
cinnamon xxi–xxii
clams
  crab and beans porial
    115–16
  sautéed with mussels
    146–7
cloves xxii–xxiii
coconut
  green chutney 242
  pancakes 252–3
  sweet with sago balls 251
  uses of x, xxiii
coffee 263
coriander xxiii–xxiv
corn
  baked 39–40
  and broccoli Usli 157–8
  with cauliflower 169–70
corn meal roti 224–5
crab
  clam and beans porial
    with egg 115–16
  stuffed (Goan style)
    114–15
cumin xxiv–xxv
curry
  masala 6–7
  masala (East Indian) 7–8
  use of the term x–xi
curry leaves xxv–xxvi
custard, baked 260–1

Dhan Daar Nay Vaghaar
  164–6
diversity xlv–xlvii
drinks see beverages
duck tikka 90–1

eggs
  akoori 33–5
  baked spicy omelette
    41–2
  crab, clam and beans
    porial with 115–16
  fried rice with vegetables
    211–12
  lamb with 81–3
  masala omelette 40–1
  masala scrambled eggs
    8–9
  with peanuts and seafood
    58
  Shikari Nargisi Kofta
    (Scotch eggs) 86–7
enoki with ginger, garlic
  and chilli 166–7

fennel xxviii
fenugreek xxviii–xxix
fish
  curry 118
  curry (Goan style)
    119–20
  curry (green) 128–9
  curry (oily fish) 122–3
  kedgeree 121–2
  marinated and fried 134
  monkfish tikka 137–8
  pomfret steamed in
    banana leaf 139–40
  sardine curry 122, 148–9
  stuffed pomfret 140–1
  in tamarind 120–1
  see also seafood
fish cakes
  Goan style 113–14
  with tomato gravy 132–4
French beans
  and cabbage foogath 160
  and cabbage jeera 159
  with cumin and tomatoes
    167–8
  with dry cooked potatoes
    186–7
fruit chaats 31

gajak 249
garam masala 2–3
garlic
  chutney 244, 245
  and ginger paste 135
  uses of xxix–xxx
geographical differences
  viii–ix
ginger and garlic paste 135
goat's meat ix
gourd, snake 182
green chutney
  coconut 242
  fresh 241–2
  masala 14–15
  South Indian 242–3

green peppercorns
  xxxiii–xxxiv

hare
  in Scotch eggs 86
  with yoghurt 89–90
health
  Ayurvedic medicine xii,
    xiii
  digestion xii
  food as medicine viii,
    xiii–xiv
  seafood hygiene 108–9
  vegetarianism and 153–4
herbal medicine xii, xiii
hygiene xiv–xv

ingredients, obtaining raw
  xlii–xliii

jalebi 249, 250
jeera lassi 268

Kasuri methi xxix
kedgeree 121–2
king prawns
  with king scallops 125–7
  masala 111–12
  source of 104

ladies' fingers (okra) 158–9
lamb
  basic recipe for 63
  with black-eyed beans
    69–70
  braised North Indian
    style 67–8
  Chutt Patta Gosht 70–1
  with coriander 80
  curry with yoghurt and
    masoor daal 83–4
  dhaansaak 76–9
  with eggs 81–3
  kebab 84–5
  khichdi 203–4
  pulao 71–4, 198–200,
    207–8
  rack of 63–5
  roasted joint of 65–7
  rolled chappati 51–2
  soup Parsee style 24–5
  use of ix–x
  vindaloo with yoghurt
    74–5
lassi 264, 266–7
lentils
  cake 55–6
  Laapsi khichdi 208–9
  lamb khichdi 203–4
  with prawns 116–17
  with rice pulao 213–14
  with rice and yoghurt
    211
  saambaar masala 16

soup (Rasam) 18–19
  tadka daal (sizzled
    lentils) 188–9
  wheat khichdi 200–1
lime and ginger cooler 273
lime water 264, 268
livers, masala 9
lobster, stuffed 130–1

mace xxxi–xxxii
mackerel 122
Madras curry powder
  15–16
mango
  chutney 245–6
  drink 272
  powder xxvii
  soup 25–6
  uses of xxvi–xxvii
masalas
  bhakhri 225
  chaas 268–9
  chaat 3–4, 30
  chicken 4–5
  chicken livers 9
  chicken (Malayan
    Poussin Curry Parsee
    style) 17
  chilli and cassia (patia no
    masala) 11–13
  chilli, coriander and
    cumin 82
  chilli, ginger and garlic
    (baffado) 10
  chôkelo 5–6
  curry 6–7
  curry (East Indian) 7–8
  fennel and mustard 18
  garam 2–3
  ginger and garlic (Peri-
    Peri) 13–14
  green chutney 14–15
  hot Madras curry powder
    15–16
  lamb dhaansaak 77
  lassi 267
  lentil (saambaar) 16
  omelette 40–1
  potato 172
  rice 203, 215–17
  scrambled eggs 8–9
  storage of 82–3
  tandoori malai 11
  tea 270
  thimi tarkari 189–90
  uses of 2, 3
meat, texture of 60–1
menu planning xlvii–xlviii
milk cake 249–50
mint chutney 243
monkfish
  with coconut and

vegetables 144–5
seafood jhalfrazi 143–4
tikka 137–8
moong beans, and
  pomegranate salad 32
moong daal and condensed
  milk sweet 253–4
mulligatawny soup 26–7
  see also pepper water
mushrooms
  with ginger, garlic and
    chilli 166–7
  in hot garlic sauce 174
  'Manchurian' 174–5
  and peas 170–1
  tossed with dry spices
    176–7
mussels
  cocktail 138–9
  with coconut and
    vegetables 144–5
  sautéed with clams
    146–7
  seafood jhalfrazi 143–4
mustard xxx–xxxi
'mutton' x

nutmeg xxxi–xxxii

oil, quantities used xlii
okra
  fried 171–2
  with mushrooms, ginger,
    garlic and chilli 166–7
  stuffed (ladies' fingers)
    158–9
onion
  bhajia 56–7
  uses of xxxii–xxxiii
  and white radish roti
    230–1
ostrich tikka 91–2

pakora
  hot channa 42–3
  potato and paneer 35
pancakes, coconut 252–3
paneer 178–9, 35
paprika xx
peanuts, with seafood and
  eggs 58
peas, and mushrooms
  170–1
pepper xxxiii–xxxiv
pepper water 21
  see also mulligatawny soup
Peri-Peri masala 13–14
pickles
  carrot 238
  mixed vegetable 239
  prawn 243–4
  uses of 236
  whole stuffed chilli 237
  see also chutneys

pomegranate and moong
  bean salad 32
pomegranate seeds
  xxxiv–xxxv
pomfret
  steamed in banana leaf
    139–40
  stuffed 140–1
poories
  with spices 226–7
  white flour 229–30
pork
  roast 95–6
  taboo on xli, 105
potatoes
  aloo chaat 30
  bhajee 179
  bhajee with apple 181
  chaat milavut 33
  with chopped spinach
    180
  cooked dry with French
    beans 186–7
  with flattened rice 205–6
  and Indian Whey cheese
    with coconut 155–6
  masala na papeta 172
  with onions (Aloo ki
    Subzee) 154–5
  and prawn soup 22–3
  with rice and cauliflower
    204–5
  spicy with prawns 135–6
  tikki 36–7
  in tomato gravy 162
prawns
  with coconut and
    vegetables 144–5
  green curry 129–30
  with lentils 116–17
  in masala with spicy
    potatoes 135–6
  patia 127–8
  pickle 112–13, 243–4
  and potato soup 22–3
  samosa 123–5
  seafood jhalfrazi 143–4
  stir-fried with rice 142
  see also king prawns
preserved foods xli–xlii,
  xliii
pulaos
  basic recipe for 214–15
  chickpea 209–10
  lamb 71–4, 198–200,
    207–8
  with lentils 213–14
  potato and cauliflower
    204–5
  seafood (Goan style)
    201–2
pumpkin
  pickled skin 240
  thimi tarkari masala
    189–90

purées 236

rabbit, with yoghurt 89–90
radish and onion roti
  230–1
raita xv
rice
  absorption method 197
  basmati 71, 194–5
  boiled 196
  and cheese croquette 49
  chickpeas pulao 209–10
  egg and vegetable fried
    211–12
  flattened, with potato
    205–6
  lamb khichdi 203–4
  lamb pulao 198–200,
    207–8
  lentil pulao 213–14
  masala rice 215–17
  with onion and tomato
    (Laapsi khichdi) 208–9
  with potatoes and
    cauliflower 204–5
  pudding 256–7
  seafood pulao (Goan
    style) 201–2
  sesame 212–13
  stir-fried with prawns
    142
  tomato 197–8
  uses of 194–5
  variety of 194–5
  with yoghurt (Dahi
    Bhaat) 217–18
  with yoghurt and lentils
    211
roasting 60–2
rock salt xxxv–xxxvi
rose water 250

saffron
  fried bread and 256–7
  uses of xxxvi–xxxvii
sago balls and coconut milk
  251
salad
  currimbhoy 48
  moong bean and
    pomegranate 32
salmon 122
salt xxxv–xxxvi
sardine curry 122, 148–9
scallops
  with coconut and
    vegetables 144–5
  with ginger 136–7
  with ginger, garlic and
    chilli 110–11
  with king prawns 125–7
  seafood jhalfrazi 143–4
seafood
  buying 106

with coconut and
    vegetables 144–5
  cooking techniques
    106–7
  with eggs and peanuts 58
  health benefits of 109
  hygiene and 108–9
  jhalfrazi 143–4
  marinating 107–8
  pulao (Goan style)
    201–2
  religious taboos on 105
  uses of 105
  variety of 104
  see also crab; fish; fish
    cakes; king prawns;
    lobster; mussels;
    prawns; scallops
seasonality xxxix–xl
semolina pudding 258–59
sesame rice 212–13
simplicity, importance of
    xxxix
snake gourd caldeen 182
soups
  buttermilk 28
  lamb broth 24–5
  lentil (Rasam) 18–19
  mango 25–6
  mulligatawny 26–7
  pepper water 21
  prawn and potato 22–3
  solkadhi (kokum) 23
  vegetable broth 19–21
soya bean flour chappaties
    234
spinach, chopped with
    potato 180
spring rolls (prawn) 123–5
squid
  with coconut and
    vegetables 144–5
  stuffed 147–8
star anise xxxvii–xxxviii
stewing 61–2
sweet corn
  with cauliflower 169–70
  see also corn
sweets
  baked custard 260–1
  banana fritters 254
  bread and butter pudding
    262
  carrot halwa 249
  coconut pancakes 253–4
  fried bread in saffron
    milk 256–7
  gajak 249
  jalebi 249, 250
  milk cake 249–50
  moong daal and
    condensed milk 253–4

popularity of 248–50
  rice pudding 255–6
  sago balls, milk and
    coconut milk 251
  semolina pudding
    259–60
  variety of 248–50
  yoghurt dessert 257

tamarind (poor man's
    food) 173
tandoor 62
tea 264, 270
Thai cuisine x
tikkas
  chicken (kala miri
    masala) 95
  chicken (malai Murg)
    92–3
  chicken (Murgh) 94
  cooking 62
  duck 90–1
  monkfish 137–8
  ostrich 91–2
tikkis, potato and kidney
    bean 36–7
tomatoes
  cauliflower and 168–9
  with fishcakes 132–4
  with French beans and
    cumin 167–8
  with potatoes 162
  with rice 197–8
  with rice and onion
    (Laapsi khichdi) 208–9
turmeric, uses of xii, xiv,
    xxxvii–xxxviii

vegetables
  curried puffs 46–7
  egg fried rice 211–12
  mixed pickled 239
  mixed, with yoghurt and
    coconut 156
  soup 19–21
  Thoran 191–2
vegetarianism ix, 151–4
venison 86
vermicelli 198–200

watermelon juice 268
wheat khichdi 200–1
white peppercorns
    xxxiii–xxxiv
wild boar 86
wine 266

yoghurt
  buttermilk soup 28
  curry (kadhi) 162–4
  dessert (Shrikhand) 257
  with rice and lentils 211
  uses of xv